GETTYSBURG

The Long Encampment

GETTYSBURG

The Long Encampment

by Jack McLaughlin

BONANZA BOOKS
NEW YORK

Foreword

"There's something about the place that gets you." These are the words spoken several years ago by a guide at Gettysburg, a man who by all rights should have been somewhat blasé from long exposure. The place, however, was still vital to him.

Ghosts? No one has ever seen one at Gettysburg, but they must be there. The land is filled with yesterday—a long, haunted history.

There are photographs of that history. They are a little one-sided—the Confederates had no photographers following their army. Those photographs are in this book. Some are faded, not too good, but they are included. Some are very good. They are in this book, also.

There is a "story" of Gettysburg. It is in this book, too. But since this is a special place and has special meaning, the facts have a way of blurring. To one, they are this; to another, they are that. Many words. Many interpretations.

No matter. There *is* something about the place that gets you.

Acknowledgments

Among the many, I am especially indebted to the following for making available to me specific information and photographs:

James Babcock, Detroit Public Library, Detroit, Michigan; Harry F. Baughman, President of the Lutheran Theological Seminary, Gettysburg, Pennsylvania; Bruce Catton, *American Heritage*, New York, New York; John J. Conlon, National Commander World Wars Tank Corps Association, Rego Park, New York; Edgar Cox, Falls Church, Virginia; Betty Doolittle, *Down East Magazine*, Camden, Maine; J. Earl Endacott, Executive Director, The Eisenhower Foundation, Abilene, Kansas; James C. Hagerty, Press Secretary to President Eisenhower; Oscar Hamlin, Milo, Maine (Mr. Hamlin is the grandson of Corporal Livermore whose picture appears on page 170); Donald H. Kent, Research and Publications Division, Pennsylvania Historical and Museum Commission, Harrisburg, Pennsylvania; Ray Mainwaring, photographer, Bridgeport, Connecticut; Tim McDonald, Bridgeport Weather Bureau, Bridgeport, Connecticut; Albert E. Minns, Jr., Curator, Medical Museum, Armed Forces Institute of Pathology, Walter Reed Army Medical Center, Washington, D.C.; W. S. Nye, Associate Editor, The Stackpole Company, Harrisburg, Pennsylvania; Frank A. Parsons, Director of Information Services, Washington and Lee University, Lexington, Virginia; M. L. Peterson, Head Curator, Department of Armed Forces History, Smithsonian Institution, U.S. National Museum, Washington, D.C.; John J. Pullen, Philadelphia, Pennsylvania (Mr. Pullen graciously offered information about photographs appearing in his book *The Twentieth Maine*); Robert L. Schultz, Aide to General Eisenhower, Gettysburg, Pennsylvania; Cynthia Stevens, Scientific Assistant, The American Museum —Hayden Planetarium, New York, New York; Richard W. Streiff, Office of the Military Aide under President Eisenhower; India W. Thomas, House Regent, The Confederate Museum, Richmond, Virginia; Frederick P. Todd, Director of Museum, West Point Museum, West Point, New York; B. Elizabeth Ulrich, Chief Reference Librarian, State Library, Commonwealth of Pennsylvania, Harrisburg.

And also, Virginia Daiker, Milton Kaplan, and other members of the staff of Still Prints and Photographs, Library of Congress, Washington, D.C.; Josephine Cobb, Forest L. Williams, and associates, Still Pictures Branch, National Archives and Records Service, Washington, D.C.; Donald C. Holmes and his associates of The Photoduplication Service, Library of Congress, Washington, D.C.; and Mary Johnson, Exhibits and Publications Branch, National Archives and Records Service.

And to those officials of the Gettysburg National Military Park who showed me courtesy far beyond the everyday amenities I am indeed grateful. In particular: J. Walter Coleman, Superintendent, who graciously opened his doors and made available the resources and data of his offices; Harry W. Pfanz, Supervisory Park Historian, who supplied me with information and who was generous enough to review and point out several glaring mistakes in the first manuscript (I hasten to add, any mistakes now extant are mine and not Doctor Pfanz's, and he may not agree with some of my premises and conclusions); Frederick Tilberg, Park Historian, who kindly identified photographs and who filled me in with definitive knowledge; and S. G. Sollenberger, Assistant Superintendent, who weathered a veritable barrage of correspondence and who without flinching faithfully answered every query.

A very special note of thanks goes to Walter Lane, Lane Studio, Gettysburg, Pennsylvania. Over a long period of time he lent his enthusiasm and diligence to this project by searching out old photographs (many of which were supplied by the Gettysburg National Military Park), and he also took all of the modern views.

And to Ira L. Williams, photographer at Gettysburg, I owe thanks. Mr. Williams supplied me with a photograph which had proven to be extraordinarily elusive.

My guides at Gettysburg were Robert D. Fidler and Jacob M. Sheads, both of whom understood their subject thoroughly, both of whom were patient.

To the members and staff of the Pequot Library, Southport, Connecticut, I wish to express thanks for allowing me to enter the stacks to locate special material; and I am likewise grateful to the members and staff of the Burroughs Library, Bridgeport, Connecticut, for assisting me in locating special books and allowing me to select and use certain photographs.

My sincere thanks go to Gordon Carroll of Westport, Connecticut, for his suggestions and encouragement.

Maps were drawn and executed by Edward Roge, Newtown, Connecticut, with valuable ideas and planning supplied by Harrie Wood, also of Newtown.

To the following publishers for permission to use excerpts and quotations my thanks:

Doubleday & Company, Inc.: From *The Glory Road* by Bruce Catton. Copyright 1952 by Bruce Catton. Reprinted by permission of Doubleday & Company, Inc.

Thomas Y. Crowell Company: From *South After Gettysburg: Letters of Cornelia Hancock, 1863–1868*, edited by Henrietta Stratton Jaquette.

The Georgetown University Press: From *John Dooley Confederate Soldier, His War Journal*, edited by Joseph T. Durkin, S.J.

Harcourt, Brace and World, Inc.: From *Abraham Lincoln: The War Years*, Vol. III, by Carl Sandburg.

J. B. Lippincott Company: From *The Twentieth Maine* by John J. Pullen.

The Macmillan Company: From *They Who Fought Here* by Bell Irvin Wiley and Hirst D. Milhollen. Reprinted by permission of The Macmillan Company.

Contents

GETTYSBURG

The Long Encampment

Chapter I

The Enemy Is Approaching

The rising tide of eastern light turned an intermittently cloudy sky into an opaque, pale red. Its faint illumination cast trees and hills into gray and black silhouettes, as though unreal in a strange summer land of only height and width. For the somewhat ragged pickets trekking through damp fields there was something alien about all of this, but the far-off sounds and near-by distinctions of dawn noises held an infinite familiarity for them—they did not differ from those they had heard on July mornings in Tennessee and Alabama.

To the rear the pickets could make out the indistinct form of their company following in a loose column along a gravelly road bounded by split-rail fences. Beyond, where the road blended and disappeared into the landscape in the west, was the dark outline of the South Mountain Range, and beyond this, if you followed the road far enough, was the town of Chambersburg, Pennsylvania. The pickets paused at the crest of a low ridge, the column still following. Suddenly there was a stir. Almost hidden in the dim light, and moving at a fast clip, a lone horseman rode down and away from the eastern approach of the slight ridge onto the flattened center land of a slow, shallow valley. There was something about him—a too-blatant urgency—which was alarming. The pickets raised their muskets and began firing at the insubstantial target, unfurling a coarse racket into the morning air.

Out on the low land the solitary rider drew up beside a scant bridge spanning the slim line of a grass-banked stream, and almost instantly several sharp flicks of light flashed out, followed by a strident *bang, bang, bang.*

A carbine! A Yankee!

As the sounds of the carbine echoed and faded, the rider turned his mount and bolted in a frantic gallop towards the far side of the valley and a second, somewhat higher ridge.

The road to Chambersburg from west of Gettysburg in 1863.

The Battle of Gettysburg had begun.

The background which led up to this exchange of shots on a July morning in Pennsylvania was wrapped up in the mystery of the past. There had been Yankee trader ships with cargoes of "black ivory"—slaves from Africa brought to toil in the New World and eventually haunt men into holy convictions of outrage or stiff-backed defense; and there had been the physical characteristic of the "peculiar institution" of slavery whereby it lent itself best to a southern climate and agriculture on a vast scale; and there had been a new country full of growing pains which were alleviated with the balm of indecisive legislation and the shortsightedness of imposing an arbitrary demarcation—the Mason-Dixon line—dividing states and territories into those which were "slave" and those which were not; and there had been, and was still, the issue of States' rights as opposed to the Federal Government of the United States. There were many things, and together they had caused a deep rift and created a North and a South.

The circumstances which impelled those men from Alabama and Tennessee to come to a little ridge in Pennsylvania had their beginnings at four-twenty in the morning of April 12, 1861, when the sovereign state of South Carolina opened fire on Fort Sumter, owned by the United States, in the bay of Charleston.

Newly elected President Lincoln, who had stated he was "morally opposed" to slavery but who as President did not intend to change its status, was not acceptable to many in the South, and therefore a case in point for the clatter of the guns at Charleston; but whatever the reasons, South Carolina had seceded from the union composing the United States, and Fort Sumter technically represented a foreign power within the state's sovereign borders. After April 12 and the later surrender of Fort Sumter the South had congealed into a confederation of ten states which then proceeded to do what the North felt it could not do: win battles.[1]

When the Confederate States of America won the first big battle of the war at a little, unheard-of place called Bull Run on July 21, 1861, the proposition for the North to put down the "insurrection" took a drastic change. It became necessary to initiate areas of operation in which the entire might of the North would be brought into play. These areas would be naval, western, and eastern. Naval operations would blockade all Southern ports. In the west Union forces would move to try to cut the Confederacy in half along a line corresponding to the Mississippi River. In the east a Union army would move through Virginia and seize the confederate capital at Richmond.

The naval blockade became one of the most successful operations of its type in history—the South was squeezed off from all but a trickle of imports from Europe. The western military operations were slow but in the main successful. The eastern operations, however, because of an obsession in Wash-

Cadillac Square, Detroit, Michigan, 1861. Michigan soldiers ready to leave for Washington.

ington with the idea of capturing Richmond, received great emphasis; and it was here that the North, despite a preponderance of strength, was completely frustrated. In its efforts to take Richmond, the North by mid-May, 1863, had lost the major battles of Bull Run, the Seven Days' Battle, Second Battle of Bull Run, Fredericksburg, and on May 1 to 4, 1863, Chancellorsville.

Only once, at the Battle of Antietam, did the North win a "victory." Here in September, 1862, by a little meandering creek in Maryland, the South's first massive invasion of the North was brought to a halt when Federal forces battered and rammed with bloody slaughter against the Army of Northern Virginia and finally forced it to withdraw. This "victory" was the moment President Lincoln had been waiting for to deliver his Emancipation Proclamation, thus changing the war from a political affair for preservation of the Union into a crusade to free the slaves. As an instrument of policy, the Emancipation Proclamation was designed to influence foreign opinion. Apart from its more lofty aspects, it was as valuable to the North as an additional army in the field: its issuance caused popular European sentiment to swing to the side of the North; and the last good hope in the South for direct foreign assistance and recognition began to fade.

High among the factors which brought Southern arms to dominate or at least check the North in Virginia was the Southern soldier. More at home with weapons and outdoor life than his Northern counterpart, he had adapted quite readily to military indoctrination. He also regarded the North as an invader, and this had produced a tenacious will to prevail.

Of equal, if not more, importance in frustrating the North was the emergence of one of the most able tactical generals in American history: Robert Edward Lee.

The term "written in the stars" could find no better embodiment than Robert E. Lee. Born to be a soldier, he was inexorably caught up by conditions over which he had no control. The fourth child of Henry "Light-Horse Harry" Lee, Revolutionary War general and hero, and his second wife, Ann Carter of Virginia, Robert E. Lee grew up in the tradition and background of two prominent families. This was his great heritage; and this, plus his own make-up, instilled in him a sense of duty from which he never varied towards all that he deemed honorable.

After a childhood which easily could have stifled his spirit—he bore a young man's mortification of knowing his father had to leave the country to avoid scandalous debts, and he patiently cared for his invalid mother over a long period of time—he entered the United States Military Academy. In

Robert E. Lee. Taken in 1863.

1829 he was graduated second in his class and without one demerit during the whole of his four years at the Academy. Twenty-three years later he returned as Superintendent.

In 1859 he was placed in charge of troops which stormed the U. S. Arsenal at Harper's Ferry, Maryland, to root out a band of antislavery insurrectionists. The day was October 16, and the first shudder of things to come could be seen in the wild eyes of the insurrectionist leader. His name was John Brown.

Robert E. Lee was a Lieutenant Colonel in the United States Army when Fort Sumter was fired upon.

On April 18, 1861, Lincoln, through the offices of General in Chief of the Army Winfield Scott, hero of the War of 1812 and the war with Mexico, offered Lee command of the Federal Army.[2] The following day Lee's home state of Virginia formally seceded from the Union. For Lee to accept Lincoln's offer meant taking the sword against his native state, friends, and relatives, against his own personal background, even against his home, Arlington, across the Potomac River from Washington and now the site of the Arlington National Military Cemetery. Lee understandably found it impossible to accept Lincoln's offer and after five days resigned his commission and rode sadly out of Washington on horseback. A man who had written his oldest son he could "anticipate no greater calamity for the country than a dissolution of the Union," Lee headed south towards history and a lost cause.

By the late spring of 1863, despite the recent brilliant victory at Chancellorsville, the star of the Confederate States had begun to wane. The Battle of Chancellorsville had cost the life of one of the South's greatest generals, Lieutenant General Thomas J. "Stonewall" Jackson (West Point, 1846), who was accidentally fired upon by his own men. (Lee exclaimed, when notified of Jackson's death, "I have lost my right arm.") Foreign recognition, so desperately needed, had not materialized. Out in the West a Union general, who had slowly and steadily proved his merit by winning, had slammed the heavy lid of siege on Vicksburg, the South's "Gibraltar of the West" on the Mississippi River. This was Major General Ulysses S. Grant (West Point, 1843), who was waging a relentless campaign to take Vicksburg and gain control of the entire Mississippi River.

Even more disastrous than the loss of Stonewall Jackson, the activities of Grant, and lack of foreign recognition, was the fact that a war of attrition had mantled itself around the South. The South, "the Cotton Kingdom," limited primarily to an agricultural economy, was slowly and inexorably losing to the artisans and abundant resources of the North. Despite battle-

6

field defeats the North was growing, expanding, until in the field of armament alone it was able to outproduce the South a thousandfold—factories in the North were turning out five thousand muskets a day as opposed to the feeble output of one hundred a day in the South.

Still, the war was far from over from the Southern standpoint, or, for that matter, from anybody's standpoint. On the firing line, in battle, and despite the North's preponderance of production, issues had a chance to be settled with finality. An invasion of the North might reap many benefits for the South: a victory on Northern soil could command foreign recognition, erase Grant's advantage at Vicksburg, and strengthen the demands by certain elements in the North for a negotiated peace. A complete defeat of the Union forces in the North would mean a victorious march on Washington and a dictated peace, and the permanent establishment of the Confederate States of America. The fading star of the Confederacy with one mighty stroke could be made to shine brighter than ever.

General Lee's Army of Northern Virginia was in high spirits. Though ill-equipped and lean and hungry, morale was excellent, while the enemy's soldiers, marching into defeat after defeat, were resigned, almost apathetic about their generals' abilities. The risks for an invasion of the North were great—the possible advantages, greater.

Accordingly, General Lee, who had taken over command of the Army of Northern Virginia in June, 1862, during the Seven Days' Battle, met in Richmond with Confederate President Jefferson Davis and his cabinet from May 14 to 17.[3] Lee's motives in invading the North were dictated not only by the overriding possibilities, but by the absolute necessity of procuring supplies for his army—the major portion of the fighting had been in Virginia

Fredericksburg, Virginia, 1863. Scene of a Northern attack in December, 1862, which ended in defeat for The Army of the Potomac.
Library of Congress

and the land had been depleted. If nothing else, it would take the war out of Virginia for a while. Davis and his cabinet approved Lee's plans by majority decision.

Sharing the jubilant feeling of his men that there was no enemy they could not whip, General Lee ordered his Army of Northern Virginia to prepare to break off from its defensive positions on the south side of the Rappahannock River around Fredericksburg, Virginia.

For the campaign Lee, handicapped by the death of Stonewall Jackson, reorganized his army of close to eighty thousand men into three large corps, totaling nine infantry divisions, and six cavalry brigades. Major General J. E. B. ("Jeb") Stuart—Lee had been commandant at West Point when Stuart graduated in 1854—was left in command of the cavalry. (Partly as it was the custom, and probably also out of a sense of vanity, thirty-year-old Jeb sported a full and luxuriant beard. It hid a receding chin which had earned him the twisted title of "Beaut" from his classmates at West Point.) Lieutenant General James Peter ("Pete") Longstreet (West Point, 1842) remained in charge of the I Corps. Major General Ambrose Power Hill (West Point, 1847) was upgraded to Lieutenant General to take the helm of a newly created III Corps. And recently commissioned Lieutenant General Richard Stoddard Ewell (West Point, 1840) was given the leadership of the II Corps, Stonewall Jackson's old command. (Ewell held a certain eminence through his great lack of hair and of course was nicknamed "Baldy." He also had lost a leg during an earlier battle of the war, and now he traveled with a horse and buggy. In battle he would mount up and have himself strapped to the saddle.)

Pete Longstreet did not share Lee's enthusiasm for this campaign. Longstreet indicated that he would assent to Lee's plans only if he (Lee) would make the invasion "offensive in strategy but defensive in tactics." This meant, regardless of circumstances, that the Army of Northern Virginia might maneuver into the North (*strategy*), but force the enemy to do the attacking (*tactics*). Lee never really concurred with this, but did acknowledge its logic. Longstreet misconstrued Lee's polite attention to his concepts as acceptance. This was fatal: Longstreet carried into the invasion a psychological block. He could not promptly and fully carry out orders which ran contrary to his idea of the right way to do things. And now, with the loss of Jackson, Lee would have to depend upon Longstreet as his most experienced officer.

Opposite the Army of Northern Virginia, on the north banks of the Rappahannock River around Falmouth, Virginia, the Union Army of the Poto-

Major General J. E. B. Stuart.

Lieutenant General James Longstreet.

Lieutenant General A. P. Hill.

Lieutenant General Richard Ewell.

mac, under General Joseph ("Fighting Joe") Hooker (West Point, 1837), was still upset about the way things had gone at the Battle of Chancellorsville. Yet it sensed that it was still an army of destiny. Despite the defeats, and they had happened with regularity, some place, some time, with the right leadership, that manifest destiny would be fulfilled. And new recruits were soon made aware that it was not the soldiers who had been licked—they were as good as any on earth—but rather the men at the top.

And if a recruit really felt put upon to ask about Hooker he probably would have gotten the stock answer of the Civil War soldier towards anything which invoked his cynicism: "Big thing! Big thing!" He probably would hear some more rather explicit thoughts, too.

Joe Hooker was just some more of the same old oats. He took good care of his soldiers, all right, but when it came to fighting he was not one whit better than his predecessor, General Burnside, at Fredericksburg. Burnside sacrificed twelve thousand boys in blue at Fredericksburg in useless infantry charges, but at least he had the decency to offer to lead a final charge himself. He was talked out of it, of course. Fighting Joe . . . Well, his uniforms came

Major General Joseph Hooker, commanding officer of the Army of the Potomac.

26th New York Infantry at drill.

from that fine Brooks Brothers Store in New York, but they weren't worth two cents to him when Bobby Lee finished with him at Chancellorsville. "May God have mercy on General Lee, for I shall have none." That's what he said before Chancellorsville. And then he swore off liquor for the campaign. And then a cannon ball struck his headquarters building. And then it struck Fighting Joe it was time to call a retreat. One thing certain, Hooker never should have sworn off liquor. That Bobby Lee was a caution, sure enough.

But whatever the gripe the enlisted soldiers had with Hooker's generalship, he was well thought of in terms of what he had done for the morale of the Army of the Potomac. Upon taking command in January, 1863, he began reorganization of the heretofore poorly grouped cavalry into what was becoming a highly efficient fighting force. And it was remembered long afterward how he had insisted on sprucing things up: clean quarters, daily inspections, drills, furloughs, and an unending supply of good and plentiful food. Freshly baked bread, meat, and vegetables seemed to overflow in a vast, unending bounty. Only in one area did Hooker's standards for food fall short. This was a patented process for dried, or desiccated, vegetables. They weren't very good, and with the age-old ability of soldiers to mispronounce in the right key, the vegetables were referred to as "desecrated."

Hooker also had inspired organizational pride by issuing little cloth badges to his soldiers. Designed in various shapes and colors and sewn to the soldiers' caps, they indicated the different corps and divisions—a practice still in effect in the form of shoulder patches on modern United States Army uniforms.

Hooker later proved he left much to be desired as a general in battle, but his efforts in lifting the tone and spirit of the soldiers under him were rewarded. Even after the defeat at Chancellorsville morale did not fall into hopelessness.

11

Officers' Mess, Company F, 93rd New York Infantry.

On June 1, Hooker had an army of seven infantry corps and eight cavalry brigades, numbering slightly more than one hundred thousand men.

The sun came up early on the morning of June 3, and before its heat could burn off the low fog of dawn, soldiers from Longstreet's I Corps took to the road and began trekking westward towards the Blue Ridge Mountains.

Lee's plans called for a westward march past the Blue Ridge, and then a right wheel down the Shenandoah Valley into Maryland and Pennsylvania with an eventual thrust to seize Harrisburg and Baltimore, and even Philadelphia. (The vernacular of the time described a movement north along the Shenandoah Valley as *down*.) The Blue Ridge would act as a screen between his forces and Hooker's.

On June 4 and 5 Baldy Ewell's II Corps joined the long lines moving west, no doubt with Ewell jogging along in his horse and buggy wondering if he could fill Stonewall Jackson's shoes.

By any standards it was a motley-looking army which stretched across the country roads of Virginia. The classic gray uniforms the South had adopted at the beginning of the war for the most part were gone, worn out. And in the South uniform replacement was a hard thing to come by—woolens had to come from Europe past a naval blockade. The men who marched for "the cause" on those early June days of 1863 were dressed in a variety of clothing, very little of which had uniformity—trousers and shirts made of homespun, colored an off-shade of brown from a dye made of butternuts, battered hats of several varieties, old civilian jackets and overalls dominated

12

the attire. And a lot of the men marched off in their bare feet. The South had courage, plenty of it, but it was no match for the North in the thousand and one things necessary to run a war. A simple item such as a canteen had to be made of cedar wood. There was no tin in the South. Yet, with their "trademark" of a toothbrush worn jauntily in a buttonhole and a blanket slung across a shoulder, these men of the Army of Northern Virginia were infinitely more than a great horde of ragamuffins. In spite of appearances, with their indispensable muskets, they were in truth the finest fighting infantrymen in the world.

With the movement of the II Corps on June 4 and 5, two-thirds of Lee's forces were on the road. If General Hooker now took it upon himself suddenly to launch an attack in a southerly direction, he would be opposed only by A. P. Hill's III Corps, still in line around Fredericksburg. And Hooker did move.

He already had definite information that the status quo of Lee's army had altered drastically. An observation balloon had been sent aloft, and the Confederates were seen marching by the left flank in long columns of infantry, artillery, and wagon trains. On June 6 Hooker threw a pontoon bridge across the Rappahannock. After a furious bombardment he sent infantrymen scurrying over the bridge, and immediately it looked as if something were up. Lee halted the advance of Ewell's corps. If this were a full-scale maneuver, it would be necessary to turn the corps about and send it back on the double. Then it all petered out. Hooker really had nothing more in mind than reconnaissance. Ewell was ordered to continue on towards the Blue Ridge, and the action, such as it was, was called the Battle of Franklin's Crossing, the first of many minor skirmishes and battles connected with the Gettysburg Campaign.

Now, as Ewell and Longstreet's men put distance between themselves and the Army of the Potomac, the invasion was fully committed. For better or worse the men of the South must push into the North, down dusty roads into

The 16th New York Infantry stands for inspection.

a land ripe with the good things Northern farmers had grown, the necessary things Northern factories had produced. There was a large plum to be plucked and they meant to have it.

It was on Monday, June 8, that Jeb Stuart, filled with the spirit of a medieval cavalier, brought to a finish what in part might aptly be termed a pageant.

Stuart and his cavalry were at a rendezvous point in the little town of Culpeper, Virginia, and on the preceding Thursday evening a full-dress military ball had been given by the officers at the Culpeper Court House, young ladies of the area swinging crinoline-covered hoops in the quadrille and making the proper gestures of helplessness to Jeb's stalwart "knights." The following day a great review of massed cavalry was held in the long, wide fields adjacent to Culpeper. Spectators were treated to the sight of the General and his staff reviewing a mile-and-a-half-long line of men and their horses. A little later on there was the thrilling and to some young ladies entirely overwhelming sight of thousands of cavalrymen, sabers drawn, horses reined to full gallop, passing in a thunderous charge, while from a nearby hill twenty-four cannon belched out stupendous noise with blank charges. As a spectacle there had never been anything like it.

That same evening there was another ball; only this time it was held under

Soldiers of 71st New York Infantry "horse it up" for the photographer.

A Northern observation balloon—Fair Oaks, Virginia, May 31, 1862.

the stars, while sparkling bonfires lit up the fields and radiated on the happy, youthful faces of officers and their ladies.

It was on Monday, however, that the more serious aspects of military life for Stuart's squadrons were realized. General Lee himself was at Culpeper to inspect the cavalry of his army. It was not the riotous demonstration of Friday, the cavalrymen passing in review at a walk, yet General Lee must have been impressed with the vastness of his mounted army: nearly ten thousand horsemen paraded in a long line under a warm, early summer sun.

Considering the fact that Lee's army was in the process of staging an invasion, the past few days had been unique, but as the late-afternoon shadows

15

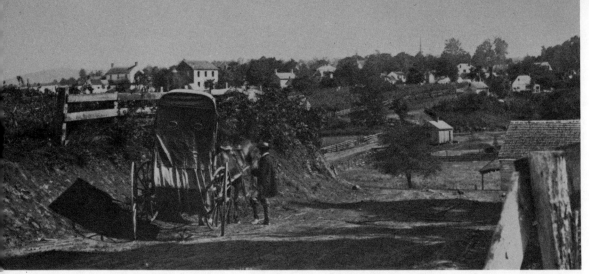

Culpeper, Virginia. In the foreground is photographer Matthew Brady, who, with his assistants and at his own expense, photographed the operations annd battles of the Army of the Potomac. Brady is standing beside his traveling "darkroom." Soldiers in the Army of the Potomac referred to his photographic wagon as a "What Is It?"

stretched over the land around Culpeper on Monday, June 8, Jeb Stuart probably had the feeling it had been time well spent.

That night, with most of their equipage stored away in wagons ready to move out, Stuart and his men slept peacefully in the fields of Virginia. And in the darkness thoughts of the Yankees and of States' rights ebbed and flowed away in the summer stillness.

One hundred miles to the north, waiting unaware, serenely peaceful, was the town of Gettysburg, Pennsylvania. Founded in the year 1781 and named after John Gettys, to whom the land had been deeded by William Penn, in its eighty-two-year history Gettysburg had grown into a prosperous farm town with the added distinction of having two colleges, Pennsylvania College just north of town, and, on a wooded ridge slightly to the west, a Lutheran theological seminary. Unlike so many little country towns dotting rural America in the 1860's, however, Gettysburg had become the hub of a network of ten roads, a fact which a traveler, or for that matter a military strategist, would rank as significant.

On the night of June 8 the bells of Gettysburg sounded the late hours. Their smooth, benign tones coasted over dew-soaked meadows, past the theological seminary, down into cool glens, and up onto wooded hills, and were lost, slowly, in the quiet drift of that long-ago night in June.

The next morning the perverse fortunes of war hit Jeb Stuart and his

16

legions with jarring and rude abruptness. Union cavalrymen—men who for
the most part had had to learn to seat a horse before they could be taught
cavalry tactics—and a few infantry soldiers, ten thousand in all, forded the
Rappahannock River and moved in on Stuart's cavalry quite unnoticed,
catching them all off guard at a little whistle stop near Culpeper named
Brandy Station. It was an audacious move by cavalry which up to this point
had suffered practically nothing but defeat and humiliation at the hands of
"born to the saddle" and hitherto superior Southern horsemen; but they were
learning—Hooker wanted information, and he was going to get it with a
vengeance.

Under the leadership of Major General Alfred Pleasonton (West Point,
1844), a dandy who wore white gauntlets and a perky little straw hat, the
Union cavalry hit the astounded Confederates with the greatest weapon of
war—surprise—and quickly began smashing them apart. With Pleasonton
were some rather unique subordinates:

Colonel Hugh Judson Kilpatrick (West Point, 1861), a young officer who
affected fluffy, unruly sideburns, and who was dubbed "Kill Cavalry" for his
knack of taking cavalry off on wild-goose chases without realizing he was
running it ragged; a soldier of fortune from England, just possibly brought in
for good measure, with the highly improbable name of Sir Percy Windham;
and a young man of twenty-three named George Armstrong Custer (West

George Armstrong Custer,
a Brigadier General
at the time
of Gettysburg.

The National Archives

Brigadier General
W. H. Fitzhugh Lee.

Library of Congress

Point, 1861). Custer, along with a rather weedy mustache and flaxen hair, which hung about his ears in what one contemporary writer described as "sparse, dry ringlets," dressed in an outlandish uniform of tight black velvet trousers with gold lace trim and the modified jacket of a Hungarian cavalry officer. He was aptly likened to "a circus rider gone mad."

But, notwithstanding idiosyncrasies and names, on this morning the Union cavalry was out to give Jeb Stuart and his men a lesson. And they did just that in what was to turn into the biggest cavalry fight of the war.

Stuart's legions rallied after the initial onslaught and counterattacked and, in turn, were almost taken in a flanking movement. And in the dust and smoke and confusion of pounding hoofs and yelling and shooting, squadrons got lost and galloped right out of the fight; overheated carbines blew up in the faces of dismounted Union cavalrymen; Confederate horse artillery blasted away at the head of an advancing column only to find they were shooting at their own men; and until late in the afternoon it was a tossup who was winning. Finally, Pleasonton's tired legions were recalled—word had arrived of the approach of a large body of Confederate infantry. They high-tailed it back across the Rappahannock with the information Hooker wanted. And they had it in spades: an officer had been captured with papers telling of Lee's orders for an immediate advance into Pennsylvania.

The Battle of Brandy Station ended in a victory of sorts for Jeb Stuart— his troopers had killed, wounded, and captured 936 Yankees and held the field at the end of the day. But it was not without costs. His forces had suffered 523 casualties; among them was one of his best officers, Brigadier

18

General William Henry Fitzhugh Lee, second eldest son of Robert E. Lee, who received a severe leg wound. And Stuart had had to suffer the galling experience of watching his horsemen not only caught off guard, but almost taking a beating at the hands of an enemy suddenly become brazen enough to attack, and attack with vigor and purpose. His legions, only a day after a grand review, had not won a thrilling, outright, story-book victory. Stuart was mortified. His exaggerated sense of chivalry would have to be vindicated.

With his plumed hat (he really wore one) and his troubadour (he actually had one) and his bold "knights" (most of whom were equipped with the same "armor" of homespun and hodgepodge dress as the infantry), he would meet the foe again and sweep him from the field.

The affair at Brandy Station created a mental kink in Stuart which was to have significant bearing on the fighting at Gettysburg, twenty-two days away.

The events of June 9 did not cause General Lee to alter his plans: Ewell's II Corps swung into the lead and cut through the Blue Ridge Mountains at Chester Gap into the Shenandoah Valley.

In Washington there was an uproar over Lee's adventure. *What was Hooker going to do?* Hooker had a plan: he would attack en masse towards

Capitol, Washington, 1863. Note that dome has not yet been completed.

Richmond. Logically, it had some merit. It would tend to force Lee to call a retrograde movement of his invasion, and would place the initiative in Hooker's hands.

The War Department in Washington, ever mindful of any threat to Washington (*If Hooker crashed down on Richmond why couldn't Lee swing around and take Washington?*), turned Hooker's plans down. General in chief of the North's combined armies, Major General Henry W. Halleck (West Point, 1839), relayed the War Department's sentiments by ordering Hooker to maintain his army between Lee's forces and the Capital. This preoccupation with the defense of Washington had created a sharp division between the military and the War Department. Generals McDowell, McClellan, Pope, and Burnside, all of whom had either once commanded the Army of the Potomac or led troops in the North's efforts to take Richmond, had been plagued with it. Hooker was no exception. With his proposal turned down, Hooker, upset about his own authority to institute and carry out plans, grew grumpy and did nothing. About this time he must have had a sense of things to come: Major General D. N. Couch (West Point, 1846) resigned in protest against Hooker from command of the II Corps, Army of the Potomac.

West of the Blue Ridge Ewell's soldiers swung into a right turn and headed down the Shenandoah Valley. As they moved they began to pick up steam, bowling over everything in their path.

By June 14 elements of Ewell's II Corps were at the outskirts of Winchester, Virginia. In Winchester there was a Federal garrison; out in front of Winchester fortifications had been thrown up.

With a dispatch worthy of his predecessor, Stonewall Jackson, most noted

Major General
Jubal Early.

Library of Congress

Pontoon bridge across the Potomac River, 1862.

for his fast, hard-hitting flanking maneuvers, Ewell sent Major General Jubal ("Jube") Early (West Point, 1837) and his division scooting around the fortifications; and, after a savage artillery duel, stormed in and crumpled the Federal troops on June 15. General Milroy, the commanding Federal officer, succeeded in escaping, but he left behind four thousand prisoners and twenty-five cannon. The "risks" of the invasion were beginning to pay off. The Second Battle of Winchester (Winchester would have three such battles before the war was over) did not delay Ewell's long-range objectives. While Confederates stormed over the parapets at Winchester, still others were streaming north towards the Potomac River where a crossing would be made into the town of Williamsport, Maryland.

Pontoon bridges were placed across the Potomac in the Williamsport area and everything proceeded with smooth, flawless ease, Ewell's artillery, wagons, and men sliding neatly into Maryland.

On June 19 the van of the II Corps reached as far as Hagerstown, Maryland, ten miles from the Pennsylvania border.

With the II Corps having its own way about things Pete Longstreet's I Corps, which had marched as far as Culpeper, now began its movements northward. Staying east of the Blue Ridge Mountains in the initial phase, the corps then plunged westward through the Blue Ridge Mountains at Snicker's and Ashby's Gaps, and followed in the general direction of Ewell's II Corps down the Shenandoah Valley.

When Longstreet's men reached the Potomac they ran into what might be termed a military ceremonial problem. The pontoon bridges were jammed with horse- and mule-drawn vehicles. But the water was low, and many

Men of the 22nd New York State Militia.

of the foot soldiers were obliged to wade across the river at a near-by ford. Soldiers removed their shoes and trousers and rolled them into bundles, which, with their cartridge cases and muskets, they held over their heads. It so happened, as one group of men approached the center of the Potomac, some young ladies from Maryland on an outing into Virginia, using the same ford, splashed across in carriages. The exigencies of the situation made it necessary for the half-clad Confederates to "pass in review" before the demure ladies. But with carriages going one way and the men another, it was a very brief "review."

On June 15, the day Ewell's men gobbled up Winchester, A. P. Hill's III Corps was directed to start a long rear-guard movement on the same general line of march Ewell had used.

And with Jeb Stuart's cavalry ranged east of the Blue Ridge Mountains, screening the Army of Northern Virginia, and trying to keep tab on General Hooker and his Army of the Potomac, all elements of Lee's forces were now moving, making the mighty stroke into the North a total reality.

And that it was a mighty stroke was fully reflected by a North suddenly seized with panic. President Lincoln issued a call for troops to serve for six months or less to put down "armed insurrectionary combinations threatening

22

to make inroads" into the North. Governor Andrew Curtin of Pennsylvania sounded the alarm with a widely distributed handbill: "The Enemy Is Approaching," in which an appeal was made for companies of state militia to come to the defense of Pennsylvania. The governors of New York and New Jersey sent over some nattily attired regiments; and after some squabbling about taking an oath to serve the Federal Government (as state militia these regiments were separate and distinct from Federal authority), these units along with those of Pennsylvania came to total the amazing number of fifty thousand men. Their effectiveness, however, in halting Lee's army was not the equivalent of much more than a few bee stings.

About twenty thousand state militia troops were placed under the command of General Couch, the same soldier who had left the Army of the Potomac in protest against Hooker. These were to defend Harrisburg, an eventuality never realized. The rest were rather loosely scattered, and this, plus sketchy and inadequate training, rendered their efforts almost ineffectual. Some units stood the test of bravery, and some started running fast and far at the approach of the Confederates. The very hard fact of the matter was that there was only one organization which, if anything were to do it, could stop General Lee and the Army of Northern Virginia: the Army of the Potomac.

And evidence indicated that the Army of the Potomac was about to try.

On the night of June 13 Hooker, finally over his pique with the authorities in Washington, sent his army marching north on a line parallel to Lee east of the Blue Ridge Mountains. He would obey to the letter his instructions to

Union soldiers at Harper's Ferry ready to move out. Note fixed bayonets.

maintain the Army of the Potomac between the Confederates and Washington.

That General Hooker was thorough (this characteristic somehow seemed to desert him in battle) was manifest in his competent handling of his army. For the march he divided it into two wings, with the I, III, and XI Corps as the left wing under the command of Major General John Reynolds (West Point, 1841). The right wing, the II, V, VI, and XII Corps, he kept directly under his own command. The cavalry under General Pleasonton was to maintain itself in the front and flanks of the army, with probing attacks towards the Blue Ridge.

That Hooker could be decisive, if he wished, was indicated in the manner in which he drove his forces north. Many veterans, recalling the events in June and July, 1863, felt the worst aspect of the entire campaign was by and large the marching. This had to be done in Government-issued shoes in which, due to the fact that mass-manufactured shoes of that era had no right and left, it was a tossup which would mold to contour first, the foot or the shoe.

Summer was over the land, and for the first few days of marching it was hot and dry. Blue uniforms soon turned white in floury layers of dust kicked up in thick swirls from the dirt roads. And sunstroke and prostration hit men by the scores.

Slowly at first, and then with alarming haste, the world would tilt, the columns up ahead would shimmer and dance about as in a mirage; and, if he could make it the staggering soldier went to the side of the road before he collapsed. A friend might help him, but regulations wouldn't allow him to stay, and the chances were good he would never see him again. Many Northern soldiers just lay down and died on the side of the road that June, victims of the enervating heat and total exhaustion.

And there was dysentery, the bugaboo of both armies. It claimed more victims than the battles and was always present—the idea of sterile water was unknown—and it marched along with the men, weakening and terrible.

And horses, too, fell victim to the broiling early summer weather. Urged on to the point of exhaustion, many of the pitiful animals were abandoned as useless. After a little rest, out of habit, they would often fall in with a passing column. For a few enterprising infantrymen they were like a well in a desert. Until spied by a ranking officer, who couldn't quite see it as the proper way to do things, there would be a "march" astride a friendly stray.

After a few days of intensive legging it across the rural countryside of Virginia the Army of the Potomac was stretched out from the Bull Run Mountains, a lesser range east of the Blue Ridge, almost up to the Potomac River, the boundary between Maryland and Virginia.

Part of the army had to pass through the Bull Run battlefield (ten months earlier Lee and Stonewall Jackson had given the Union forces a thorough going over at Bull Run) and there were gruesome reminders for the soldiers that at the end of their hard march among the many things they could expect was Death. Hastily dug graves had come uncovered, and the remains of bodies with bleached, dry bones, sunlight filtering through disoriented ribs and tatters of rotting clothing, beckoned spectrally. The soldiers kept walking.

And if you could have listened to all the chatter and cussing and imprecations against the weather, this officer and that officer, the Rebels, and especially the marching, you would have heard the voices and dialects of many European nations. The Army of the Potomac had many recruits from foreign lands, immigrants who had come to the New World to take their chances and found themselves caught up, one way or the other, in an ever increasing war effort. Very often these men would be "bounty soldiers." In an effort to raise armies, both the North and the South used the bounty system, whereby various sums, depending upon length of enlistment, were offered as an inducement to volunteer. In the North, the sum grew to a fairly stable figure of three hundred dollars. Three hundred dollars was a fortune for a new arrival in this country, and with a base pay of thirteen dollars a month, plus board, it was not a bad deal. Also, the Homestead Act had been passed by Congress in 1862, whereby for a very nominal sum a man could own 160 acres of land in the West. If a man were willing to hazard the terrible risks of battle and disease, with three hundred dollars to his credit and the opportunity to settle on his own land after the war he had the opportunity for a mighty good future. Many American families got their start with this combination.[4]

On Wednesday, June 24, advance elements of the Army of the Potomac were at Edward's Ferry, Virginia, on the south bank of the Potomac River.

It was on June 25 that the Battle of Brandy Station began to come full round. The humiliation Jeb Stuart had suffered at the hands of Yankee cavalry on June 9 was suddenly to be rectified, or at least Stuart saw it in this light.

Stuart and his cavalry were east of the Blue Ridge Mountains, blocking off passes and screening the Army of Northern Virginia over in the Shenandoah

Thomas T. Munford,
cavalry officer
under Jeb Stuart.

Valley. At Aldie, Middleburg, and Upperville, Virginia, there had been spirited cavalry clashes. But, as at Brandy Station, Stuart found that the Union cavalry was aggressive and more than willing to fight. It was good. Very good. What Stuart needed was something big, something spectacular. The almost daily cavalry ·tilts had proved no more than the insolence of the Yankees.

On June 23 Stuart had received a rather vague written order from General Lee advising him the sooner he crossed north of the Potomac River into Maryland the better, but that he was to use his own judgment on how this could best be done. There was a suggestion in the order that Stuart might ride around the Army of the Potomac and connect up with Ewell's II Corps in Maryland or Pennsylvania. This latter suggestion presupposed certain conditions, the foremost being that the Army of the Potomac was not moving. (There was intelligence to the fact that the Army of the Potomac was stationary at the moment. Stuart and his men could slip through or below the various elements. If the Army of the Potomac were on the move, long-drawn-out columns would block all the roads.) There was implied discretion in this order, but its most important feature was that Stuart was to cross the Potomac River as soon as possible.

A ride around the Army of the Potomac! The idea fitted Stuart's temperament like his plumed hat. This was that spectacular something Stuart had yearned for. And what could be better than a hell-bent-for-leather sweep around the Yankees? It would brighten his tarnished ego and dispel any doubts that his cavalry was anything but superior. There was no question of discretion—the cavalry would maneuver around the Army of the Potomac!

In concept it was not too far-fetched. The year before, during the Peninsular Campaign, Stuart had led his troopers in a wild ride around the Federal forces, pursued with singular lack of success by a pack of cavalry under General Philip St. George Cooke (West Point, 1827). Cooke was Stuart's father-in-law.[5]

During the evening of June 24 five thousand Southern cavalrymen gathered at a staging area near Salem, Virginia, and waited for the command "to horse." A moon in its first half hung for a while in the western skies and then settled slowly back of the rim of the Blue Ridge, leaving the land mantled in darkness. In a week the moon would hang high and full and slow above Pennsylvania hills and valleys. A lot of men would remember that moon the rest of their lives—and others would never have the chance to remember.

Finally, at one o'clock in the morning of June 25, the order was passed, and Stuart's edgy legions headed east. General Lee would get one message from Stuart, and then not hear from him again until the afternoon of the second day's fighting at Gettysburg.

The role of cavalry was multipurposed in the Civil War, to stage raids, guard communications and supplies, mask army maneuvers, and occasionally act as a fast striking force; but its greatest service was reconnaissance—to be the "eyes and ears" of an army. Stuart's service to Lee in this last function was now suddenly reduced to zero. The Army of Northern Virginia would have to grope its way blindly in relation to General Hooker and the Army of the Potomac.

Technically, General Lee had enough cavalry to render adequate reconnaissance: Stuart had left behind two cavalry brigades, and there were two

Southern cavalrymen captured at Aldie, Virginia.

detached cavalry brigades with the Confederates in the Shenandoah Valley. But Lee had come to depend upon Stuart alone for intelligence of the enemy. Stuart was gone, and General Lee had lost his eyes and ears.

At dawn of June 25, under a mizzling, gray sky, Stuart's cavalry passed through the Bull Run Mountains and bumped into thousands of blue-jacketed soldiers wearing trefoil badges in their caps—men of the Army of the Potomac's II Corps. They were moving north, on the line of march Stuart intended to follow. Stuart sent a few shells lobbing into the nearest troops of the II Corps, and then withdrew and made camp as the skies opened up in a heavy rain. It was at this point he sent his only communication to General Lee during the circuit of the Federal army, this to the effect that Hooker's II Corps was moving north.

June 26: Stuart made a quarter wheel and headed southeast—he would get below the moving columns. His prime purpose was to move north, and now he was pushing in an opposite direction.

By midmorning of the twenty-seventh his columns had been on the roads better than fifty hours and had covered only thirty-four miles. Horses began to weary. And the countryside was plucked clean as a bone by the passing Federal troops.

At last the rear-guard elements of blue-clad soldiers passed Stuart's front, and his anxious horsemen reined their mounts in a long arc which eventually put them in a northeast direction into a region untouched by predatory Yankees. Forage was the order, and more hours of delay were spent in resting and feeding the horses.

On June 28 the plodding campaigners at last forded the Potomac River and crossed into Maryland. But they were far to the east of the Blue Ridge from whence they had started, and the Maryland border follows the Potomac in a southeast direction; hence actually they were only fourteen miles farther north than they had been three days earlier.

This same day they ran into another obstacle to any sort of a prompt juncture with Ewell's II Corps: the spoils of war.

Chasing a Federal wagon train almost into the outskirts of Washington, Stuart's soldiers captured 125 spanking new wagons, complete with sleek mules. And the wagons were loaded with goodies: oats and corn, welcome enough for the horses, crackers and hams and bacon—and whiskey. It was a wonderful, marvelous, fantastic haul.

Stuart viewed the captured wagons as tangible evidence of his cavalry's prowess. The wagons, mules and all, would have to be taken back to Virginia.

The booty-burdened cavalrymen pushed deeper into Maryland, wagons in tow, and time had already begun to run out.

On the night of June 28 the light of the moon caught the glint and shimmer of scabbards and bridle rings as the Southern horsemen kept to the road. Tired, falling asleep in their saddles, they plodded along with their captured wagons and their now paling dream of a heroic and stirring ride around the enemy.

Shortly after midnight they made camp, and with lonely, sleepy sentinels thrown out on guard mount, the exhausted men sprawled in fields and forgot about the war and the Army of the Potomac amidst the familiar, musky odors of animals.

Once dawn broke the troopers would lean to their saddles, leather rubbing in a muffled rasp, and would push up through Maryland, past Cooksville to Hood's Mill, to cut telegraph lines and tear up railroad tracks. They would learn that Ewell's II Corps had reached Pennsylvania, and find themselves

Railroad tracks torn up near Gettysburg. Note broken telegraph wires.

attacked by the 1st Delaware Cavalry at Westminster. The attack would be beaten off, and Westminster would have supplies, and a night's stop to replenish would further slow them down.

June 30: Hanover, Pennsylvania, will fall into the line of march, and an old antagonist will appear—Judson Kilpatrick and a command of Union cavalry. Kilpatrick will attack and nearly capture Stuart himself.

July 1: The presence of Kilpatrick's cavalry will force a detour. In a wide arc which brings the groggy troopers almost due north of Gettysburg, they will arrive at Carlisle too late to connect up with Baldy Ewell, who had left Carlisle the day before. Men of the horse artillery, too tired to remember how or where they unlimbered their cannon, will destroy a Federal cavalry barracks at Carlisle. And Stuart will get the fateful word there has been heavy fighting at Gettysburg. . . .

And General Lee would be, as he stated in his official report, "embarrassed" by Stuart's continued absence. . . . The moon on the morning of June 29 retreated westward in a precise line, and in the short, quiet hours before dawn its light angled gently in a misty sheen over the fields of Maryland and over Stuart's ghostly legions in a time when men of war owed much to their horses. . . .

The gray light of dawn cut up through a sheen of fine mist on the morning of June 24, the day before Stuart and his men rode off into the blue. It spread over twinkling fields and captured the glint of muskets at "right shoulder." It grew over long strung-out columns of men, plodding along damp country roads. The morning air, clean and moist, lent a snap and vigor to the "route-stepping" soldiers, and before eight o'clock they had put a lot of distance between themselves and last night's bivouac. These were men of Ewell's II Corps, and they had come all the way down the Shenandoah Valley into its upper reaches in Pennsylvania where the name changes to the Cumberland Valley, and which curves slowly to end near Harrisburg and the Susquehanna River. These men of Ewell's had crossed the Mason-Dixon line, the symbolic line established to separate the nonslave states and territories from those maintaining slaves, and they were now in the country of the North.[6]

Right and left of them were lands bursting with the fruits of early summer, the efforts of prosperous hard-working Pennsylvania farmers. Country boys from the back sections of North Carolina and Georgia who, when they first had been called to arms, thought they were going off to fight the British, and whose only association with slavery consisted of once or twice seeing a slave auction in the "city," viewed with the delighted eye of those who understood the soil the neatly fenced fields of grain ripening into a yellow gold, the vast, rolling expanse of ripe cherry orchards, the sleek dairy herds and trim, spick-and-span farm buildings. And there was even enough to allow fields to fallow with mantles of white daisies. *This beat all hell out of that piece of "bottom land" back home. Still, you could do a lot with the right land....*

Up ahead the sound of a regimental band cut through the ever-present treading and clumping and shuffle. A church spire hove into view. They were coming to the town of Chambersburg, Pennsylvania, key town in the Cumberland Valley, and some officer with a flair for the dramatic had ordered those "tootling fellows" to strike up an appropriate tune.

The citizens could hear the music, too—"Bonnie Blue Flag" rendered with pomp and flourish. These weren't the first Confederates to pass—the day before a brigade of cavalry had stomped through and camped north of the town. And the day before the arrival of the cavalry, like a drove of geese, citizens from below Chambersburg piled through the town with horses, livestock, and personal belongings heaped high into wagons—civilians fleeing the terror of an avenging host: *The Confederates are coming and they're taking everything. Oh, they don't plunder! General Lee won't allow it. They just requisition everything and pay you with Confederate money.*

Many citizens of Chambersburg took heed of the type of payment Lee's soldiers handed out and went north with as much of their earthly goods as they could take. Others hid flour and bacon and anything else worth hiding in cellars and back rooms. One enterprising Confederate investigated this latter fact and nearly had his head bashed in by an irate, ax-wielding girl who caught him snooping in her father's cellar. He was Major Todd, President Lincoln's brother-in-law.

At nine o'clock the van of Ewell's corps passed the town square and headed out to encamp north of Chambersburg. Throughout the day immense mule-drawn wagon trains, cattle (meat was an "on the hoof" business in both armies), artillery, and long columns of infantry (about ten thousand soldiers) passed through Chambersburg. Baldy Ewell himself arrived in a buggy drawn by two horses with a mounted escort; and then it began for the citizens still in Chambersburg. Requisitions. And they were quite fantastic:

Five thousand suits of clothing, ten thousand pounds of sole leather, fifty thousand pounds of bread, eleven thousand pounds of coffee, one hundred thousand pounds of hard bread, twenty-five barrels of sauerkraut. (Sauerkraut was an antidote for dysentery, and the Confederates felt that as long as they were in a section of the country heavily populated by citizens of Dutch and Germanic origin, sauerkraut should be found in abundance.) The list seemed endless—so many currycombs, this many horseshoe nails, ad infinitum.

The items, which of course could never be furnished in the amounts requested, were an indication of the desperate need Lee's army had for supplies.

The authorities of Chambersburg to whom the requisitions were directed pointed out the impossibility of compliance. And if the Confederates were going to burn the town they had only to do it.

No . . . the Confederates weren't in Pennsylvania to burn and plunder. The shops and stores, then, of Chambersburg must be opened and goods exchanged for Confederate money. And so it was. Soldiers descended on the merchants and bought and bought and paid and paid with Confederate money. (The burning of Chambersburg would come a year later when two Confederate cavalry brigades, upon the inability of the citizens to supply $100,000 in gold as reprisal for Federal vandalism in West Virginia, would set the torch to the place.)

Chambersburg in 1864 after Confederates burned it.

Another odd requisition, which was realized, was a printing press. The Confederates, certain of ultimate success, printed thousands of paroles with the intention of issuing them to prisoners of war after they had defeated the Army of the Potomac.

On June 25, during a drizzling rain, more soldiers of Baldy Ewell's II Corps slogged past the Chambersburg square. And behind this vast array of soldiers were immense wagon trains loaded with plunder. And behind the wagon trains, "so completely was the country through which the Confederate army passed robbed and plundered," wrote Lieutenant Colonel Fremantle, a British observer with the Army of Northern Virginia, "that, all the cattle and farm horses having been seized by General Ewell, farm labor had come to a standstill."

And down the road a bit were the corps of A. P. Hill and Pete Longstreet converging on Chambersburg. The following day the Army of Northern Virginia, using Chambersburg as a pivotal point, would begin to divide and fan out into lower Pennsylvania, some elements following the long curve of the Cumberland Valley and others wheeling right to cut through the South Mountain Range towards Gettysburg and York on the Chambersburg Pike. (As with the change in name of the Shenandoah Valley in Pennsylvania, the Blue Ridge Mountains in the northern extension become the South Mountain Range.)

On this day, Friday, June 26, General Lee rode into Chambersburg. One citizen, remembering Lee long after the war, wrote that Lee looked every inch a soldier as he sat on his horse by the town square, and ". . . his whole appearance indicated dignity, composure and disregard for the gaudy trappings of war and the honor attaching [to] his high station." Whether Northerner or Southerner, Lee never failed to impress all who saw him.

Lee immediately set up headquarters in a grove just east of town and followed the movements of his forces, all except for Jeb Stuart's cavalry. No one had heard from Jeb in the last thirty hours. But Lee was confident. He understood his soldiers and felt "there were never such men in any army." This confidence was not misplaced. They would go any place and do anything asked of them. This they had proved time and time again. It was also reasonably safe to assume Hooker's army was far back in Virginia. Lee was entirely aware of the Federal Government's predilection for guarding Washington at all costs.

As General Lee arrived at the town square in Chambersburg, Jube Early's Division of Ewell's II Corps, cutting due east through the South Mountain

General Lee astride his horse Traveller, 1862.

Range, came upon the ironworks of Congressman Thaddeus Stevens, an uncompromising foe of the South. (Stevens would become the leader of a faction in Congress which would implement harsh terms for the South after the war and also try to impeach President Andrew Johnson for his adherence to Lincoln's policies of a "soft" peace.) The ironworks were burned to the ground.

Still later in the day Early's men bumped into a group of Pennsylvania militia just west of Gettysburg along the Chambersburg Pike. After a brief and rather mild exchange of shots, they gathered in 175 prisoners and continued their march into the streets of Gettysburg, a village of no more than twenty-five hundred people. The usual requisitions were made and, as usual, could not be met. But it really was not important: Jube's soldiers were tired, and besides they were en route to York, which would probably yield much finer booty. They camped outside town that night; but they didn't know, nobody knew, that they would remember Gettysburg better than any place they had seen in the entire campaign.

In Chambersburg, on June 27, Pete Longstreet's I Corps trudged into town, and the citizens, among them a strong contingent of women, still curious about Southern soldiers, lined the streets and doorways to see them. If nothing else, the number of Confederates attested they had strength, and they were in Pennsylvania to prove it. But for some of the women spectators the mighty host held no awe.

One young lady hurled a biting remark at the passing soldiers when she likened them to the Pharaoh's army marching to the Red Sea. And as the division of Major General John B. Hood (West Point, 1853) clumped by the town square, it was met by jeers and catcalls. The corps was composed of men from Texas, Alabama, Arkansas, Georgia, and South Carolina, who had marched hard and long and were muddy and grimy and, as so many other Confederates, were dressed in ragged clothing and barefooted. Lieutenant Colonel Fremantle, who kept a record of his observations, tells of a rather alarming woman who decided to give visible proof of her exact feelings:

> One female had seen fit to adorn her ample bosom with a huge Yankee flag, and she stood at the door of her house, her countenance expressing the greatest contempt for the barefooted Rebs; several companies passed her without taking notice, but at length a Texan gravely remarked, "Take care, madam, Hood's boys are great at storming breastworks when Yankee colors is on them." After this speech the patriotic lady beat a precipitate retreat.

Notwithstanding the venom of the women of Chambersburg, Lee's forces continued to spread out. There was no stopping them, and there was so much to be requisitioned it was unthinkable to call any kind of halt.

Part of Ewell's corps streamed towards Carlisle with Baldy himself in command. The farm lands were fat with everything, and, immensely satisfied, the Confederates collected staggering amounts of supplies by requisition.

With wagon trains crammed to overflowing, the plunder-laden columns trundled into Carlisle. And Ewell immediately made plans to seize Harrisburg, fifteen miles to the east. He sent a cavalry brigade and some engineers to reconnoiter the defenses of Pennsylvania's capital city.

Ewell's immediate problems with Carlisle, however, were not much more than receiving a number of clergymen: Would General Ewell object if they included a prayer for the President of the United States in their Sunday prayers? Ewell answered them adroitly: "Certainly not. Pray for him. I'm sure he needs it."

With Ewell at Carlisle, Jube Early moved from the vicinity of Gettysburg toward York, and as his determined campaigners moved along country roads they were greeted with stony stares and sour countenances. But here and there they were confounded by farmers standing before their houses making weird, ritualistic motions. It seems some imaginative and enterprising scoundrels had revealed to the gullible farmers, for a "consideration," the proper mumbo-jumbo, a fraternal sign, which the Rebels respected to the point of not molesting their farms. And for all these farmers ever knew, it was worth the effort and cost—Jube's men weren't taking out much time for forage and requisitions with their objective so near at hand.

Jube had no problem with York. A committee of townspeople formally surrendered the town. The Confederates marched in with a band playing "Yankee Doodle" and requisitioned twenty-eight thousand dollars in Yankee money. One of Jube's brigadier generals made a little speech and, receiving some scattered applause from the civilians, warmed up to the occasion by stating that he and his men were in York to do no harm; in fact, they were there on sort of "an outing." His speech slowed up the columns to the rear. Asked by an irate General Early why he was impeding the movements of the troops, the brigadier replied he was having a little fun, which he contended was good for everyone.

The speech-making over, Early's men moved on to Wrightsville to take a long wooden bridge crossing the Susquehanna River. But in this they were frustrated. Before they could capture it, Federal militia set it on fire. And Wrightsville represented the end of their "outing." Something had happened to frustrate *all* their plans.

On the evening of June 28, at Chambersburg, Pete Longstreet brought to General Lee's attention a startling bit of information. Old Pete, ever mindful that the whole invasion was a terrible risk, had hired a spy on his own. And the spy had collected this startling intelligence:

36

Hooker had moved his army up past the Potomac River, all the way to Frederick, Maryland. Units were heading for the Pennsylvania border. And ever more surprisingly, Hooker had been relieved of his command and replaced by General George Gordon Meade.

If this information were true, then a rapid recall of the widespread Army of Northern Virginia would have to be made. There was no way of confirming the report—Jeb Stuart's cavalry, the only really effective reconnaissance Lee had, had not been heard from in two days. General Lee had no recourse but to accept the intelligence of the enemy's movements. It would be too dangerous to leave his forces deployed as they were. An attack by the Army of the Potomac would give it the opportunity to smash into the Confederates piecemeal. The order was given. And at Wrightsville, Carlisle, and York the word was received on June 29 to begin a retrograde movement back towards Chambersburg. Then a second order was sent: the Army of Northern Virginia would concentrate east of the South Mountain Range, around Cashtown, eight miles from Gettysburg.

This second order helped lay the framework for the Battle of Gettysburg. General Lee, observing his maps, concluded it would be better to concentrate east of the South Mountain Range. If the enemy attacked, Lee would have the advantage of the mountain passes in his possession, and thus free communication with his reserve and supply wagons. And in case of the almost unthinkable possibility of retreat the mountains formed an admirable barrier —a small force could easily defend a pass.

With Ewell's forces notified, Lee moved his headquarters from Chambersburg east to a little mountain town called Greenwood, and the corps of A. P. Hill and Longstreet began crossing the South Mountain Range. The finale of a lot of marching, hopes, worry, and planning was about ready to be played.

Lee's converging forces, due to straggling, sickness, and the exigencies of campaigning, which always seem to give commanding officers less soldiers than the roll call indicates, now numbered, including Jeb Stuart's cavalry, about seventy-five thousand men.

Chapter II

The Commanding General Requests

If there was any doubt in Lee's headquarters concerning the northward movement of the Army of the Potomac, there was none among the weatherbeaten, blue-jacketed Federal soldiers. They had been going north, marching hard through mud and rain, and then, when the sun came out bright and hot, over suddenly dried roads, ankle deep in loose, dusty earth. One regiment, the 20th Maine, marched forty miles in two days and had crossed the Potomac River and was nearly up to Frederick, Maryland, on the twenty-eighth, tired and disgruntled with the whole idea of chasing after Bobby Lee and his boys.

Longstreet's spy had been absolutely correct when he disclosed that General Hooker had been replaced by General Meade.

Hooker, still upset with the officials in Washington and their constant rejection of his plans, found one more irritating denial enough to cause him to get off a hasty wire to Washington asking to be relieved as commanding officer of the Army of the Potomac. This stemmed from his request to move a Federal garrison out of Harper's Ferry and incorporate the troops into his own forces. He was denied permission. Annoyed by his orders to guard Washington without being able to exercise complete command, Hooker finally decided to find out who was going to run things.

The request to be relieved had some of the overtones of a gesture, the type of thing men sometimes do to exert pressure from what they feel is a secure position, then to their great and unhappy enlightenment they find the offer quickly snapped up and accepted. The officials in Washington were not only quick in accepting Hooker's resignation, they immediately dispatched Colonel James A. Hardie from the War Department by fast train to Frederick, Maryland, and the headquarters of Major General Gordon Meade (West Point, 1835), commanding officer of the V Corps, to inform him he was, without recourse of refusal, the new commander of the Army of the Potomac. Without shilly-shally Colonel Hardie took Meade to Hooker's tent early in the morning on June 28, and there General Meade told a groggy Hooker what had happened. That it was Hooker and not so much his plans the officials in Washington distrusted was shown in the prompt permission given Meade, upon taking command, to remove the troops in question from Harper's Ferry and station them under their commanding officer, Major General William H. French (West Point, 1837), at Frederick, Maryland.

It must be said for Hooker that he took the early morning news gracefully. He wished Meade success and brought in his Chief of Staff, Major General Daniel Butterfield, to confer with Meade. Butterfield's greatest contribution to the war had not been in battle but rather in composing a new and softly nostalgic bugle call. It is still used today, and anybody who has ever served in U.S. Armed Forces will recall the nighttime quiet which descends when Taps is sounded.

Hooker explained to Meade the general position of the Army of the Potomac, and that was that for Fighting Joe Hooker. In his one great test at Chancellorsville he had failed, and from then on nobody ever quite trusted him to come up with the right answers. Fighting Joe would go out West

Harper's Ferry, Maryland.

and serve under Grant, and help in a brilliant victory at the battle of Chattanooga; he would march with General Sherman to Atlanta, and resign for the last time.

Who thinks of a soldier in a war fought one hundred odd years ago? Who reads in the history books the little fearful things that could have gnawed at a man who wanted victory as desperately as anyone else? What war? The Civil War. Oh! They built a statue in Boston to Fighting Joe. Made of bronze. And it is tarnished and filmed over in a lusterless patina....

When the news of Meade's appointment reached the men in the ranks it created very little stir. They had seen generals come and go. General Meade was good enough. The men of the V Corps seemed to like him. He might just as well have a crack at it. And maybe the nickname some of his soldiers had tagged on him, "The Ol' Snapping Turtle," meant something more than just a reference to his looks and reported terrible temper.

But the change in generals didn't alter certain basic things for the enlisted men. More marching, forced marching, was the only way to bring Lee and his Confederates to some kind of showdown. And so the leg-tiring, back-wearying marching went on and on up through Maryland. On June 28, the very day Meade took over, the II Corps marched thirty-two miles in thirteen hours and men, fatigued beyond their own comprehension, found, much to their own surprise, that they very often had walked great distances either asleep or in some sort of hypnotic trance, induced by weariness and the rhythmical sound of tramping feet.

And as they moved over the roads of Maryland there was a general awareness that The Ol' Snapping Turtle, Meade, was not one to concern himself with the frills and goodwill of the ranks. He pushed them vigorously and long; and if all this toe-and-heeling meant anything, then, maybe this time, on Northern soil, it would be different and the Army of Northern Virginia would taste the gall of defeat.

There seemed to be a purpose in back of the marching, the continued, unrelenting marching. Meade was heading everybody right up through Maryland without delay in a broad front which veered slightly to the east, thus keeping the entire army south and east of the general area where reports had placed the columns of General Lee. This was in accordance with his orders from Washington—the same in many respects which had plagued Hooker—

Major General George Gordon Meade, commanding general of the Army of the Potomac.

to maintain the Army of the Potomac as a cover between Lee and Washington.

With his seven corps and cavalry spread out in an arc of about twenty-five miles, Meade maintained Hooker's provision of a right and left wing. The right wing stayed under his personal command, the left again under Major General Reynolds, who once had refused command of the Army of the Potomac for the reason that he would have too much interference from Washington. It was anticipated by Meade that the left wing would probably make the first contact with Lee's forces, and he wanted the best possible commander to handle this portion of the army. He had him in forty-three-year-old John Reynolds.

On June 29 most elements of the Army of the Potomac were up to within striking distance of the Pennsylvania border. While the army had tended to spread out, Meade had used his maps judiciously enough to insure that roads were available to link up one part of his army to the other. Thus, if one corps were attacked, all other corps could use connecting roads to maneuver in support.

If planning and lines of movement concerned the high command, their attendant anxieties seldom, if ever, filtered down to the men in the ranks. There were much more mundane things to contend with and somehow solve.

Evening mess, especially after a long day of it and after the order finally was given to fall out, created little problems of how to prepare the food. Rations for marching were a far different thing from the food Hooker had insisted upon when he had taken over in January and the Army of the Poto-

Soldiers of the 4th Michigan strike a pose.

mac was in its quarters around Falmouth. Each soldier usually carried his own rations, consisting of coffee, a slab of pork, and hardtack. It was in regard to the last that the soldiers' preoccupation with culinary talents came to the foreground. How to prepare it? Fry it with the salt pork? Soak it in the coffee? No matter what you did it came out the same way. Hardtack, made of flour and water into a flat biscuit about three inches square, was anything but palatable, and as it aged it took on some of the consistency of concrete. But, from the standpoint of energy, a great deal of mileage was derived from this griped-about ration.

Another item was fuel. This wasn't difficult to locate. The land abounded in split-rail fences. The wood was seasoned and cut and burned beautifully. (Some farmers, unwilling to accept what appeared inevitable, made available their wood piles instead, and by way of afterthought hastily hid their chickens. Such action usually saved them the task of rebounding their fields, although, hidden or not, the chickens just seemed to disappear.)

After a tin or two of hot coffee there was a mellow cigar or pipe, lighted with a "lucifer," a current form of friction match, and most probably a spell of undivided attention to an occupation which was almost an obsession in both armies—whittling, and of a variety no more complex than sharpening the ends of twigs or sticks. General Lee, himself, had succumbed to its therapeutic effects. If nothing else, the mark of a passing army could be seen in the thousands of wood shavings littering the ground around every bivouac.

The whittling done, the tobacco smoked, the chances were there was suddenly a lot of cussing: word was passed there would be more marching. And rising on aching limbs, they would shoulder their muskets and sling their knapsacks, rolled blankets on top, and trudge off in the darkness.

One evening men in a division of the III Corps solved the problem of darkness, or more probably relieved their own monotony, by placing lighted candles in the barrels of their muskets. And until the candles burned out it all looked like some sort of political torchlight parade, or even a procession of Druids tramping through the countryside invoking ancient and mysterious spells. The goddess of sleep, however, was around everywhere, and officers, those of them who were not ready to fall out on the side of the road, tried to keep her at a distance, and the procession moved on and on. But somewhere up ahead she prevailed, and even the die-hard officers gave up and everybody turned in for a brief bivouac, and tired bodies heaved down in fields full of piping insects and the agreeable smell of damp, crumpled grass, and everything went away and disappeared in a dreamless sleep.

Drummer boys of the North. A few of the forty thousand boy musicians who served in the Union armies.

Morning would come all too soon, and it would start all over again. But each mile north brought a perceptible difference in morale. The men passed into a land of long, rolling, green fields and acres of swaying wheat and waist-high corn. And in little villages there were the spirit-raising cheers of citizenry. Some regiments were greeted by townspeople selling cold lemonade, milk, cookies, pies, and cakes at little, quickly erected roadside stands. After partaking of the welcome refreshments, there would be great and profuse thanks followed by a good-by of "charge it to Uncle Sam." It was noted, however, as the soldiers drew nearer Lee and his army, that the refreshments were offered quite free of charge.

Another great morale-raiser was the cheers of young girls who came to wish "the boys in blue" well and give them moral support. And a nice-looking girl was apt to evoke the phenomenon of widespread coughing and clearing of throats, as though an entire regiment had spontaneously come down with a severe respiratory condition—the Civil War soldiers' "wolf-call."

The diversions were passing things, however. They came and they went, adjuncts to an underlying hard core of effort. Company by company, regiment by regiment, brigade by brigade, division and corps, the Army of the Potomac moved hour on tired hour towards an unknown fulfillment.

When the main elements streamed across the Mason-Dixon line, represented by the Maryland-Pennsylvania border, on June 30, regimental flags were unfurled, bands struck up jaunty marching tunes, and drummer boys, some no more than thirteen years old, who probably had gone off to war with an older brother, uncle, or some other relative, and who when their legs gave out usually picked up a ride on an officer's horse or the back of a strong foot soldier, rattled their sticks across taut drum heads. For a little while there was cheering and singing, and then the flags were furled and the drums and music stopped, as though even this effort were costly and only put a minor wedge in an overriding monotony of marching.

On June 30, because of laggards and men who just couldn't go on—the result of the intense forced marching of the past few days—and the fact that terms of enlistment had expired for many men just prior to the campaign, Meade's forces, including his cavalry, now numbered considerably less than at the outset—approximately eighty-five thousand.

"The Commanding General requests that, previous to the engagement soon expected with the enemy . . . commanding officers address their troops, explaining to them the immense issues involved in the struggle . . . Corps and other commanders are authorized to order the instant death of any soldier who fails in his duty at this hour." These grim words, plus an appeal to the issues of "homes, firesides and domestic altars," were the keynote of a circular issued by General Meade on June 30. The Ol' Snapping Turtle was not much given to high-sounding rhetoric or impassioned appeals to the men who would, after all, have to do his fighting. ". . . instant death of any soldier who fails in his duty at this hour," spelled out his cut-and-dried attitude about soldiering. At best it was different than anything the ranks had ever heard from the previous generals, who either boasted or let themselves be seen with all their trappings at gigantic reviews.

As the men of the Army of the Potomac heard Meade's words read to them, the first rumbling, the initial tug of Gettysburg began to make itself felt in the left wing of the army.

Meade had examined his maps, and there was Gettysburg eight miles north of the Pennsylvania border, with ten roads extending out as the spokes on a wheel. Lee was probably north and west of this town. It should be held by Union forces. Possession would insure use of those roads.

General Reynolds was ordered to move his forces to Gettysburg.

It was not Meade's intention to bring about any major fighting at Gettysburg. This was primarily a probing movement with the end result to be the securing of Gettysburg in Union hands. He issued a standby plan to set up a defense line along Pipe Creek, considerably to the east and south of Gettysburg. If his lead elements were hit by Lee, they were to fight a delaying action and fall back on this line. Meade was displaying the marked talents of a careful general who, while moving in on his enemy, was allowing for contingencies. There was nothing audacious in his plans; but, then, only a fool would risk everything in a daring move when he was confronted by General Lee. Lee had an unparalleled ability of turning the best-laid plans to his advantage.

In advance of the left wing of the Army of the Potomac was a cavalry division of about four thousand horsemen under thirty-seven-year-old Major General John Buford (West Point, 1848). Buford and his men went clattering and thumping into Gettysburg at eleven o'clock in the morning of Tuesday, June 30. Out on the Chambersburg Pike was a brigade of Confederates. It quickly withdrew as a detachment of Federal cavalry moved beyond the streets of town and encamped on a small ridge about one mile to the west.

Buford knew something was up. Before he and his cavalry arrived they had to make a circuit around a large body of Confederates at Fairfield, southwest of Gettysburg; and now there was this body of Confederates which had withdrawn down the Chambersburg Pike. Orders were given to maintain a brigade west of town in position, and a second brigade was placed to the north straddling the road to Carlisle. Vedettes were thrown out in a long arc extending from southwest to northeast of Gettysburg.

With this defense perimeter established Buford set up his headquarters in the Lutheran Theological Seminary building. The fact that it was a Tuesday and the last day in June held little interest for Buford. The fact that he had seen Confederates around Gettysburg was so significant to Buford that he became convinced with the advancing afternoon his forces would be attacked by Confederate infantry the following morning.

The moon rose bright and full over Gettysburg on that last night in June,

Cavalrymen of the 1st United States Regular Cavalry who rode into Gettysburg on June 30 with General Buford.

Library of Congress

Major General
John Buford.

The National Archives

and Buford's command turned in early. Faintly visible in the nighttime sky, Mars and Jupiter and Saturn, ancient and superstitious signs of the zodiac, held to an immemorial pattern—age-old spectators of other nights, other times, when men contemplated battle. There was a tenuous expectancy in the air and the cavalrymen listened, but they heard only the crickets and occasional stir of horses, and the night sounds mingled into dreams and faded and were gone. . . .

To the north and west, gathering Confederates looked beyond smoldering campfires and ground-hugging mists and saw the land which for some would become an end, and for others a memory to be carried to the last moment.

Southeast, down by Littlestown and Taneytown, Union foot soldiers, still plodding along, pressed through dusk into moonlight and the cool, scented sorcery of a summer night. And somewhere a rumor, an eerie "fact," began circulating among the soldiers, pushed on by no more than a wish for a hopeful sign: *the ghost of George Washington had been seen riding a white horse leading the columns—the Other World was going to help them.* Swaying blue ranks of enlisted men—really boys averaging only eighteen years of age—pushed towards tomorrow, and down pale, moonlit roads Destiny's outstretched hand held July 1, 1863.

The next morning the rising tide of the eastern light turned an intermittently cloudy sky into an opaque, pale red. Its faint illumination cast trees and hills into gray and black silhouettes as though unreal in a strange summer land of only height and width. For Corporal Alphonse Hodges of Company F, 9th New York Cavalry, there was something alien about the hills and rolling land. He had seen them yesterday for the first time, but now in the early morning it was hard to distinguish anything familiar. It was not important. In a few minutes he and his three-man squad would be relieved from picket

47

duty. Somebody would have breakfast started. There would be hot tins of coffee waiting.

Corporal Hodges looked westward, past a gravelly road which dipped, crossed a little stream, and then climbed to disappear over a low ridge. On the ridge was the dark outline of a house. Corporal Hodges could make out nothing which particularly distinguished it from other houses dotting the Pennsylvania landscape. His eyes swung to the road. There was something there! And out in the fields! Shadowy figures—and they were moving. Hodges reined his horse down over the little stream and up onto the rising land at the base of the western ridge. Confederates! Without waiting for more confirmation, Hodges swung his horse back in a full gallop. Suddenly, the sharp, startling crash of musket fire burst through the calm morning air. They were firing at him, and the high whine of nearby bullets indicated a certain accuracy and intent on the part of Confederates.

At the stream Hodges pulled up by a small bridge and shouldered his carbine. Quickly now he squeezed off several shots and then loosened his rein. Hodges and his horse skedaddled back to spread the alarm. The time was five thirty on the morning of July 1, 1863, and Corporal Alphonse Hodges had just fired the opening shots of the Union side at the Battle of Gettysburg.

The Lutheran Seminary building, July, 1863.

Chapter III

Feed It to 'Em!

The land west of Gettysburg is good farming country. In the early summer it is swollen with great expanses of flowing yellow wheat and rugged green corn, and stone barns with heavily timbered roofs are crammed with pungent hay. This is a gently rolling country, the earth expanding into long, rounded swells which extend north and south all the way out to the South Mountain Range, the high points of land sometimes wooded with poplar and elm and hickory trees. As points of high ground, however, they are not much more than gentle waves; yet, locally, they are known as "ridges." Between the ridges are wide, shallow valleys, usually punctuated by small wandering brooks, banks all heavily garlanded in overhanging sedge and spear grass. Cutting across the streams, the valleys and ridges, almost at a right angle, is U.S. Route 30—the Chambersburg Pike.

One mile west of Gettysburg is McPherson's Ridge, named after the owner of some farm buildings which occupied its crest, and it was here that General Buford deployed his cavalry when Corporal Hodges spread the alarm.

In reality, Buford's soldiers were mounted infantrymen. Whenever there was heavy fighting they would dismount and follow the maneuvers of foot soldiers. Buford strung his men out north and south of the Chambersburg Pike as it crosses McPherson's Ridge, and with one man in four to the rear holding the horses, his line strength was a little less than three thousand. Astride the Chambersburg Pike he posted a battery of six cannon. Vedettes were maintained north and northeast of Gettysburg on the Carlisle and Harrisburg roads.

West of McPherson's Ridge, three-quarters of a mile, is Herr Ridge, and here a Confederate division under Major General Henry Heth (West Point, 1847), A. P. Hill's III Corps, formed into a loose and rather slipshod battle

Major General Henry Heth.

Library of Congress

formation. The most persistent story as to why Heth's division was headed towards Gettysburg on this morning is that Heth had heard there were shoes at Gettysburg and had directed his division to go there and get them. Whatever the reason, Heth and his men were on Herr Ridge, and both he and his officers felt they had run into nothing more serious than some State Militia.

After contact was made at 5:30 A.M. there was sporadic firing and shifting and probing by pickets and skirmishers for fully two and one-half hours. Then, shortly after eight o'clock, Heth pushed his troops forward in what he termed in his official report a "forced reconnaissance." This brought his men past the little stream, Willoughby Run, where Corporal Hodges had first fired at the Confederates, into the land leading up to McPherson's Ridge, and there they ran into a labyrinth of gunfire which effectively contained their advance.

Buford's men were armed in part with the most advanced small weapon of the Civil War: the Spencer Repeating Rifle. Termed as Lincoln's "secret weapon," as it was he who had enthusiastically pushed for its use, the Spencer fired seven rounds of .52-caliber copper-rimmed cartridges. These were loaded into a tubular magazine which passed through the stock. By pulling down the trigger guard, the breech block was dropped and the used shell extracted. Closing the trigger guard placed a live round in the breech. The Confederates claimed the Spencer was "loaded on Sunday and fired all week."

Despite the superior strength of Heth's division—it outnumbered the cavalrymen two to one—the presence of the Spencer Carbine in Buford's ranks lent a vastly greater firepower over the enemy, who used a single-shot muzzle-loader. For one Confederate this was a tragic reality.[7]

50

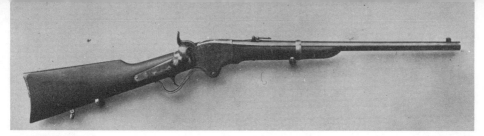

The Spencer Repeating Rifle.

Edging forward with the rest of his company on hands and knees into a wheat field, Henry Raisin, Company B, Seventh Tennessee Regiment, heard the snap and buzz of bullets above, and sometimes among, the swaying shafts of grain. The feel of his musket was reassuring, but it didn't offer much defense against the enemy, who seemed to have the wheat field zeroed as a prime target. Suddenly, there was an astonishing punch that went *thuck* inside him. He never heard the bullet that reached him. He never felt the damp wheat on his face. Henry Raisin was the first Confederate killed at Gettysburg.

With his reconnaissance contained, Heth called for his artillery, and here he held a wide edge over Buford. Nineteen horse-drawn pieces came rattling up and were detached from their limbers, the vehicles used to transport them, and wheeled into position along Herr Ridge. Behind the guns came the cais-

July, 1863. Photographer Matthew Brady surveying area where Confederate and Union forces first clashed.

Culver Service, New York

Looking down the Chambersburg Pike in 1863 from the position where Buford placed his artillery. On the left is McPherson's barn, used as a hospital during and after the battle. Same view today. (*Below*)

Lane Studio, Gettysburg, Pennsylvania

sons, the ammunition carriers. (Both the limbers and caissons carried ammunition in a box set between the wheels.)

Civil War field artillery, far different from the long-range cannon in use today, was used primarily as an antipersonnel weapon, very much as machine guns are employed by modern armies. Although utilized as a counter-weapon to enemy artillery, its short trajectory precluded effective bombardment of communications and supply. Several types of muzzle-loading fieldpieces were included in the weaponry of both armies. The Ordnance Gun and the Parrott, both having rifled barrels, were widely used and had effective maximum ranges of about four thousand yards, but the basic cannon was the smooth-bore Napoleon. Cast in either bronze or iron, the Napoleon was 4.62 in caliber and had an effective range of fifteen hundred yards. The Napoleon fired a variety of projectiles—solid shot, shell, grape, and canister. The latter two, both similar, were a savage cluster of iron or lead balls all packed together that scattered immediately after leaving the muzzle. In the case of shellfire, cannoneers were required to cut the fuse to what they deemed the right length for it to burn and set off the charge when it was on target. The fuse was usually either a paper or wooden tube filled with a combustible which ignited when the cannon was fired. Despite the intricacies involved, the Civil War cannoneers averaged pretty well with their "art."

A bugle sounded along Herr Ridge and Heth's cannons roared into life, rearing back on their stocks, and spurts of dust and sudden flashes of orange-red light along McPherson's Ridge showed the barrage was reaching its mark. And for one soldier of the 12th Illinois Cavalry the Confederate aim was all too perfect: a piece of shrapnel sliced the life right out of him. Ferdinand Ushner became the first Northern soldier to die at Gettysburg.

With cannon banging away at the Yankees, Heth's foot soldiers continued to apply pressure, but Buford's soldiers held. Men from Tennessee, Alabama, Mississippi, and North Carolina were checked with almost baffling ease: State Militia had never fought like this before. Seemingly, all the muskets in the world couldn't dislodge them.

The musket of the infantrymen in both armies was in reality a rifle. While not so intricately engineered as the Spencer Carbine made available to the Yankee cavalrymen, it was, even so, a highly potent weapon. Spiral grooves, "rifling," along the interior of the barrel made a .58-caliber slug rotate in flight, giving it a high degree of accuracy over considerable distance. It packed plenty of wallop, and the lead slug had a tendency to flatten out on impact and leave a large hole.

There was, however, a great deal more to do than just aiming this weapon and pulling the trigger. As with the close-order drill of Civil War soldiers, which was necessary for maneuvering large, closely ranked bodies of infantry into battle formations, and which makes the drill instruction of modern soldiers look about as complicated as running to first base, there was the time-consuming and intricate task of loading. Muskets were loaded through the muzzle, and during his basic training the infantryman had to learn a procedure called "Load in Nine Times" whereby the movements were organized into nine steps. Among the many requirements were these: take a cartridge, which was made up of powder and a lead Minié ball all wrapped in paper; tear open the paper with the teeth, place the powder in the barrel, and insert the Minié ball; take a ramrod and tamp the ball in, take out the ramrod and then put a little cap (the explosive device that triggered off the gunpowder) in a "nipple" situated over the breech; and finally cock the hammer. In the heat of battle, often enough to earn themselves a few rounds of cussing, soldiers sometimes would forget one of the steps and the muskets would misfire, or ramrods left in the barrels would go sailing off in the direction of the enemy as soon as triggers were pulled. A well-trained soldier, nevertheless, was expected to get off at least one round a minute.

For all of this, Heth's infantrymen were throwing plenty of lead at Buford's horse soldiers, ramming Minié balls into their muzzle-loaders by the count. *Pop . . . pop . . . pop . . . pop.* And mixed in with this staccato beat, piling up

Monument of the 17th Pennsylvania Cavalry. The 17th Pennsylvania was deployed on the Union right at the opening of the battle. Veterans were especially impressed with the accurate portrayal of the horse's expression as seen in battle.

Walter Lane

A Federal gun crew practicing with their twenty-pound Parrott. Parrott guns were easily identified by a band of iron around the breech as a reinforcement to withstand the pressure of a rifled barrel.

into the morning air, was a steady *bang, bang, bang,* the almost rhythmical fire of the Yankee carbines.

Also piling up into the air was a thick churning cloud of smoke. The gunpowder of the Civil War had not changed much from its earliest forms. It burned improperly and left a high residue. Made of saltpeter, sulphur, and carbon, it added to the visible evidence of battle by enveloping the land in a mantle of smoke—smoke which for all the world smelled like rotten eggs.

With the Confederate infantrymen pouring it on the Yankees, twelve of Heth's cannon zeroed in on Buford's artillery and began knocking the props out from under it. Infantrymen were "queen of battle," but artillery was "king," and the weight of metal was all in favor of the Confederates. Buford sent couriers galloping off with messages to General Reynolds at Marsh Creek, five miles below Gettysburg, and General Meade at Taneytown, thirteen miles southeast of Gettysburg, to the effect that he had encountered a strong body of Confederates and that immediate help was needed.

Five hundred yards east of McPherson's Ridge, back towards town, the Lutheran Theological Seminary building stands atop a long, narrow wooded ridge. Deriving its name from the Seminary, the ridge extends south of Gettysburg, and its northern contours reach up past the Chambersburg Pike to a prominent knoll of heavily wooded land called Oak Hill.

Twelve-pound "Napoleons." Developed under Napoleon III, this gun became standard equipment in the United States Army in 1856.

A dig of a spur, and Buford and his horse rushed in a soaring gallop towards Seminary Ridge. At the Seminary building horse and rider came to a dismounting, clattering halt. Buford, one hand steadying his sidearm, raced into the building. Cool, dark corridors and stairways, smelling faintly of years of polishing with pine oil, echoed to the sound of his urgent steps as he sprinted up to the tower-like cupola on the roof. With field glasses aimed towards McPherson's Ridge he confirmed his suspicions: his troops were slowly giving ground now but still maintaining an orderly line of battle; the sheer number of Confederates, however, was about to spill over the flanks.

It was after nine thirty, and the dismounted Yankee cavalry had given a good account of themselves, but if reinforcements didn't come up quickly Buford would have to call a retreat.

At nine fifty-five General Reynolds, responding to Buford's pressing request and drawn by the sound of fighting, led his horse in a swift canter into the streets of town. Behind him, and coming up fast on the Emmitsburg Road, were units of the I Corps. A scout told him Buford was at the Seminary building. Another full-tilt ride and there was General Buford running down the steps of the Seminary building crying, "There's the devil to pay!"

After a hasty briefing Reynolds sent a dispatch to General Meade in which he promised to hold off the Confederates by barricading the streets of Gettysburg if necessary. (There is strong evidence that Reynolds never received Meade's order about the proposed line of defense at Pipe Creek, southeast of Gettysburg. Meade had told him to occupy the town in order to have use and access of all the converging roads, and apparently Reynolds viewed this as mandatory: Gettysburg was to be held by Union forces.) Reynolds was going to make a fight of it, although in a short time the barricading of the streets, the battle itself, would have no meaning to him.

Colt 1860
Army Model
Revolver.

Connecticut State Library Museum

Muskets of Confederate infantrymen. Top to bottom: Palmetto musket, Richmond rifle-musket, Cook infantry rifle, Morse musket.

Smithsonian Institution

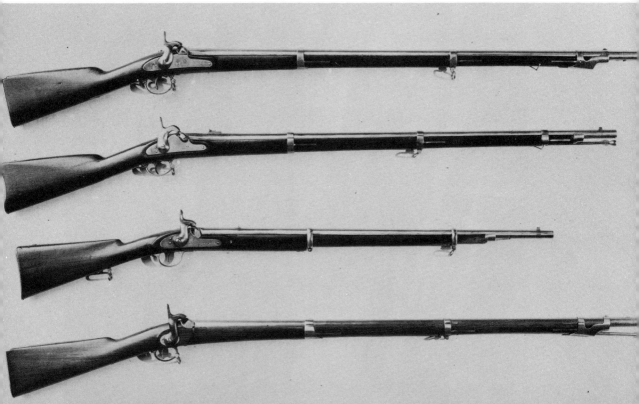

Reynolds sent off a second hasty dispatch to Major General Oliver O. Howard (West Point, 1854) to bring his XI Corps up from Emmitsburg, ten miles south of Gettysburg.

With his messages sent, Reynolds cantered back to the Emmitsburg Road and intercepted the vanguard of the approaching soldiers of the I Corps. He directed them to cut cross-country and hook up with Buford's men on Mc-Pherson's Ridge. Muskets were lowered and powder and lead slugs tamped down long barrels, and men removed their "kepi" hats, the full-moon insignia of the I Corps emblazoned on the fronts, and wiped sweaty brows and contemplated the coming ordeal—*no matter how often, you just never get used to battle.*

A regimental band struck up the bright notes of "The Campbells Are Coming," and two brigades headed across wheat fields and over fences towards the stomach-tightening sounds of battle.

One unit, the Iron Brigade, composed of men from Indiana, Wisconsin, and Michigan, plowed straight ahead south of the Chambersburg Pike, catch-

Soldier musicians of the North.

Major General
John Reynolds.

Library of Congress

ing a Confederate brigade in flank in some woods just in front of McPherson's Ridge. One soldier from the 2nd Wisconsin saw a heavily braided Confederate officer who somehow had managed to get marooned from the rest of his outfit. It would have been a simple thing for the soldier to raise his musket and shoot the Confederate, but the Fates tempted him and he took out after the officer with his bare hands. Private Patrick Maloney, big and brawny, knew just what to do when he caught up with the Confederate officer and his nice shiny braid. He clamped his hands around his throat and started to throttle him—it is not often a private gets a chance to choke an officer, either one of his own or the enemy's. Maloney was finally dissuaded from his savagery, and examination of his prize of war revealed he had reached high up: he had captured Brigadier General James Archer, former resident of Maryland and the first officer holding the rank of general captured since Lee had taken command of the Army of Northern Virginia.

They passed Archer to the rear under escort, his bruised feelings at the explosive point. At a headquarters site he was spotted by Major General Abner Doubleday (West Point, 1842), division commander in Reynolds I Corps. (With Reynolds in command of the left wing of the Army of the Potomac, Doubleday now held temporary command of the I Corps.) Archer was an old friend of Doubleday's. Doubleday extended his hand and told Archer he was glad to see him. Quite suddenly, traditional Southern courtesy went by the boards when Archer refused Doubleday's hand and blurted, "Well, I'm not glad to see you by a damned sight!" All things considered, a very understandable reply.

It was as Private Maloney mauled General Archer that the Confederates suddenly realized they were not fighting State Militia. The Iron Brigade was

59

A young officer and en-listed man from Michigan, recruited from the same town. The officer wears the type of hat worn by the Iron Brigade.

The National Archives

not only well known by the way it fought, but also because of its distinctive nonregulation black headgear. A Confederate man in the ranks, seeing the caps, yelled, "Here are those damned black-hatted fellers again . . . 'Tain't no militia—that's the Army of the Potomac!"

For a few moments longer everything went in the North's favor. Reynolds positioned the second brigade north of the Chambersburg Pike, and pulled Buford's tired horsemen out of the line. Still full of fight and proud of what they had done, the cavalrymen mounted up and trotted off to positions of reserve and guard.

But all at once the tide swung around to favor a brigade of battle-tested Mississippians under the command of thirty-three-year-old Brigadier General Joseph R. Davis, Jefferson Davis' nephew. Driving in with everything they had—musket fire, artillery, and bayonets, and the raw courage which allows men to wade into pointed guns—the Mississippians broke into the right side of Reynolds' line, north of the Chambersburg Pike, and everything started flying apart in a swift avalanche of Confederates, kicking up a steady crashing roar under a low pall of smoke. A bugle sounded retreat. Then another. And the bluecoats streamed back toward the momentary safety of Seminary Ridge, a battery of Maine men, which had been squeezed in, following, limbers, caissons, drivers, and horses all heaving and bouncing and rattling. The withdrawal was so rapid that one regiment, unaware of the orders, was stranded and almost completely surrounded by Davis' men.

The converging roads of Gettysburg offered the enemy great tactical advantages for movement which could carry him easily and rapidly into the flanks and rear of the Federal line. And south of the Chambersburg Pike Abner Doubleday, in anticipation of this possibility, ordered a squadron of Buford's horse soldiers to move out on the left-flank area around the Hagerstown Road. In a few minutes the possibilities, the contingencies—the over-all battle—would occupy Doubleday's thinking and energy. (Doubleday, who as a captain had given the nod for the first return fire from Fort Sumter back in April, 1861, would find his name passed over as a general at Gettysburg, although he gave a creditable account of himself, but history would best remember him as the man who was keen on a new game evolving out of an English pastime known as "rounders," and eventually he would be dubbed the Father of Baseball.)

At ten minutes past ten a Confederate soldier took a bead on a Union officer astride his horse, pointing and giving directions. The soldier squeezed his trigger and General Reynolds, one of the best generals of the North, fell from his horse mortally wounded fifteen minutes after he had arrived on the field. As senior officer, Abner Doubleday immediately assumed all responsibilities, and his problem was acute: the retreat of the forces north of the turnpike exposed the rest of the line to attack from both frontal and flank fire.

In the game of war, however, what is an advantage is often, if not equally, subject to a counterstroke. When the Confederates rushed after the retreating Union forces on the right, some of them piled into a long unfinished railway cut running parallel to the Chambersburg Pike, and their advantage was

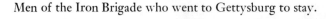

Men of the Iron Brigade who went to Gettysburg to stay.

quickly turned when Doubleday threw in reserve troops along with soldiers brought over from south of the Chambersburg Pike, among them the 6th Wisconsin, part of the Iron Brigade. The reinforcements charged into the cut, pouring a deadly fire down the length of the Confederates milling between the sharp banks. Then a Union battery was placed squarely on the end of the cut and opened up with a lethal enfilade fire, and hundreds of suddenly baffled Southerners were compelled to surrender. A Union officer shouted over to a Confederate colonel to give up. The stunned and unhappy colonel walked forward and turned over his sword. Six subordinates followed him, swords proffered in a token of surrender, and the amazed Union offier found his arms loaded with the clanking accouterments.

The counterattack reversed the tide, and Davis' men were forced into retreat, leaving all of McPherson's Ridge once more in Union hands. It was not without cost, however: the Yankee regiment which had become stranded lost two thirds of its men. But all in all, it was a Federal victory. The Confederates had been stopped west of Gettysburg.

As the main bulk of the I Corps filed onto McPherson's Ridge shortly after eleven o'clock, the fighting subsided into a distinct lull, and an odd sort of calm held as the morning ebbed towards noon.

It was as this unsteady slowdown prevailed that the men of the Iron Brigade began to notice an elderly man in their ranks all done up in a swallowtail coat with brass buttons and carrying an outmoded musket, vintage 1812. He was John Burns, seventy-year-old citizen of Gettysburg and veteran of the War of 1812, who had come out to volunteer his services as a fighting soldier —the Confederates had driven off his cows and he avowed he was going to "get even."

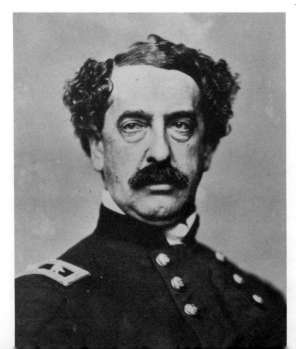

Major General
Abner Doubleday.

The National Archives

Gettysburg National Military Park—Walter Lane

Railway cut.

Neither General Lee nor General Meade anticipated or wished to bring on heavy fighting at Gettysburg. Lee did not want to engage in major battle until his army was completely assembled; Meade had already decided on Pipe Creek, considerably to the southeast, as his choice of site for battle. The elements which had just fought, in spite of this, showed no inclination to disengage. The winning side, then, would be the one which could bring up additional troops first. Reynolds, the commanding officer of Meade's left wing, had already made it plain he intended to fight it out before he was killed by calling for Howard's XI Corps to move to Gettysburg.

To the west, along the Chambersburg Pike, an entire Confederate Division

63

was moving up from reserve. General Heth, whose soldiers had received such a decisive check, maintained his battle formation and grimly prepared for a renewal of attack, waiting until the new division was fully in support.

Thus, it was through the actions of field officers, rather than of the High Command of either army, that the events of Gettysburg were initiated.

At eleven thirty General Howard arrived on the streets of Gettysburg astride a great snorting and prancing stallion, and minus an arm lost in an earlier battle of the war. Both Howard and horse had pressed hard to get to the scene of the fighting, leaving behind the XI Corps to double time up the Emmitsburg Road south of Gettysburg.

The shocking news of General Reynolds' death altered Howard's role drastically. As senior officer he immediately took command of all Union troops; and while the fighting had ebbed, the situation he was faced with was undergoing a formidable change. Scouts located in the large cupola of the Pennsylvania College building north of town were reporting ominous signs from the Carlisle direction. Swirls of dust, obviously kicked up by thousands of shuffling feet, could be seen hanging low on the near horizon.

With this alarming information, Howard instructed Abner Doubleday to hold the I Corps in its present position along McPherson's Ridge: the soon-arriving XI Corps would move north of town and then swing west past the road to Mummasburg and effect a hookup with the I Corps.

It had grown quite warm, the temperature climbing into the mid-seventies under an intermittently cloudy sky, when at one o'clock the first elements of the XI Corps streamed into Gettysburg. They had been moving fast, covering the last mile at a running trot. Citizens were out in the streets with pails of cool water, and as the panting soldiers slacked their thirst frantic couriers from Buford's cavalry brought in confirmation about the swirls of dust. Confederates in great numbers were bearing down on Gettysburg from the north. If Buford's horse soldiers could have extended their observations into the ranks of the approaching Confederates, they would have found out these were men of Ewell's II Corps—the Rebels who had had such a field day with requisitions in Chambersburg and then moved on to Carlisle. Baldy Ewell had had some difficulty in deciding where to hook up with the rest of Lee's army when he received Lee's message to begin a retrograde movement on July 29; but there was word Yankees had been seen around Gettysburg, and it was assumed that was where the II Corps should head.

Howard sent a dispatch with feverish urgency to Major General Daniel

Sickles near Emmitsburg to bring his III Corps to Gettysburg as rapidly as possible. Another messenger galloped off with the same plea to Major General Henry Slocum (West Point, 1852). Slocum and his XII Corps were five miles southeast of Gettysburg on the Baltimore Pike. Now Howard ordered two divisions of the rapidly assembling XI Corps to move north of town and execute his plan for a hookup on McPherson's Ridge, their front facing north in anticipation of the approaching Confederates. A third division, plus some artillery, was held in reserve on Cemetery Hill, a high rise of land just south of town with a quiet village cemetery on its brow. (The choice of Cemetery Hill as a reserve point would later earn Howard a formal vote of thanks from Congress.)

The XI Corps had quite a few soldiers of German descent in its ranks, men who had fled to this country during the early 1850's after an unsuccessful revolutionary movement in Europe. These new Americans made fine soldiers, but their numbers in the corps hardly constituted a majority, or even much of a minority; still, to the rest of the Army of the Potomac, the XI Corps was the "German Corps."

And the German Corps, with its crescent-moon insignia, was just plain unlucky. Somehow, someway, or so it seemed, whenever the Confederates managed a beautifully executed military maneuver on the Yankees it was this corps which caught it. On July 1 the German Corps' luck was running true to form.

When the two forward divisions moved out into the flat, open country north of town and began to set up their line, they were not given much time. Baldy Ewell was driving his proud Rebels hard, and backed with artillery and a fierce enthusiasm to give the Yankees a thorough trouncing, they pushed into the new line, leaving the stunned bluecoats no choice but to try to counter as best they could; and with even more dire portent, there was no time to effect a hookup with Doubleday's troops holding McPherson's Ridge. The new line terminated at the northwesterly road to Mummasburg, and there was a quarter-mile gap between Federal troops to the west and those to the north.

Civilians by this time had fled to the safety of their basements, but many of the soldiers of the XI Corps recalled afterward how, as they trotted out to the front along the street leading to the Carlisle Road while a few shells burst overhead, a young lady, all alone, stood on a porch waving her handkerchief, cheering them on.

Her gesture and hopes for success, however, were no more than wishes.

65

Major General Robert E. Rodes,
division commander
in Ewell's II Corps.

Library of Congress

The division Baldy Ewell had slammed in so propitiously was under the command of Virginia Military Institute graduate, thirty-four-year-old Major General Robert Rodes. As elements of his division pushed the German Corps off balance, still more swarmed far out and followed a line which brought them up by Oak Hill. As with Seminary Ridge, Oak Hill overlooks the northern end of McPherson's Ridge, both ridges tending to converge at this point. Very quickly, Rodes' men had the proper measure on the Yankees, and were ready to throw a right hook: they were squarely on the flank of the entire western Federal line. Rodes ordered an attack to go banging in and roll it up. It might have been overconfidence engendered by their sudden thrust into battle, but the attack was broken up by an adroit maneuver of pulling Federal troops back and letting some cannon near the Chambersburg Pike change front to rake the oncoming Confederates. In turn, the Confederates were swept savagely by musketry fire—some Yankees had hidden themselves behind a long stone fence and caught the Rebels in the awful punch of surprise, and all in all, Rodes' men were stopped, suffering fifteen hundred casualties.

For the moment the Federal troops were holding, but the Confederate line was linked up in a great semicircle from the southwest all the way around to the northeast, and it was all afire with crashing cannon and skirmishers and pickets moving in close to let go with their muskets. The weight of numbers now—it was a little after two thirty—was heavily in favor of the Confederates; and there was for General Howard the additional disagreeable news of a brigade of Buford's horsemen hotly contesting the advance of a new Rebel column pile-driving in from the northeast over by Rock Creek, a flowing stream which edges east of Gettysburg. The column belonged to Jubal Early's division.

Old Jube was bringing his boys in rapidly with their "swag" of twenty-eight thousand dollars from the citizens of York, and the timing could not have been better if a general staff had sat down and drawn diagrams. The Confederates had the Yankees in a giant pincers.

As the catastrophe of facing overwhelming numbers of Confederates was building up for the Union forces, General Lee arrived on the field.

Throughout the morning near Cashtown Lee had heard the muffled, far-off booming of cannon rolling over the land from the east like a distant summer storm, and he had waited anxiously for word of what it was all about. Under normal circumstances a courier from Stuart's cavalry would have had the information, but Stuart and his men were yet to be heard from, and nobody seemed to have news of any kind. The insistent rumbling had continued, and Lee, at last drawn by the sound of battle, had reined Traveller in a long, loping canter down the Chambersburg Pike towards a now irrevocable place in history.

Somewhat later in the afternoon, far to the southeast on a ride of parallel urgency to Lee's, with a cloud of dust swirling behind them, a party of horsemen galloped over the Taneytown Road towards Gettysburg. Leading the group astride a pounding sorrel was Major General Winfield Scott Hancock (West Point, 1840), commanding officer of the II Corps, with special orders from General Meade assigning him full authority over all the Federal troops assembled at Gettysburg. Meade, still planning his defenses at Pipe Creek, had received a message from General Buford which told of Reynolds' death, and that there seemed "to be no directing person." Without any idea of the magnitude of the buildup taking place at Gettysburg—by now the events already had outraced plans—he designated Hancock to substitute for himself at the scene of fighting. The choice would prove prudent: Hancock, a career soldier, tall (six feet two inches), and easily one of the handsomest men in the Army of the Potomac, had all the qualities necessary to lead and was an excellent tactician.

It started first in the line north of town with the men of the unlucky German Corps. The division on the right was under the command of Brigadier General Francis Barlow, a boyish-looking soldier who had enlisted as a private in 1861. Barlow had extended his line so that his right flank rested on a small knoll near Rock Creek. (When the fighting was all over and men began to fashion the battlegrounds into a military park, they would give the name Barlow Knoll to this bit of land.) Along with support infantry, Barlow posted a battery of four Napoleons on this elevation—as a vantage point it was good, covering the flat ground around it.

For a while the battery under the command of First Lieutenant Bayard Wilkeson gave a good account of itself, flailing into massed Rebel troops on its front. Then it happened. Jube Early's men! They had battered and slugged their way past Rock Creek and came on yelling and whooping, pouring a lethal rain of bullets into the front and flank of the knoll. Rebel foot soldiers snaked in and struck with vicious fusillades of hissing lead, while a Confederate battery swerved into position and unlimbered its cannon, horses all wide-eyed, foam-flecked mouths snorting and fluttering.

From the moment Early's infantrymen struck it was no contest, but when the Confederate battery got the range it was all over. Exploding shells smothered the position. General Barlow, just south of the knoll issuing orders and trying to hold his men together, went down, fearfully wounded. Lieutenant Wilkeson, seated on a white horse, made a beautiful target. And in a few moments an exploding shell knocked him and his mount to the ground, both mortally wounded. Then the supporting infantry caved in and there was nothing else to do but limber up the cannon and get out of there as best and as fast as possible. Early's men had done it! They had squeezed hard, and the Yankee line was cracking.

For Wilkeson there was a slow agony followed by death that night back

Four generals of the Army of the Potomac, all wounded at Gettysburg. Standing with sword is Brigadier General Francis Barlow, division commander in the XI Corps; seated is Major General Winfield Scott Hancock, commanding officer of the II Corps; behind Hancock is Major General David Birney, division commander in the III Corps; and on right is Major General John Gibbon, division commander in the II Corps.

The National Archives

of the Confederate lines, while his father, assigned to Meade's headquarters as a correspondent for *The New York Times*, anxiously sought out news, and with more than equal anxiety, wondered what was happening to his son.

With the knoll overpowered, the rest of the line held by the men of the XI Corps was only moments away from overwhelming defeat.

In the midst of smoke roiling up in a thick cloud and an unending bedlam of earsplitting noise, Confederate infantrymen smashed forward, and one section after the other of the line yielded. A new line was hastily formed a few hundred yards to the rear, but the Rebels roared in and rattled it loose, and the Yankees went into full and final retreat. Some artillery which had been shoved into the gap separating the XI Corpsmen from the I Corps over on McPherson's Ridge was forced to make a run for it, joining the foot soldiers in a wild scramble for the reserve position on Cemetery Hill.

Two divisions of the German Corps had had another bad day with Lee's great soldiers, and they tumbled and floundered into the streets of Gettysburg, groups of panicky, demoralized men darting down blind alleys and side streets—anything to get away from the closely pursuing Rebels—only to find themselves trapped, forced either to fight their way out or surrender.

After the two divisions north of town collapsed, nothing in the world could save the I Corps. The indefatigable men who had done so much to stop the Confederates driving in from the west during the morning now were presented with the impossible task of holding a line flanked at both ends and assaulted in front.

At four o'clock General Lee gave the nod for his forces to attack en masse. A solid double line of infantrymen surged forward, guns blazing, their sights set on annihilating the Yankees. Lee had not wanted to bring on any kind of a major battle until his army was fully assembled, but the opportunity to break up part of Meade's troops was presented to him and he did not hesitate.

The I Corps hung on, grimly inflicting terrible casualties on the enemy, raking their advance with musket and artillery fire. But the fierce might of the Rebels was overpowering, and loaded with the spirit and courage which kept a color bearer waving his flag after a shell had torn his arm almost off, the Confederates were not to be denied.

From Cemetery Hill, where the reserve elements of the XI Corps were digging in, the plight of the I Corps was obvious, and General Howard sent word for the sorely pressed soldiers to retreat back to this high ground. Somehow Howard's message became garbled and was interpreted by part of the corps south of the Chambersburg Pike as an order to fall back on Seminary

This composite photograph taken soon after the battle shows exactly how the Confederates saw Gettysburg on the afternoon of July 1 after they had overwhelmed the Union forces west of town and driven them back through the streets and south of Gettysburg. At the left is the "Old Dorm" of Pennsylvania College (now Gettysburg College). The tower of "Old Dorm" was used as an observatory both by the Federals and Confederates.

Ridge; and soldiers and artillery streamed back to the ridge and set up a new defense line. And for a few minutes it held, the indomitable Iron Brigade right in the middle of it, firing furiously at the front ranks of Rebels, melting their line with devastating accuracy, but the rear elements kept coming and finally everything broke.

Over on the north of the pike, Confederates cut into the Yankees from front and side, and in some instances from the rear.

On each side of the railway cut, three Napoleons to the left and three to the right, was Battery B, 4th United States Artillery. Cannoneers were required to fight out in the open—they had no protection beyond what the wheels and metal parts of their pieces offered—and the men in Battery B, ramming armloads of canister down the hot muzzles of their pieces, were taking a heavy beating from the eagle-eyed Confederate infantrymen. Lieutenant James Davison, commanding the three guns on the left, caught a bullet in the ankle,

The fields immediately in front of "Old Dorm" swarmed with retreating Union soldiers. (Note the broken fences.) The unfinished railway cuts from the extreme left up through the center. On the right is the Chambersburg Pike. Cemetery Hill, the Union rallying point, is visible as a sharp rise on the horizon line at center right.

but he hobbled about cheering his men and yelling at the top of his voice: "Feed it to 'em. God damn 'em. Feed it to 'em!"

Battery B, its anxious gunners sweating, jackets off, sleeves rolled up, unloaded hot, metallic death at the Rebels, but it was no use. There were too many of them. Soon Lieutenant Davison collapsed from loss of blood, and there was nothing to do but move out. The railway cut was overrun, and up the line a bit a stubborn, white-haired brigadier general, trying to rally his men, suddenly fell to the ground when a bullet burst through both of his eyes. West Point graduate Brigadier General Gabriel Paul lost all vision permanently. With Paul out of it, the brigade was overpowered; and the possibilities of a last-ditch stand west of Gettysburg dissolved in an overriding tide of triumphant Confederates.

The entire I Corps went into complete and final retreat, and as though in a last gasp of helpless defiance Confederates saw the remnants of the 143rd

Pennsylvania Regiment cluster around its color bearer, smoke pouring from their muskets as they triggered off a futile volley. The color bearer was shaking his fist at the dominate enemy, and admiring cries went up from the Confederates: "Don't shoot him! Don't shoot him!" But someone had drawn a bead on the plucky soldier and he went down, flag and all, and the retreat continued.

In the precipitate withdrawal were the remnants of the 151st Pennsylvania Regiment, 130 men out of an original 467. Company D of the 151st was composed mostly of students and teachers of Lost Creek Academy, a secondary school in McAlisterville, Pennsylvania; thus the entire regiment was known as "The School Teachers' Regiment." The Pennsylvanians had been thrown in in a last desperate effort to block the Confederates. It was a futile try, but the 26th North Carolina Regiment had found out before it managed to pry them loose that booklearning wasn't all these men had—their muskets, with those of a Michigan regiment, had removed 584 North Carolinians from action.

Not in the retreat was Private Maloney, who had captured a general with his bare hands. His body lay somewhere in the rubble on Seminary Ridge.

Swarming through the streets of Gettysburg, horses and men caught in a jumble of colliding disorganized regiments, Confederate shells whining and bursting between houses and buildings, here-and-there bricks and debris falling, converging troops of the XI Corps, the added, if somewhat amazing, pandemonium of a few panic-stricken citizens begging not to be abandoned to the onrushing Confederates, the Yankees found themselves hopelessly snarled. Somebody managed to bring some artillery out in a street near the town square, and the Rebels were held up for a time. Even so, five thousand Yankees were cut off and taken prisoner on the streets of Gettysburg. Among them was old John Burns who had taken his musket to "get even" with the

Monument of the 143rd
Pennsylvania Infantry Regiment.

Walter Lane

Confederate dead of the first day about to be covered over in a shallow grave near McPherson's Ridge.

Union dead of the first day. Note how they have been stripped of shoes by the Confederates.

Confederates, three minor wounds in his hoary body. (Burns, before his release, was nearly hanged as a combatant out of uniform.)

For those who made it back to Cemetery Hill, with cannon and men lined up beside tombstones, there was the fearful reckoning of what the rout had cost. The I Corps had gone into battle with better than ten thousand men; about one-half were left. (The Iron Brigade was reduced to a shadow, two-thirds of its original eighteen hundred gone.) The XI Corps sustained casualties which left it with less than four thousand of an original nine thousand, and a lot of these men were cast aside in the retreat and were out of the battle. Including Buford's cavalry (Buford had his men back in the thick of things, making a demonstration down on the left of Cemetery Hill), no more than ten thousand disoriented Federal soldiers were left to fend off the Confederates. General Lee had at hand better than twenty-four thousand effective troops to continue the fight.

When the fatigued remnants of the I and XI Corps pulled themselves up onto Cemetery Hill, they were met by General Howard, a battle flag tucked under the stump of his right arm as he rode back and forth shouting encouragement, and General Hancock, just arrived with his special orders of command from Meade. There was a continuing friction about just who was in command, but Hancock was able to put the point across to Abner Doubleday at least when he ordered him to take his troops over and occupy Culp's Hill, a heavily forested height off to the right of Cemetery Hill.

Doubleday objected. His men had had a bad day of it, and many of the officers were dead or missing. *It might be better if Hancock were to send someone else over to Culp's Hill.*

It is not recorded whether Hancock swore or not, but in an army noted for its profuse and protracted imprecations, it was acknowledged by all who had ever come within earshot of Hancock that when he let go, he was by and large the champion of precise cursing with all the proper shadings. Cussing or not, Hancock stood up in his stirrups, raised one hand towards Doubleday,

The Sheads' home in Gettysburg. A spent shell is still lodged in the upper wall just under the eave.

Walter Lane

the sleeve of his shirt spotlessly white (no one seemed to know how he managed it, but Hancock always had clean linen), and roared, "Sir! I am in command on this field. Send every man you have got!"

Abner Doubleday obeyed.

General Howard's selection of Cemetery Hill as a reserve area had been auspicious: the Yankees were afforded the tactical advantage of defensive fighting from high ground. This advantage, of course, was offset by the vastly preponderant amount of Confederates—a good shove would send the Yankees stumbling off the hill and once more into retreat.

Yet the Confederates did not renew the attack. And in this error of omission they lost their greatest opportunity to finish off the two Federal corps at Gettysburg. This failure stemmed from the type of orders issued by their high command.

General Lee maintained a policy of instituting over-all plans and leaving tactics to his generals. Rarely, if ever, did he issue direct orders, but rather would suggest. This had worked beautifully when Stonewall Jackson was his chief lieutenant. A suggestion and Jackson would be quick to act upon it. But there was no Stonewall on the field this day. For fifty-six-year-old General Lee a precise moment had arrived; and as things turned out, it would have been better had he taken a tight rein on his army and given more specific orders.

Watching the rout of the Yankees north and west of town, and the subsequent entrenching at Cemetery Hill, Lee sent a message to Baldy Ewell

74

stating it was only necessary "to push those people" off the hill; that "if practicable" he was to attack.

Lee's message was discretionary, and Ewell did not act upon it. He wished to await the arrival of one of his divisions, not yet on the field, before he committed his forces to an assault, and there was the added problem of not knowing if the Yankees had reinforcements back of the high ground—intelligence which, if Stuart's cavalry had been present, might have been gained quickly. As it was, the awaited division did not arrive until after dark, much too late for Ewell to do anything.[8]

What hitherto had operated efficiently for General Lee—the policy of suggestions and discretionary orders—was now evolving into a problem.

And a second and more serious flaw began to manifest itself in the late afternoon: General Longstreet.

Pete Longstreet had ridden forward in advance of his I Corps, still back near Cashtown, and on Seminary Ridge with General Lee had observed the frantic efforts of the Federals to set up a new defense line.

Longstreet still clung to the idea of a defensive battle and was under the impression that this was Lee's attitude. Lee informed Longstreet of his message to Ewell, and that he intended to wage an offensive battle. Indicating the Federal disposition, he stated, "If Meade is there tomorrow I will attack him."

Longstreet replied, in effect, that if Meade were there tomorrow, it would be because he wanted the Confederates to attack—a good reason, in his judgment, for not attacking.

There were ponderables for Lee to weigh. Maneuvering would not necessarily force Meade into attacking. Lee was deep in the enemy's home ground. His forces would have to live off the land in a confined area, whereas the enemy could easily receive shipments of everything it needed. Protracted maneuvering would work in Meade's favor. It was, therefore, from Lee's point of view wisest to attack and defeat Meade without delay.

Thus, there was as the fateful day drew towards a close a seed of discord between the commanding general and his top field officer.

It was General Hancock who saw more than anyone else just how favorable the Federal position around Cemetery Hill was for defense.

On the right was Culp's Hill. (Abner Doubleday's men were already moving out to occupy it.) On the left and rear was a long, low fold of ground stretching due south for two miles—its conjunction with the southern base of

The gate of the Citizen's Cemetery on Cemetery Hill in July, 1863.

Cemetery Hill had led the citizens of Gettysburg, over the years, to give it the name of Cemetery Ridge. There were already a few troops of the I Corps positioned along the upper portion of the ridge. (In the retreat, these troops had swung southwest of town and fallen into a defense line here.) An attacking force, hoping to dislodge the enemy from Cemetery Ridge, would have to group along Seminary Ridge, almost a mile to the west, and then move over a shallow valley, which offered no more cover than fields of wheat and corn and a few orchards, cross the Emmitsburg Road, angling slowly in a northeasterly direction, and finally, up the rising ground in front of Cemetery Ridge. At the extreme southern end of Cemetery Ridge was a prominent elevation—Little Round Top. Beyond, and higher, was Big Round Top. Occupation of Cemetery Ridge and the two elevations, especially Little Round Top, with enough Federal troops would give the Army of the Potomac an almost impregnable position.

Despite Hancock's authorization from General Meade to take command, General Howard objected strenuously—*Hancock did not rank him, and therefore could not give him orders.* Hancock acceded a little in Howard's direction by saying he would second any order Howard issued, but that Meade had directed he (Hancock) select a field in the rear of Pipe Creek in which to fight. However, he felt the line now held "seemed the strongest position by nature" for Meade to concentrate his forces. General Howard concurred. "Very well, sir," replied Hancock. "I select this as the battlefield."

A message was sent to Meade at Taneytown stating the conditions, and Hancock's belief this was a good place to wage battle. General Meade immediately scrapped his plans for Pipe Creek and sent word to all elements of the Army of the Potomac to march for Gettysburg.

With the arrival of General Slocum's XII Corps between five and five thirty, less than an hour after the tumultuous regrouping on Cemetery Hill, followed by units of General Sickles' III Corps, Hancock, by sundown, was able to seize the high ground, and the tactical arrangement of battle quite dramatically swung back to favor the North.

In a continuous three-mile line, the Federal position now encompassed two main highways—the Taneytown Road and the Baltimore Pike—and extended in the shape of a great "fishhook" from Culp's Hill on the right, over Cemetery Hill and back down Cemetery Ridge to Little Round Top on the extreme left.

Assured the new position was formidable, and with command turned over to General Slocum, now ranking officer on the field, Hancock rode back to contact Meade at Taneytown.

There were low, scattered clouds that night, and there was an eerie brightening and dimming of the land as the moonlight modulated from clear to muted half-tones. In the village of Gettysburg the pulsing light flowed over a country town whose citizens had never imagined, never dreamed, of a time when the outrage of war would come to their very doorsteps.

Everywhere were triumphant Southerners; and the debris of recent fighting—canteens, cartridge cases, muskets, dead soldiers—littered yards and streets and back alleys; and in every household occurred the startling innovation of unwanted "guests." A loud rap on the door was followed by the explicit information that beds and food were to be made available to the conquering host.

Squads of Confederates searched for hidden Yankee soldiers who had escaped capture by leaping into cellars, or had been concealed by citizens eager to do anything which frustrated the Confederate cause. (A considerable number of Federal soldiers were successfully hidden by the citizens until after the battle.)

The Seminary building, Pennsylvania College, warehouses, churches, public halls, even some private homes, all were converted into hospitals full of torn and mutilated Yankees and Confederates awaiting the grisly efforts of Confederate and a few Yankee surgeons—the latter being men who had elected to stay with the wounded prisoners of war.

And in the ironic backwash, a Union chaplain—he, too, had chosen to remain with the wounded—was mistaken for an escaped prisoner of war and shot dead on the steps of a church by a nervous sentry.

One young citizen, however, thirteen-year-old Billy Bayly, was presented with a most unusual surprise as the night grew older. Billy had been out picking raspberries along Seminary Ridge when the fighting started during the morning, and until things became too hot, he had had a gallery seat at the spectacle of battle. Later in the day, when the Confederates had broken the Yankee lines, his father's farm was swarmed under by the Rebels, all intent on converting the family chickens into soup. Billy had developed "foot

Seated beside her damaged house on the Chambersburg Pike is Mrs. Thompson. General Lee's headquarters was in a tent pitched opposite the Thompson house.

trouble," as he later wrote, and was told he "did not amount to a hurrah as a chicken catcher." But the cherry trees out in back of the house were bursting with ripe fruit, and Billy had been put to work collecting cherries by the bucketful for the insatiable Confederates.

It was just after midnight when Billy heard a knocking on the kitchen door. With his mother, he opened the door and saw a "little fellow in a gray uniform" scarcely older than himself. He was from North Carolina, and claimed he "never wanted to see another battle." Pathetically frightened, he asked Billy and his mother to hide him until the battle was over. He was given a suit of clothes and sent to the safety of the attic.

The moon had moved into early morning when General Meade finally arrived on the battlefield and took full control. (With Meade at last at Gettysburg, the Federal forces at Gettysburg, due to the piecemeal arrival of troops and seniority, had had seven successive commanders during the day: Buford, Reynolds, Doubleday, Howard, Hancock, Slocum, and finally Meade.) In the soft July moonlight, Meade made a reconnaissance of Cemetery Hill, where young soldiers were nestled among the tombstones; where, of the countless nights, for many this was the last night of all.

Over in the Confederate lines General Lee held a conference at his headquarters tent set up on Seminary Ridge near the Chambersburg Pike. Lee had remarked earlier to one of his officers: "The enemy is here, and if we do not whip him, he will whip us."

They made plans at Lee's headquarters.

And as the moon waned and a rising pink light in the east signaled sunrise, the long fingers of sorrow and anguish were spreading into New England, out to the wide farmlands of Minnesota, down to the intricate bayous of Louisiana, into the Carolinas and Georgia—the bleak casualty lists, North and South, would be long. And when the time came to erect monuments on the greens and squares, in the country towns, the villages, the cities, the name GETTYSBURG would be chiselled deep and sharp in the granite bases.

Chapter IV

Let Us Shout, Too!

It was four forty in the morning of Thursday, July 2, when a hazy sun began climbing over the eastern horizon. The air was thick and sultry, and there was some indication it might rain.

As dawn brought things into focus the dominant military factors were position and initiative.

During the night the Confederates had extended their line to conform in a great outside arc with Meade's "fishhook" perimeter. This line at sunrise stretched from a point northeast of Rock Creek opposite Culp's Hill, through the streets of the town and partially down Seminary Ridge. With the advent of daylight, skirmishers swung off the ridge and went forward until fired upon and then moved by the right, thus ascertaining the position of Meade's line and its length. By late afternoon the Confederate line would reach to a point opposite the Round Tops and Lee's over-all position of battle would measure almost six miles.

Once General Hancock had disposed the Federal troops into the "fishhook" line, Meade was given the tactical advantage of superior position, plus the benefit of interior communications. A courier riding from one flank to the other would have to traverse only a mile and a half. A courier moving from one flank to the other in Lee's fully extended line would have to travel by an outside route the entire six miles.

Neither army was totally assembled at sunrise, however, and the number of soldiers on both sides was about equal—between forty-five thousand and forty-six thousand each.[9]

The initiative, nevertheless, still belonged to Lee. He had his artillery up, plus his II and III Corps, and part of the I Corps. (Not yet heard from were Stuart and his cavalry.) Meade, on the other hand, was awaiting the arrival of

Cemetery Ridge looking south. Visible in the center background is Big Round Top.

his Artillery Reserve, ordinance wagons, two brigades of the III Corps, the V Corps, the VI Corps, and two cavalry divisions.

On the basis that there is no such thing as a total defense—it is impossible to maintain optimum strength at all points, while an attacker can mass a decisive strength at a point of his choosing—Lee's forces could have been grouped for an all-out assault during the early hours of that morning with a very good chance of knocking the Army of the Potomac out of its defenses. The fact that this was not done involved the Confederate top-command policy and its implementation.

During the night General Lee had concluded his conference by saying, "Gentlemen, we will attack the enemy as early in the morning as practicable." When specific directions were given they called for an assault on Meade's left with a simultaneous "demonstration" on Meade's right around Culp's Hill. The main effort was to be in the form of an "oblique attack." In military terms, this is an assault whereby the attacking columns strike in succession, one after the other, progressively moving along the enemy's line and rolling it up.

The indecision of yesterday afternoon about attacking Cemetery Hill was still in the air. And now at daybreak of July 2, General Lee, for all practical purposes, lost direct control of his army. His policy of making only an over-all plan and leaving the tactics to his generals was about to be interpreted by one of them that he had something to say about the battle and how it should be conducted.

It was to Longstreet and his I Corps that Lee had entrusted the attack on Meade's left; but Longstreet, still full of his idea of forcing the enemy to attack, stalled. In hopes, possibly, that General Lee might alter his viewpoint, Longstreet brought about a series of incredible delays. One of his divisions, Pickett's, was still in Chambersburg. Longstreet decided to wait for it. He couldn't, as he put it, "fight with one boot off." (As it was, he had to begin his attack with this "one boot off." Pickett's division did not arrive at Gettysburg until late in the afternoon and was held in reserve.)

In deference to Longstreet, General Lee postponed the attack until eleven o'clock.

The hour of eleven came and went, and still Longstreet did not make his move. Noon. One o'clock. Two o'clock. Now Longstreet further delayed by countermarching some troops, which were moving down to the southern end of Seminary Ridge, the jumpoff point of attack. He thought they had been observed by the Yankees on Little Round Top. The troops were turned about, retraced their steps, and then sent back to the same destination by a different route.

The opportunity to smash into Meade's army while it was still assembling and, equally important, being placed in position, was completely gone by now. Meade's artillery reserve, ordnance wagons, cavalry and infantry corps, except one—the VI Corps, en route from Manchester, Maryland, in an incredible thirty-five-mile march—were all safely within his lines.

Three o'clock. Three thirty. Now there was a shift in Longstreet's attitude. He would attack exactly as General Lee wished; *but no more than that.*

Confederate reconnaissance, vastly hampered by Jeb Stuart's continued absence, was in serious error about Meade's true position. Yankee pickets had been spotted along the Emmitsburg Road, and it was assumed Meade's left rested here. In reality, Meade's main line was considerably to the rear. The called-for "oblique attack," then, was designed to roll up the Emmitsburg Road and "turn" what was thought to be the Federal left.

Around noon the brigade of Brigadier General Evander M. Law—part of Longstreet's corps—had arrived along Seminary Ridge after a gruelling twenty-eight-mile march from the Cumberland Valley. Despite the long march, Law got some of his men clear below Meade's lines, and they made a startling discovery: the left flank of Meade's line was unguarded. *If Long-*

street took his troops and moved below and around the left end of Meade's line, he could get his men around the flank and rear of the Army of the Potomac. This news was relayed to Longstreet. But with obdurate stubbornness he stuck to Lee's "oblique attack" by saying, "General Lee's orders are to attack up the Emmitsburg Road." And right or wrong, that was the way it was going to be.

As the hour of four o'clock approached the stage was almost set, but not quite. General Meade was having a few problems.

When General Lee heard Meade had been appointed commanding general of the Army of the Potomac, he remarked, "General Meade will commit no blunder in my front." It was an honest appraisal of a man he had known in the prewar regular United States Army. By inference this indicated the Army of the Potomac was going to be well led. It did not imply by projection that all elements of the Army of the Potomac were now suddenly to be oriented into a perfect fighting organization. It was a compliment limited to Meade alone. But even by inference, by the most tenuous of minor premises, it would have been stretching things far beyond the breaking point to have General Lee's statement sift down and include Major General Daniel Edgar Sickles, commanding officer of Meade's III Corps.

In both armies there was no other man quite like Dan Sickles. A "graduate" of Tammany Hall politics in New York City, he had risen to become a congressman in 1858. And there were some who claimed he had been headed for the White House; but Sickles, a few cuts bigger than life, unstable, always operating with a full head of steam, upset his political future by shooting

Major General
Daniel Edgar Sickles.

The National Archives

and killing his wife's "lover," Philip Barton Key, son of the composer of "The Star-Spangled Banner," on a Washington sidewalk. In the ensuing trial Sickles was defended by Edwin Stanton, later famed as President Lincoln's controversial Secretary of War. Stanton won an acquittal for Sickles by reason of "temporary insanity." It was the first time such a phrase had been heard in an American court.

Sickles' detractors, and they were legion, stated flatly that he was using the war to bolster a reputation which was not only tarnished but totally corroded. (In a life constantly laced with all sorts of breaches of the accepted norm Dan had committed the unpardonable "sin" of taking his wife back to his bed and board after the Key affair.)

When the hostilities between the North and South had erupted in April, 1861, Dan was out of Washington, back in New York practicing law. And, over a drink or two with a Tammany Hall crony, Captain William Wiley, at his favorite restaurant, Delmonico's, one of the most famous dining establishments ever seen in America, Dan decided to raise a volunteer regiment— Captain Wiley would help. With an authorization from the Governor of New York to raise a regiment and five hundred dollars from a local Union Defense Committee, handbills were printed and before long volunteers began to appear.

In the peculiar process by which the North raised an army, a man who mustered a volunteer regiment was usually commissioned a colonel, a man who formed a volunteer brigade stood a better chance for a Brigadier General's commission. Not one to miss such an opportunity, Dan soon had a volunteer brigade and promptly dubbed it the Excelsior Brigade.

In a melee of confusion—the governor of New York tried to force Sickles to disband most of his volunteers and maintain his organization at regimental strength, and some of the volunteers attempted to desert—the Excelsior Brigade was moved to Staten Island by permission of the authorities in Washington. It was, nevertheless, still an independent military organization and supposed to pay its own way. Debts began piling up at an alarming rate. But money and bills and Dan Sickles long had had an understanding: somehow, some place, these things took care of themselves, and of course without Dan's having to make any personal sacrifice. Among his many facets, Dan was a first-class moocher. Undaunted by a host of creditors—unflagging energy was also one of his characteristics—Dan hired a circus tent, on credit, naturally, from P. T. Barnum, America's great circus entrepreneur, got his men under shelter, and then proceeded to badger Lincoln and anybody else who would listen to have the Government swear his troops in as United States Volunteers.

84

Philip R. DeTrobriand, brigade commander in the III Corps. (This seems to be the only portrait photograph out of thousands taken of Civil War soldiers in which an attempt at an artistic pose was made.)

When the First Battle of Bull Run went against the North, a desperate cry went up from the capital for more troops, and shortly, the Excelsior Brigade was sworn in and entrained for Washington.

Various figures ranging from $250,000 to $400,000 were submitted as owed by the brigade, but Dan's concept of money and debts was correct: he left Captain Wiley holding the bag (Wiley, who had to placate a host of creditors, became a bitter enemy of Dan's), and his tenacity in maintaining a volunteer brigade was rewarded when Congress passed on his commission as a Brigadier General.

Dan's detractors, and they were always busy, couldn't come up with much about Dan's valor: he led the Excelsior Brigade with perseverance and the resoluteness of a man whose personal courage was beyond question, although these did not necessarily qualify him as a capable tactician. But in an army heavily watered with politics Dan was one of the best swimmers, and he flawlessly made his way to command of the III Corps with the attendant rank of Major General.

On July 2, 1863, Daniel Edgar Sickles, thirty-eight years old, bombastic and filled with himself, came face to face with history, and in Dan's book he was not found wanting—at least he was going to stress this fact the rest of his life.

When the last elements of the III Corps pulled into Meade's line shortly after 9 A.M., Sickles was directed to position his troops along the lower end of Cemetery Ridge and up onto Little Round Top. (A division of the XII Corps had held this section of Meade's defense perimeter since the preceding evening, and Sickles' corps was to relieve it.) The western face of Little Round Top was clear of trees and most underbrush and therefore offered a strong site for defense. Where Cemetery Ridge hooks up with Little Round Top, however, it is a ridge in name only. With scattered woods and rocks, Cemetery Ridge in its southern portion settles and sags until it is no more than a boggy heave of earth. Along with Little Round Top, this was the extreme left of the Federal defenses. Dan Sickles, of course, didn't like it.

He threw out some skirmishers to his front. They passed over a little stream which meandered out in front of Cemetery Ridge, known locally as Plum Run, and reached some high ground in and around a peach orchard bordering the Emmitsburg Road, about a half mile beyond the position assigned to the III Corps. This was the ground Sickles liked. As he saw it, it was the proper place to station his troops.

All morning Dan fretted over that high ground. It beckoned to him with all the allure of a Lorelei. At last he rode over to Meade's little headquarters house just behind the central section of Cemetery Ridge and requested Meade himself to come and take a look.

Earlier in the day Meade had proposed launching an attack from Culp's Hill, but the terrain would not allow good artillery support, and his plans were now one hundred per cent defensive. *Let Lee do the attacking and he would counter. The army was to stay where it was.* Sickles' incursion with a tactical problem, and one which would tend to alter his defensive plans, hardly did anything to help Meade's frayed nerves. Not caring very much for Sickles in the first place, Meade refused his request. Sickles was to place his men where the order called for, and that was that. Meade finally did give in a little and had his chief of artillery, Brigadier General Henry J. Hunt (West Point, 1839), ride over to see just what it was that was bothering Sickles.

Upon returning to his troops, Sickles grew even more concerned over his position when confronted with the information that he was totally unsupported by any force on his left. Through some mix-up in orders Buford's cavalry, which had been stationed along the left flank of Meade's defense perimeter, was gone, and no unit had moved in to take its place.

86

Shortly before noon Hunt suggested Sickles send out a reconnaissance party to find out what the Confederates were doing west of the Emmitsburg Road. Sickles promptly dispatched Berdan's Sharpshooters, an elite unit of soldiers all garbed in European green and picked for their uncanny shooting accuracy, to go forward. Supported by an infantry regiment, the Sharpshooters pushed out beyond the high ground on which Sickles had set his sights and edged across the Emmitsburg Road into a farmyard near Seminary Ridge. By a barn was a little boy, excited and all agog over what he had seen. He pointed to some woods and, with an exclamation of extreme excitement, blurted out, "There are lots of Rebels in there—in rows!"

Somewhat skeptical, the Sharpshooters and the support infantry regiment headed towards the woods. Suddenly, shots rang out and the high whine of bullets bracketed the entire patrol. The little boy had been right. There were plenty of Confederates, and "in rows."

After a nasty little fight, the patrol pulled out and doubled back to inform Sickles what it had seen. This was all the impetuous Sickles needed: his troops would have to occupy that high ground out by the Emmitsburg Road before the Confederates grabbed it. He had previously asked General Hunt if he could move his corps forward and Hunt had warned him that General Meade would have to be consulted and then rode off to inspect another portion of the field. Sickles now issued orders anyway. Bugles sounded, flags were unfurled, and the entire corps moved forward in a mile-long line.

For the men of General Hancock's II Corps, stationed along Cemetery Ridge to the right of the III Corps, the sight of the diamond-insignia III Corps soldiers moving out, regimental flags and guidons fluttering, must have been both alarming and confusing. It indicated that orders had been issued from General Headquarters for either an attack or regrouping. No such orders had been received at any level in the II Corps. They were all quite unaware that this was an undertaking initiated solely by Dan Sickles.

However, the III Corps was rolling forward for the last time. (When the afternoon was over the III Corps would be so decimated that what was left would have to be disbanded and the men reassigned.) And the land of Gettysburg was in its first phase of becoming the foremost battlefield in American history. Despite the fact that thousands upon thousands of other men had something to do with the battle, Gettysburg was about to evolve into something special in the person of Major General Daniel Edgar Sickles. Before the afternoon was over he would reach the high point of his life by losing his leg, and whether because of this or merely because of his character, he would somehow conceive the notion that he was the "hero" of the battle, the man who had "turned the tide" at Gettysburg. This idea, which proved durable and impervious to facts, would tantalize Dan the rest of his long and somewhat notorious life and would have great bearing in setting up the battlefield as it is seen today. Dan Sickles, more than any other individual, was responsible for promoting and nurturing the plan to turn the Gettysburg battlegrounds into a National Military Park.

As the III Corps assembled along its advanced position and the men of Hancock's II Corps tried to fathom what was happening, the sun moved well into afternoon. The skies, which had threatened rain in the morning, had cleared considerably, and with sunlight streaming down it had grown hot, the temperature reaching into the high seventies. Slowly, inexorably, the mainspring of battle had been wound into a tight coil of energy. And shortly before the sun's westerly position indicated four o'clock it received its last turn.

With fifty-year-old Major General John Sedgwick (West Point, 1837) at the helm, soldiers with a Greek Cross insignia on their caps began streaming into the Union lines—the men of the VI Corps. Arriving along the Taneytown Road, fifteen thousand infinitely weary soldiers were placed in reserve

Soldiers of the 6th Maine, VI Corps, lined up for inspection.

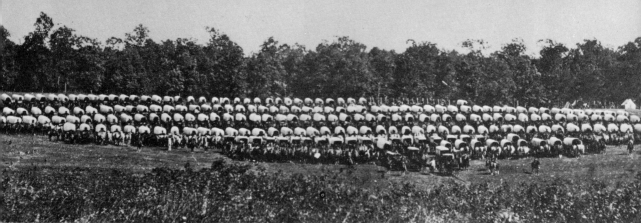

One of the wagon trains of the VI Corps.

to the rear of the Round Tops. They had marched thirty-five miles with only one break, and it is quite plausible to assume a great portion of the men heaved themselves down to the earth, cursed "Uncle" (behind his back) John Sedgwick for marching them so hard, and went to sleep, battle or no battle.

Meade's army was now totally assembled, but it is doubtful he was given the opportunity to gasp a sigh of relief. At General Headquarters there was a conference of corps commanders. In walked Meade's chief of engineers, thirty-three-year-old Major General Gouverneur K. Warren (West Point, 1850) with the word on Sickles and the new position of the III Corps. From the vicinity of the Round Tops a steady hum of musketry and cannonading could be heard. Up rode Sickles, and before he could dismount, he was curtly ordered to return to his corps and informed that Meade would follow him. Major General Sykes (West Point, 1842) was ordered to move his V Corps from a reserve position on the right and file into support of the III Corps.

It must have been a wrathful Meade who rode over to see what Dan Sickles had done; and when he saw, it must have made his heart skip. In regrouping his corps, Sickles had fashioned a defense line forward of the rest of the Army of the Potomac in the shape of an inverted V. Tactically, this formation is one of the worst possible for defense: the apex can be hit with frontal and flank fire from both sides. But that wasn't all Sickles had done.

In setting up his new line he had angled his right along the Emmitsburg Road. But there were just not enough troops to effect a hookup with Hancock's troops. Thus there was a gap between the two corps. The left cut back from the peach orchard scouted earlier by the III Corps skirmishers, through a wheat field and over a boulder-strewn, craggy hill appropriately named Devil's Den. As with his right, however, Sickles did not have enough manpower to occupy Little Round Top. And now, beyond a few signalmen, Little Round Top was unoccupied. (The higher eminence of Big Round

89

Major General
Gouverneur K. Warren.

Top offered, militarily, no advantage as it was covered by a dense mantle of woods.)

If the Confederates were to get control of Little Round Top, their artillery firing from this height would be squarely on the flank of Cemetery Ridge. The resultant enfilading fire down the ridge would once and for all end the Army of the Potomac's grip on the high grounds south of Gettysburg. It probably would mean the destruction of the Army of the Potomac as well: Confederate control of Little Round Top would also gain domination of the Taneytown Road. Meade would then have only the Baltimore Pike through which to extricate his army, and with thousands of men, wagons, artillery. and horses bunched onto one road it would be a rout. Little Round Top, then, was the key to the entire Union position.

It might have been that for once in his cocksure life—prompted, perhaps, by an irate glint in Meade's eyes—Sickles felt he had acted a little too impetuously, for he offered to recall the III Corps if Meade so wished. Whatever doubts may have clutched at Dan at that moment were quickly dissipated in a sudden avalanche of sound. The energy of battle which had been sputtering with nervous little flare-ups of artillery and musket fire began to uncoil as forty-six Confederate cannon suddenly opened up with a crashing roar on Sickles' salient; it was too late to do anything but stay and fight it out. The time was four o'clock, and the attack General Lee had entrusted to Pete Longstreet early in the day was finally under way, fully five hours later than Lee had anticipated.

The shattering crash of Longstreet's guns caused Meade to inform Sickles tersely that he was to maintain his advanced formation, and that he (Meade) would see that the rest of the army supported him.

For Meade, a career army man of forty-eight, born of American parents in

Spain—his father was in a debtors' prison at the time of General Meade's birth—who regarded Pennsylvania as his home state, the supreme moment had arrived. He could lose the battle right here and now, and with it the war.

And as though Sickles' ill-timed and badly conceived move were not enough, the Fates decided Meade's equilibrium needed one more jab: a Confederate cannon ball went thudding by his bay horse, Baldy. The horse bolted, and Meade and the frightened animal streaked first one way and then the other and finally in the direction of the Confederate lines. And for a few seconds it looked as if the Southerners were going to capture the commanding officer of the Army of the Potomac by default. But Meade managed to regain control of his mount, and this near disaster was averted—the first of an afternoon which was going to pile crisis upon near calamity for the Yankees.

Longstreet's artillery, heaving great boiling clouds of rank smoke into the air, flailed away at Sickles' lines in a murderous rain of solid shot and shell, mangling men and horses, and blowing a Rhode Island battery clean out of action. But General Hunt, who had warned Sickles about advancing his troops without permission, dug into his artillery reserve and began piling battery after battery just in behind the peach orchard where Sickles had anchored the apex of his salient. Concentrating twenty or thirty guns at a time on one Confederate battery and then shifting to the next, Hunt's guns managed to silence five of Longstreet's artillery emplacements in quick succession. And added to this give and take of the opposing artillery was the strange sound of music. Somewhere to the north along Seminary Ridge a Confederate regimental band was playing lively polkas and waltzes. And as if all this weren't enough, there was a hullabaloo of wild mooing. Confederate artillery had inadvertently found the range on a herd of cows feeding in the valley between Devil's Den and Little Round Top, sending the demoralized animals into a flouncing, swaying stampede for safer ground, and

Emmitsburg Road. In the foreground, in front of the white house, is the Peach Orchard.

Gettysburg National Military Park—Walter Lane

in the process nearly trampling General Hunt to an ignominious death under frenzied, cloven feet. For one farmer, at least, the blame for fluttery and upset cows and less, if not sour, milk could be pinned quite definitely on the unsympathetic Confederate artillery.

Then came another note. One Yankee officer described it as sounding "like demons emerging from the earth." The Rebel Yell!

Major General John B. Hood's division, the same which had listened to the taunts of the women in Chambersburg, came charging out of the fields and woods from the southwest and drove straight in on Sickles' left. Longstreet had pulled the first string of the "oblique attack," and due to the inverted V formation of Sickles' corps, Hood's men did not make contact with the enemy until they reached Devil's Den, the extreme left flank of the III Corps.

The Yankees in Devil's Den offered stubborn resistance in this eerie place of rocks and gullies, and, if anyone happened to be looking, poisonous snakes. Someone jerked the lanyard of a cannon and a shell went whizzing out, exploding near Hood, and a piece of hot iron cut into his arm, crippling it permanently. Hood was out of the fight within twenty minutes. Even so, the

Baldy, General Meade's bay horse. Baldy survived four wounds during the war. The last, a bullet in the ribs at Gettysburg, put him out of action for the rest of the war, but he survived Meade.

Major General John B. Hood,
division commander
in Confederate I Corps.

Library of Congress

Confederates kept smashing in hard, and despite reinforcements brought in on the double from the wheat field area, the Yankees could not hold the position and were driven out, losing three cannon in a wild confusion of sulphurous smoke and yelling and shooting and cursing and dying.

With Devil's Den gone, the men in the wheat field were suddenly exposed to flank and rear fire. The wheat field was quickly plowed under and the whole of Sickles' left from near the peach orchard back to the base of Little Round Top began breaking up. Now a full brigade of yelling Rebels swung out and burrowed straight for Little Round Top.

When the Confederate barrage opened, Meade's chief of engineers, General Warren, and some aides had ridden over to the crest of Little Round Top. Warren felt Sickles' troops were, as he later described it, "badly disposed." He quickly found out they were not merely "badly disposed" but placed without regard to military logic: Sickles' line stopped at the eastern end of Devil's Den, and that was all. Little Round Top itself, apart from a few blue-jacketed signal personnel, was completely undefended.

Warren called upon a battery near Devil's Den to lob a shell out into some woods west of the Emmitsburg Road. The sound of it whistling through the air caused Confederates to turn and look, and the resulting glint of sunlight on gun barrels and bayonets told Warren a catastrophic story. Confederates were forming for an attack; their ranks extended until they were below the Union left. Their line of advance would then press straight into Little Round Top unopposed. This discovery was "appalling" to Warren, and he directed the signalmen to make a demonstration—anything to impress upon the Confed-

93

Joshua Chamberlain,
commanding officer
of the
20th Maine Regiment.

The National Archives

erates that the hill was occupied—while he dispatched an aide to ride off and get help. As the excited aide galloped away the Confederate infantry assault was launched, and the Confederates overran Devil's Den and the wheat field area.

Warren's aide located General Sickles, but Sickles, his hands more than full, could spare no troops. Then up rode curly-headed General Sykes in advance of a division of his V Corps filing into support of the beleaguered III Corps. The aide managed to communicate to Sykes the extreme urgency of the situation on Little Round Top, and an order went out to send a brigade from the newly arriving division up onto the hill.

With the V Corps Maltese Cross insignia sewn to their caps, the men of the brigade dispatched to Little Round Top were just in time. Composed of regiments from New York, Michigan, Pennsylvania, and Maine, the brigade found the top of the hill buzzing and reverberating in a lacework of shellfire and smoke, while Confederate infantrymen clawed at the western slope.

Colonel Strong Vincent, commander of the hastily commandeered brigade, curled his regiments in a line just below the crest of Little Round Top, facing them west and south. At the extreme southern end of the newly formed line he placed the 20th Maine Regiment. And if anyone took a measuring stick at that moment and worked out just where the extreme left flank of the entire Army of the Potomac lay, it was exactly here, in the hands of 358 men, the "down easterners" of the 20th Maine.

Leading the Maine regiment was thirty-five-year-old Colonel Joshua Chamberlain, a one-time theological student and more recently a professor at Bowdoin College who had asked for two years' leave of absence, ostensibly to study in Europe, and then enlisted as a volunteer at Bangor, Maine. Instinctive and capable in the arts of a field officer, he had proved to the more skeptical professional soldiers that there were men from civilian life who, with training, were admirably suited for command. For his work on this afternoon he was going to receive the Medal of Honor.

Chamberlain placed his men into a defense line facing due south, and made certain his two brothers, one a lieutenant, the other a member of a charitable organization who had chosen to accompany the 20th Maine, were sent to the opposite ends of the line—if they were all to stay together one shell burst might, as Chamberlain put it, "make it hard for Mother."

On the right of the 20th Maine, stretching around the west face of Little Round Top, were the other regiments of Vincent's brigade. Out in front was a shallow valley, strewn with boulders and great oak and pine trees. Beyond the valley, looming above the 20th Maine, was densely forested Big Round Top. On the left there were more trees, but that was all—no troops, no support of any kind. With no soldiers on this flank, Chamberlain took the precaution of sending out Company B to get down where the ground leveled off a bit and watch as best it could for any signs of a flanking movement—there was no telling what the woods might conceal.

When John B. Hood's division went booming and yelling at the Yankees, Law's brigade of Alabamians, which had made the unrelieved twenty-eight-mile march during the morning, went streaming in with the attack, and its line of assault carried it right for the Round Tops.

The 15th Alabama and 47th Alabama regiments shoved into the short valley between Big Round Top and Little Round Top and were clearly below the Army of the Potomac. Leading the regiments was Colonel William C. Oates. Both he and some of his men had taken a quick climb up the steep

Company C, 20th Maine Regiment.

Down East *Magazine and* The 20th Maine (*J. B. Lippincott Company*)

slopes of Big Round Top to drive off a group of detached Yankee sharp-shooters who were peppering their ranks with astonishing accuracy. The sharpshooters disappeared, but from the vantage of Big Round Top it was easy for the Alabamians to see Meade's wagons parked in the rear of the Army of the Potomac. To his dying day Colonel Oates would deplore the fact that Longstreet's obdurate orders allowed for nothing but an "oblique attack." He fancied if he could have chopped down trees and dragged some artillery up on Big Round Top it would have dominated Little Round Top and thus have rendered the Yankee portion there untenable. An interesting idea, and it might have altered the course of the battle drastically; but the "ifs" of a battle are the pregnant joys of later-day tacticians, to be mulled over and propounded and pondered. Things happen as they happen, and Colonel Oates' orders did not include chopping down trees on Big Round Top on the after-noon of July 2.

The 20th Maine was struck first by a swarm of yelling Confederates driv-ing in from the right, pouring in volley after volley of deadly Minié balls. The Maine men returned the fire, and the woods sounded to the snarl and snap of lead slugs whacking trees and careening off rocks, and the peculiar *whoosh*

A youthful "volunteer" poses for the cameraman amid the hastily erected entrenchments of Little Round Top on hot July afternoon in 1863.

—c-thump of bullets breaking into flesh. But this action had only started when Colonel Chamberlain's attention was directed to a column of Rebels moving past his front behind the attacking forces. It was the 15th and 47th Alabama regiments, and they were maneuvering to get beyond Chamberlain's left. These two regiments outnumbered the 20th Maine better than two to one.

The company Chamberlain had sent out to watch for just such a contingency was quickly cut off and presumed lost. Normal tactics called for a swinging back of the entire line in the threat of a flank attack, but Chamberlain quickly saw he could not perform this maneuver: his front was under direct attack and fighting for its life. Considering his regiment was so beleaguered and that any maneuver would be hard to carry out, Chamberlain issued an amazing order.

The left half of the regiment was to bend back in a straight line and extend itself. The right half was to sidestep in order to maintain contact with the left and continue firing to the front to conceal the movement. Even for Civil War soldiers, drilled and redrilled in complex combat maneuvers, it was a highly sophisticated piece of tactical movement. But somehow, twisting and hopping behind rocks and trees, the Maine men managed it. The result was that, while stretched extremely thin, Chamberlain's troops on the right now covered the ground previously held by the entire regiment, and a new line was formed by the men on the left which reached back and faced east.

When the 15th Alabama came to the front and surged in on what they thought was the enemy's flank, they suddenly were struck with a withering hail of lead. Alabamians began falling, and momentarily the attack faltered. But these Confederate veterans were tough as nails and they charged in again, and this time the firepower of the 20th Maine was not enough to stop them. Using their bayonets, the Alabamians waded right into Chamberlain's line and began a grim hand-to-hand battle of bayonet thrusts answered by rifle butts wielded as clubs.

Acting out, perhaps, an ancient instinct which has elevated man above his fellow creatures but which holds an awful curse—the instinct of weapons—the men from Maine and Alabama slugged it out toe-to-toe in a hell of hazy smoke clinging around rocks and trees like a dank curtain of thick mist. In the peculiar rising ecstasy of battle, which can transport men into primitive and brutal killers, they battered and shot the future out of each other. Men jumped behind rocks, trees, anything which offered momentary concealment, and bit off paper cartridges and rammed lead Minié balls home in the long barrels of their muskets and fired willy-nilly into the confusion, and often as

Union dead at Little Round Top.

not they had to turn around to beat off a wild-eyed soldier running in with an outthrust bayonet—some were not able to counter in time.

Finally, there came a lull, and the Alabamians drew back for regrouping. Colonel Oates believed his men drove the Yankees from their position five times, only to have them rally and drive back. And if anyone needed proof there had been bitter fighting, he had only to look around.

The smoke lifted a little and revealed men lying in grotesque heaps, rocks covered, to use Colonel Oates' word, with "puddles" of blood. Here, a Yankee with a neat hole in his head, dead from a bayonet thrust; there, a groaning Confederate clutching his belly, warm blood cascading through his fingers, no doubt wondering in torment why he was here on some damned hill in Pennsylvania—he would stop wondering quickly enough. Trees were gashed and stripped by hastily aimed bullets. One tree four inches in diameter was chopped completely through and toppled about two feet off the ground. And those men who were still ready for more fight bore the typical look of Civil War soldiers: exhausted faces, traced with little rills of grimy sweat, punctuated by blackened teeth and lips where gunpowder had spilled over from frantically bitten paper cartridges.

Over on the right of the 20th Maine, clear around on the open west slope of Little Round Top, the rest of Vincent's brigade was hard pressed. Leathery, battle-hardened Confederate soldiers were boring in fast. Clambering over rocks and shooting and yelling, they drove into the Yankees, quickly chewing up the defenders until the right end of the line sagged and fell apart. Again it was touch and go. And this time it was General Warren himself who rode off to get help. He found the 140th New York Regiment moving in from reserve. The regimental commander protested he was under orders to take his troops elsewhere. "Never mind that ... I'll take the responsibility," Warren cried out, and the New York regiment moved up Little Round Top on a dead run, not stopping to fix bayonets or load. The weight of their running bodies cresting the hill and then tumbling down into the enemy was enough to turn the tide. Amazed Confederates wavered and drew back, and the Federal line on the right of Little Round Top was stabilized.

As the 140th New York began its improbable charge Colonel Vincent, the brigade commander who had so hastily curled his troops in a line below

Look closely at this photograph taken at the base of Little Round Top—the dead are mingled with the rocks.

the crest of Little Round Top, fell with a bullet in his groin, and litter bearers carried him out of the fight and out of the war and eventually out of everything.

Some Yankee gunners managed to drag six three-inch cannon by block and tackle up the heavily wooded back side of Little Round Top and face them in the direction of Devil's Den. This was Battery D, 5th United States Field Artillery. (Created during the Revolutionary War, Battery D is still in existence today, and is the only unit of the American Armed Forces which dates back to Washington's armies.)

The men of Battery D didn't have much of a go at it at first. They put their cannon in place all right, and even managed to get off a few rounds, but Confederate infantrymen down in Devil's Den, some of them using telescopic sights, took a bead on the battery and began firing with a murderous precision. Twenty-nine-year-old Brigadier General Stephen Weed (West Point, 1854)—the 140th New York Regiment was part of his brigade—was dropped as he gave orders to the gunners. The battery commander, bending over to assist Weed, was shot dead, and the swirl of Confederate bullets silenced Battery D.

But it was only momentary. The desperate cannoneers brought in some sharp-eyed infantrymen of their own, and they effectively covered the position while the battery blazed into action once more. And this time it erupted with fearful vengeance on Devil's Den, firing round after round of growling shells which caromed off rocks, metallic, shrieking noises tearing the air, and

Battery D, 5th United States Field Artillery at drill.

Little Round Top from Devil's Den.

exploded in great orange and red bursts with the violence of lightning, smothering the men in Devil's Den in flying iron.

The soldiers of the 20th Maine could hear the *thump, thump, thump* of Battery D, yet it was hardly reassuring. It meant, simply, that the rest of the brigade was under heavy pressure and no help could be expected. And if ever the 20th Maine needed help, it was now.

Obviously, the Alabama regiments were making ready to try it again. This time there could be no doubt about the outcome. The 20th Maine was greatly outnumbered. It had suffered casualties, including the cut-off Company B, which amounted to one-third of organizational strength, and it now numbered about 260 men.

And added to the overwhelming odds against the 20th Maine was another

Dead Confederate sharpshooter behind his barricade.

The same site today. Little Round Top in background.

problem. Up and down the line there were desperate cries of "Ammunition!" The fighting had been going on for about an hour and a half. Each man had had sixty rounds when he went into battle and they were pretty much used up. This meant nearly twenty thousand rounds had been fired off by the 20th Maine.

General Lee was only moments away from victory. Collapse of the 20th Maine would uncover Little Round Top. With Little Round Top gone, General Meade's entire position would be flanked, and that would be the beginning of the end for the Army of the Potomac.

There was nothing very much Chamberlain could do. His men were digging into the cartridge boxes of the dead and wounded, looking for new sources of ammunition; but the firepower they could offer hardly matched that of the Alabamians.

Suddenly, the electrifying cry went out: "Bayonets!" The 20th Maine was going to attack! The regiment was outnumbered, almost out of ammunition; Chamberlain had called for the impossible. And to complicate everything his left, bent far back, would have to swing forward in a "right wheel," have to swing out much as a folding ruler opening into a straight line, and come abreast of the rest of the regiment.

Bayonets clanked on barrels. Soldiers nerved themselves. A lieutenant sprang to the front of the line, his sword raised high, and yelled, "Come on! Come on, boys!" Men began to follow. Regimental flags were held up. Now there was shouting. The left wing, already fighting off a renewed Confederate effort, swarmed down the side of the hill straight into the disbelieving Alabamians. It caught them completely off guard and rolled them back until Chamberlain's line was all at once straight, and then there was no holding it.

Pivoting, as an officer to the right of the 20th Maine described it, "like a great gate upon a post," the regiment rammed into the Alabamians, shocking them into surrender or precipitate flight. One Alabama officer, striving to fathom what was happening, fired a revolver at Chamberlain, and missing, ceremoniously handed him his sword in surrender. The completely unanticipated foray into their ranks was too much. It just was not in the books. Outnumbered men did not do these things. But Chamberlain and his 20th Maine had other ideas.

Luck had been against the Alabamians from the start. When they had lined up for the general attack, back on Seminary Ridge, the 15th Alabama had sent a squad with all the canteens of the regiment looking for water. The general attack was launched before the squad returned, and then the squad had the misfortune to be captured. Tired by a twenty-eight-mile march, the 15th Alabama always felt it was the lack of water—one of the little things upon which battles hinge—which had cost them the fight. This obvious necessity was not there when they needed it, and the men were required to wage battle weakened by an overriding thirst.

That was not the only bad luck, either. As they pulled back from the initial impact of the 20th Maine's unlikely attack, the 15th Alabama encountered the nightmare of every line officer: bullets began cutting into them not only from the front, but from the rear as well. They were caught in a trap.

Company B, which Chamberlain had sent out to guard his flank and which had been cut off, suddenly popped up from behind a stone wall, guns blazing, sights leveled with tragic accuracy. And Company B was not alone. The sharpshooters Colonel Oates and his men had chased up Big Round Top at the start were there, too. Oates thought he was surrounded by an entirely new unit of Yankees. He gave the order for full retreat, but, despite strong efforts

Statistics at Devil's Den.

Library of Congress

110th Pennsylvania Regiment, part of III Corps.

to cut their way out, the Confederates lost some four hundred prisoners and were handed a defeat which did not fit into the rules of military logic.

Whatever Fates had acted in behalf of Meade, he was blessed with two strokes of luck at Little Round Top. First, was General Warren and his quick estimate of the situation; and second a group of woodsmen, fishermen, and farmers from Maine, all under a college professor, who had managed to pull off an incredible victory and saved Meade's army in one of the most dramatic actions of the war.

A breeze began to stir, not strong, not yet perceptible, as the Confederate prisoners were herded to the rear; but it was there, curling lightly around the rocks and through the trees of Little Round Top. In time it was going to blow fair and full for the Army of the Potomac.

As the 20th Maine denied Confederate occupation of Little Round Top, out in the open valley where Sickles had his III Corps dangerously exposed the Rebels were swamping the Yankees in a wild, surging mass of infantrymen and storming blasts of artillery fire.

The III Corps line running from the peach orchard back through the wheat field to Devil's Den was under the command of Alabama-born Major General David Birney, and Birney, who was to feel the sharp sting of two minor wounds as the fighting progressed, had seen this part of the III Corps knuckle under almost at the outset of the Confederate attack. Devil's Den had

The Trostle farm, Sickles' temporary field headquarters, with its casualties of battle.

gone first, and the Yankee-held real estate at the wheat field changed owner-ship, and Birney's line, what was left of it, had all but fallen apart.

In a continuing effort to stall the Confederate drive and re-establish a solid front, Birney shifted entire companies from one sector to the other, but it was a losing race, as both the enemy and time worked to drain away available manpower. When Birney sent word to Colonel Philip DeTrobriand, a French-born New York newspaperman turned soldier, to detach troops from his brigade for another portion of the line DeTrobriand replied he had none to spare—in fact, he himself would need all the troops he could get in the next few minutes. DeTrobriand, in what can be termed a vast understatement, afterward wrote, "The Confederates seemed to have the devil in them."

Devil or not, they were giving the Yankees a taste of hell and, worse, a first-class beating.

In this riot of noise and prospective calamity Dan Sickles, astride a fever-ishly nervous stallion, sought to reinstall battle order to his already perishing corps. Dan had stationed himself near his field headquarters located in the yard of a farmer named Trostle. Now, as Sickles barked out orders to saluting couriers between the *hiss, hiss, hiss* of flying cannon balls, a specific moment in his life arrived. Forward you could have heard it as it passed by, but the only thing General Daniel Sickles heard was the ghastly crunch of the cannon ball which struck his right leg above the knee.

They carried Dan into the Trostle farmyard, where Dan himself directed the buckling of a saddle strap to his thigh in an improvised tourniquet. Even a most cursory glance revealed the dire effect of the cannon ball—the leg would have to be amputated.

When a greatly alarmed General Birney rode into the Trostle farmyard Sickles called out in a loud, clear voice: "General Birney, you will take command, sir."

Birney acknowledged the order to assume responsibility of the III Corps and rode off as they lifted Dan as carefully as possible into an ambulance, a cigar perched jauntily in his mouth, waving to his soldiers—personal fortitude of a high order was also one of his characteristics.

As Dan was a major general, the surgeons saved his dismembered leg for him to dispose of as he saw fit. He found a rather interesting site for the interment.

Dan Sickles was carried out of the battle and what was to prove the rest of the war, and surgeons took one of his legs; but they couldn't take Gettysburg —the high-water mark of his life—away from him.

With Sickles gone, Meade told General Hancock to take charge of the over-all operations on the Federal left, and in particular to see what he could do to stop the rapidly deteriorating III Corps from a complete rout.

Hancock immediately ordered an entire division from the II Corps to move out to the wheat-field area.

Before the division double-timed towards its hopeless mission a brigade of soldiers from Massachusetts, New York, and Pennsylvania, "the Irish Brigade," felt there was one piece of business which should be attended to without delay.

In both armies chaplains of all denominations administered to the spiritual needs of the soldiers, although the Civil War chaplain held no rank. Impiously known as "Holy Joes" by men of both armies, men who sinned on a level seldom duplicated, and who swore so much and so profusely that their words even rubbed off on a few chaplains who were recorded as hurling the vilest epithets at the enemy, the chaplain at time of battle suddenly took on his rightful importance. The Irish Brigade, feeling the closeness of the Hereafter, knelt in an open field—it was no different than the rest of the army, and there were sins aplenty to sorrow over—and its Catholic chaplain climbed up on a rock and pronounced absolution to one and all, kneeling non-Catholics included.

The division—the Irish Brigade at least momentarily in a state of grace— marched over behind the wheat field, and the necessity of final spiritual preparation quickly was manifested in a spot of earth gone mad. Men fell over dead without a word next to men screaming their dying lungs out; and others, the living, kept up a running babble of swearing as they sighted their muskets and sought to pronounce final judgment on the enemy with their trigger fingers.

The division checked the still pressing Confederates for a while, driving them back across the wheat field, only to have them return in a strong counterattack. Meade pushed in two brigades from the V Corps, and the wheat field turned into a maelstrom of continued slaughter. When it was all over, on the basis of area involved, the wheat field marked the site of the largest number of casualties ever sustained by Americans in any battle.

Now Meade dipped heavily into his reserves and pulled up two more brigades of regulars from the V Corps. (The regulars, unlike the volunteer state regiments, were permanent units of the U.S. Army.)

When the regulars swarmed towards the wheat field they passed Plum Run, the meandering stream in front of lower Cemetery Ridge, and they saw an incredible sight: the water was running red with the blood of wounded soldiers. One of the severest side effects of a wound is drastic dehydration, and badly hurt Federals had dragged themselves to Plum Run to get a drink. Many simply fell over and died in the water or along the banks, and Plum Run was rechristened during the afternoon of July 2 to "Bloody Run."

The regulars fell into position at the wheat field, and it looked for a while as if Meade's soldiers were there in enough numbers to contain the Rebels, but all at once the brigades first sent in by Meade from the V Corps noticed bullets were winging into them from the right and rear.

"Bloody Run."

Walter Lane

Major General
Lafayette McLaws,
division commander,
Confederate III Corps.

Library of Congress

A soldier of the ranks turned to his brigade commander and shouted, "Colonel, I'll be damned if I don't think we're faced the wrong way. The Rebs are up there in the woods behind us on the right." The colonel sent an aide to advise division headquarters what was happening, but where division headquarters was supposed to be the aide found nothing but Confederates.

Pete Longstreet had pulled the second string of the "oblique attack." At six o'clock he had given the nod to Major General Lafayette McLaws (West Point, 1842) to take his division into battle, and two heavily massed brigades of Mississippians and Georgians had smashed into the peach orchard in a torrent of yelling, bayonet thrusts, and mayhem, knocking aside a regiment of Pennsylvania Zouaves dressed in Turkish uniforms of pantaloons, gaiters, and

Pennsylvania Zouaves, in uniforms patterned after the Zouaves of mid-nineteenth century French colonial armies, with turbans, gaiters, and short jackets in varied colors. Used by a number of volunteer regiments of both North and South.

Library of Congress

turbans. (These picture-book outfits had held quite a bit of popularity in both North and South at the beginning of the war. Composed usually of fraternal orders, fire companies, and various home-town drill teams which enlisted as units, the Zouave regiments' bright uniforms after a few battles became kind of tacky, causing one British observer to call them "seedy pashas.")

The Pennsylvania Zouaves rendered impotent, McLaws' Mississippi and Georgia boys had kept right on going, straight through the peach orchard, defying a furious fire from Union batteries, until they had opened a hole in the III Corps. It was these men who had moved in behind the Federals at the wheat field.

The division sent over by Hancock was the first to give way. And when it went, it was all at once, enlisted men and officers scrambling for the rear in a frantic effort to escape the catastrophe of envelopment. But even this was only partially successful. The division sustained staggering casualties, among them two brigade commanders, Brigadier General S. K. Zook and Colonel E. E. Cross, both mortally wounded. (Cross, only a few hours before, had shouted to an ambulance chief that as far as he was concerned there would be no necessity for one of the "dead carts" on this day. It was a "dead cart" which carried Cross on his final trip.)

When Hancock's division gave way the brigades wedged in from the V Corps were quickly exposed, and in a few minutes they joined the pell-mell dash for the rear, leaving behind a trail of dead and wounded all the way from the wheat field to bloody Plum Run. The regulars sustained the shock of almost eight hundred casualties, a major heading up the 11th United States Infantry claiming he lost half his men, and these "without inflicting the slightest damage upon the enemy."

What had been Birney's line was gone, and in the melancholy process two new proper names took their place in American history. At the Peach Orchard only the Rebel yell now could be heard; at the Wheat Field, despite five hundred dead Southerners sprawled among the broken shafts of grain, no living Yankee contested its occupation.

After the Peach Orchard fell, the entire right leg of the III Corps' line was doomed, the final blow falling when Major General Richard H. Anderson (West Point, 1842) sent his division of A. P. Hill's III Corps, stationed along the center of Seminary Ridge, barging across the Emmitsburg Road.

There is a story about a young girl, Josephine Miller, who, when Sickles put his troops in a forward position, found herself surrounded by the 1st Massachusetts Regiment as they crowded into her grandfather's farmyard along the Emmitsburg Road. The story goes that Josephine Miller baked bread and biscuits for the hungry soldiers, and refused to stop baking even when Confederate shells began bursting nearby. It must be a true story, for Josephine Miller was made a member of the III Corps Veterans' Association, and there is a monument to the 1st Massachusetts still standing in the farmyard.

The men of the 1st Massachusetts were not able to linger over the hot biscuits and bread very long, for the division under General Anderson came crashing in, turning their line inside out, shaking it up and tossing it aside.

Anderson's weatherbeaten, battle-seasoned soldiers from Florida, Alabama, and Georgia seemed to have found the right combination to unhook everything. Besides the 1st Massachusetts, they bowled over the entire right of the III Corps, mixing everything up in a chaos of heavy smoke and wild noise.

In a continuing effort to contain the Confederate attack, Meade kept piling in more troops, and now he "borrowed" soldiers wearing the five-pointed star insignia of his XII Corps, located in position at Culp's Hill.

These troops were just arriving when the right leg of the III Corps broke, and in a snarl of confusion, reinforcements bumped into hastily retreating regiments. Everything started piling up in a jam of quickly limbered cannon, horses, and entire companies, caught in the indefinable yet very contagious panic of precipitate retreat. And the Confederates were right on top of everything, prodding and pushing with the rod of fear and the more persuasive effect of firepower.

A New Jersey regiment trying to extricate itself lost first its colonel, next the major, then a captain, another captain, and another. Four men trying to carry the last captain were shot down, and command finally devolved into the hands of a corporal who managed to rally what was left of the regiment and get it into some sort of line back of a hedge.

A New Hampshire regiment pulling back from near the Peach Orchard became caught in the vast mass of confusion, and the Confederates caught up with it in front and flank and churned the regiment into a disorganized mob of yelling, lost men.

The Excelsior Brigade, the outfit with which Dan Sickles had launched his military career, was chewed up and digested by the voracious Confederates. Yet it wasn't all one-sided. The Confederates were getting it, too. Here and there companies and regiments rallied and turned to let go, long tongues of flame spewing from their muskets, catching the Confederates in a deadly hail of flying lead, knocking them down in platoons. One Yankee brigade general noticed an important-looking Confederate officer pushing his men and waving them on without regard to hazard. The Yankee officer detailed an entire company to aim its fire at the Confederate, and at last he was knocked over with five bullets in his body. Later they found they had inflicted fatal injuries on Brigadier General William Barksdale, a former congressman from Mississippi.

When Meade had appointed General Hancock to take over-all command of the Federal left he made a good choice, but there was nothing Hancock or anybody could do if the soldiers in blue didn't rally. They were being pushed around by an enemy which smelled victory, and yet Meade had brought up enough reserves in terms of numbers to smother the best efforts of the Confederates.

The battle had raged almost four hours now, and the sun was dipping low into the western rim of the South Mountain Range. Lurid flashes of light, the bright streaks of thundering cannon and snarling muskets, cut through the hastening twilight, and the inferno of stench and noise and death in a hundred varieties continued relentlessly.

General Meade had drained his reserves deeply, piling in troops until he had stripped Culp's Hill down to one brigade. Now Meade was using troops from the I and II Corps, all of the XII Corps, less the one brigade, in position on Culp's Hill, and all of the V Corps. Including the III Corps, this meant that as the fighting progressed, in order to counter Longstreet's attack, the number of Federal troops in action grew to twenty-two thousand. Longstreet by this time had committed about eighteen thousand troops in the attack.

The breeze which had been stirred up earlier by the 20th Maine finally drifted out from Little Round Top onto the lower end of Cemetery Ridge and caught up with a brigade of Pennsylvanians from the V Corps. Suddenly there was a shout, and the brigade swarmed off the ridge straight at the Confederates, driving them back to the Wheat Field and keeping them there.

The breeze picked up a little and moved by the "right oblique" out to Plum Run where a long line of cannon hastily set up from reserves and those which could be salvaged from the Peach Orchard and along the Emmitsburg Road were roaring at the advancing enemy. The Confederates came in strong here and the cannon blazed furiously, gunners cramming double loads of canister into the barrels, cutting the fuses short so they would explode almost instantly on leaving the guns. Even so, a Mississippi regiment managed to wade straight into one battery, and hand-to-hand fighting broke out with handspikes and rammers used as clubs, the men swearing and cursing and clobbering each other. For a few moments it had the appearance of a street brawl, but it was finally broken up as the continued fire of the other batteries forced the rear elements of the Mississippi regiment to withdraw.

The breeze—it was a wind now—cut over by General Hancock to the right and north of the cannoneers. It was late and the sun rested squarely on the horizon, and Hancock saw coming up out of a low swale the murky outlines of a Confederate brigade advancing unopposed right at Cemetery Ridge. This was the brigade of Brigadier General Cadmus Marcellus Wilcox. (On a November day seventeen years later, General Wilcox would call on Hancock to express his regrets that Hancock had lost a Presidential election to James A. Garfield by just 7,023 popular votes. On this day, however, a different defeat was infinitely more important to Hancock.)

Wilcox and his men had charged by chance into the gap left between the II and III Corps back when Sickles rearranged his lines, and they were headed for pay dirt. Once past Cemetery Ridge they would be in the rear of the Army of the Potomac and would have in effect sliced it in half.

Hancock reined his horse over to a regiment of approaching soldiers. It was the 1st Minnesota Regiment. Hancock pointed to the brigade flag of the advancing Confederate column and yelled, "Do you see those colors?" The men from Minnesota did.

"Well, capture them!" roared Hancock.

Two hundred and sixty-two men ran down off the ridge and took on the brigade. It numbered about eighteen hundred. The 1st Minnesota never captured the colors, and Wilcox's men flailed into them, inflicting 215 casualties, 82 per cent of regimental strength, the highest casualty figure for one outfit in the entire war. But the regiment bought the thing Hancock was after: time.

Union artillery on the left saw what was happening, and several batteries changed front and began pounding the Confederates, and Hancock found some more troops and rushed them in behind the heroic Midwesterners. All at once it became too hot for Wilcox and he had to withdraw, and when he pulled his men back on some open ground Union artillery zeroed in on them, turning the withdrawal into a full retreat.

The men who paid the full price for time. Dead soldiers of the 1st Minnesota Regiment.
Library of Congress

It was not all over yet. North of where Hancock had called on the 1st Minnesota to take the enemy's colors was General Meade. The sun, big and dark red, was setting, throwing out long, darkening shadows, and Meade could see quite clearly the intense flashes of artillery fire and exploding shells lighting the land and catching long streaks of low smoke like a nearby thunderstorm. Meade and a few members of his staff had ridden in a frantic rush from headquarters when they received the erroneous news that there had been a breakthrough. (Meade was on a fresh mount. Baldy had been wounded and put out of combat earlier in the afternoon as Meade rode him back of the lines.) All at once Meade and his aides saw the dismaying sight of a brigade of determined Confederates moving clear up onto Cemetery Ridge. And it was making a shambles of a Union battery, even preparing to turn captured cannon on the defenders.

Then one of Meade's aides noticed it—a column of Yankee infantry coming forward on the dead run. The aide shouted to Meade, "There they come, General!" Meade dug his spurs to his horse, waved his hat, and galloped forward, ready to lead the countercharge himself, crying, "Come on, gentlemen!"

The aides succeeded in stopping Meade from such a rash act, but the advancing bluecoats charged into the Confederates and drove them completely off Cemetery Ridge into full retreat.

This particular brigade of Confederates, under the leadership of Brigadier General Ambrose Wright, a Georgia lawyer, had made the deepest penetration into Meade's main lines.

The wind blew steady now. Longstreet's attack was over, and while it had succeeded in knocking out the salient set up by Sickles, it had not breached Meade's main line, and Little Round Top and Cemetery Ridge were still in Federal control.

Lieutenant Frank A. Haskell of the II Corps, a thirty-five-year-old lawyer with a touch of sensitivity on a manly face, had watched the shift in the tide of battle, and with the sun setting on the eerie waves of acrid smoke billowing over men who under other circumstances would have been regarded as insane, he found the scene inspiring enough to write about it:

It is now near sundown, and the battle has gone wonderfully long already. But if you will stop to notice it, a change has occurred. The Rebel cry has ceased, and the men of the Union begin to shout there under the smoke, and their lines advance. See, the Rebels are breaking! They are in confusion in all our front. . . . Let us shout, too!

The day's victory was clearly Meade's. He had handled the grave problem set up by Sickles very well, maneuvering troops to contain as much of the attack as possible. This fact probably engendered the idea in Sickles' mind at a later date that it was his forward move which had helped defeat Longstreet—the Confederates were required to move through his entire III Corps and the troops Meade moved in later before they even reached the main Federal lines along Cemetery Ridge. The fact that the III Corps suffered four thousand casualties and would have to be disbanded, and that it was Meade and not he who made the countermoves, did not seem to enter into Dan's thinking.

When Longstreet opened his attack General Lee was stationed near the center of Seminary Ridge, listening carefully for the sound of cannonading on the Union right at Cemetery Hill and Culp's Hill. The sound would signify that the "demonstration" called for in the over-all plans was under way.

Lee listened. Nothing. Then he heard it. Muffled and toned down, coasting in on the wind, the sound of cannon fire. Baldy Ewell's II Corps artillerymen were firing on the Union right, and the "demonstration" was in operation.

As it was, it did not turn out to be very much of a "demonstration." Union cannon returned the fire with terrible accuracy and a much heavier weight of metal. Firing solid shot and shell, they smothered the Confederate batteries. One battery was totally smashed on Benner's Hill, a high hump of land north of Culp's Hill, when Federal artillerists using an optical range finder imported from France made a near-perfect sighting.

Whatever it was, especially with the Union cannon dominating everything, that gave Ewell the idea he should launch an infantry attack is not clear. But fixed notions seemed to be a part of Confederate thinking on this day, and Ewell sent word to the division of twenty-nine-year-old Major General William Dorsey Pender (West Point, 1854), A. P. Hill's III Corps, that he

Major General
William Dorsey Pender,
division commander,
Confederate III Corps.

Library of Congress

Rock Creek, photographed long ago—circa 1890.

would like assistance in his attack. Pender's division, stationed just west of town, linked the Confederate III Corps with Ewell's.

Unfortunately for Ewell, and for General Lee as well, General Pender had been wounded in the leg by an exploding shell earlier in the day. (The wound turned out to be one which wouldn't heal; Pender would lose his leg and, finally, when that didn't work, his life.) The temporary division commander, Brigadier General James H. Lane, felt his orders did not give him the latitude to attack unless there was every chance of success. He sent a message to Ewell to this effect.

Couriers with messages and dispatches went back and forth between Ewell and Lane, and in the meantime the "demonstration" of artillery petered out into desultory and half-hearted exchanges which lasted throughout the late afternoon and early evening. But Ewell was not giving up his idea of an infantry attack, and he issued orders to his division commanders to make ready.

It was as Ewell cogitated on his plan of assault that Jeb Stuart arrived on the field and located General Lee. There was now no chance that his thoroughly exhausted cavalry could be put to any practical use. Stuart and his men were a day and a half too late as it was, and General Lee, in what must have been a masterful display of restraint, looked at Jeb and remarked, "Well, General Stuart, you are here at last."

The Confederate cavalrymen were placed in reserve and given, depending upon who viewed it, a much deserved rest.

In the meantime Ewell, almost at the moment Longstreet's attack ground to a halt at Cemetery Ridge and the sun was setting, sent his troops storming across Rock Creek up onto the heavily wooded slope of Culp's Hill.

The sole defensive force of one brigade left by Meade when he depleted Culp's Hill to reinforce his left down in front of the Round Tops was in behind some stout breastworks of trenches with heavy logs thrown up in front when Ewell's men came crashing through the underbrush. Though desperately pressed, the lone brigade managed to beat back four determined charges of an entire division. They were proving what some military men already suspected, but, strangely, none of the top-ranking generals of either army seemed to understand: with rifled guns and fortifications a small body of men could hold off exposed attacking forces of vastly superior numbers almost indefinitely.

One brigade of Confederates on the southeastern portion of Culp's Hill completely overlapped the lone Federal brigade and occupied some abandoned trenches; but, suspecting a trap in the darkness, they made no further move. These men of the South did not know it, but victory, total victory, was theirs if they had but moved forward. There were no Federal troops in their front, and a few hundred yards away was the Baltimore Pike and the rear of the Army of the Potomac.

Unable to dislodge the lone brigade, the Confederates dug in and settled down for a restless night on the base and eastern slope of Culp's Hill. In the morning, when there was daylight, they would try again.

The fighting for the day was not quite over. There was one final gasp of energy on East Cemetery Hill, where the land dips down to a shallow ridge and then climbs to meld into Culp's Hill.

A brigade from North Carolina and one from Louisiana charged the area. The momentum of their attack carried some of the Louisianans right into sweating Union artillerists and infantrymen. Grappling and swearing at each other, the irate Yankees and elated Confederates resorted to all sorts of weapons. Rocks were hurled, muskets were seized by the barrels and swung furiously, and handspikes and rammers were used to bash in the heads of careless Confederates. Some of the men just switched to the most primeval fighting of all, doubling up their fists and letting go, or grabbing somebody to wrestle him into a heap. But for a moment the boys from Louisiana were having the better of it, and they succeeded in putting a neat dent in the Union line. Then out of the darkness they saw the flicking tongues of musketry fire from a new mass of men, and bullets started whistling past. More Yankees.

General Hancock had heard the noise and confusion around East Cemetery Hill. Thinking help might be needed, he had sent a brigade over to see what it could do. The Louisianans withdrew, and finally, at last, the day's fighting, which had reached well into the night, was over.

By and large, after the final tally of battle, this day would stand out as the biggest of all the three days' fighting, although on the morrow the Confederates were going to stage a charge both futile and heroic.

It was not a night of rest for either army. Meade was shifting his XII Corps back to Culp's Hill. And there was a great deal of stirring and shuffling. When the men of the XII Corps worked their way back to their old positions they found some of them had been taken over by Ewell's Confederates.

It was at Spangler's Spring at the southern base of Culp's Hill that a few bluecoats inadvertently set off a small explosion. Unaware that the Confederate lines included the spring, the Union men were looking for water. Some of them were telling fellow soldiers how the Rebels had been given a warm reception down by the Round Tops. A voice from the darkness popped out: "Hell—those are Yankees!" A musket was fired. Another. And then muskets crackled all over the place until some Union officers rushed up and pulled the disgusted Yankees off, minus the hoped-for water.

This kind of brushfire war kept on all night. A nervous picket would hear something stirring out in the darkness. It could be anything—the wind turning a leaf, a jumpy rabbit. All noises sounded the same to the picket: *the enemy!* And his musket would roar. And somebody would fire at the man who took

An old photograph of Spangler's Spring.

Gettysburg National Military Park—Walter Lane

Union ambulance wagons and medical corps men. Each wagon was equipped with whiskey, a keg of water, a supply of beef stock, two leather benches, and two stretchers.

the pot shot, until muskets were going off all around, bright, quick streams of light whipping out in the darkness. It would all die down almost as soon as it happened, only to start up again somewhere else along the line.

Over by Cemetery Ridge and the Round Tops, out by the Peach Orchard, by the Wheat Field, at Devil's Den, medical corpsmen and friends of the wounded were out seeking, looking for those left on the field. They did not have far to go. Casualties were all over the place. And as tenderly as they could, they were carried back to face another horrible ordeal: the surgeons!

For a Civil War soldier, death, from the standpoint of pain and mutilation endured, was sometimes better than the surgeons. True, doctors had anesthetics, but when you woke up a simple wound on the leg resulted in the fact you had no leg. Surgery, such as it was, was a massive sort of thing, directed at amputation. The idea of saving a wounded leg or arm seemed never to occur to the surgeons. *Amputate!* At least the patient had a chance—maybe the infection would not spread. What was it that with puzzling perseverance would take a perfectly healthy man, wounded but otherwise hale and hearty, and reduce him to a fever-ridden wreck bound for the cadaver heap? Infection, its causes and cures, was an unknown factor to Civil War surgeons. The man wounded in the chest or stomach was best left alone—hemostats for checking bleeding were yet to be designed, and abdominal surgery had not progressed much beyond the use of a probe to dig out bullets and bits of metal.

In Confederate-occupied Gettysburg, the already filled churches and buildings were crammed that evening with screaming, tragically wounded Southerners; back of Cemetery Ridge, in what were euphemistically called "field hospitals," the hoarse ravings of Northerners filled the woods and meadows with the piercing tones of pain.

General Meade called a council of war late in the night. His army had taken a lot of punishment in the two days' fighting; there was fear in Meade's mind that another day's fighting might cause his army simply to dwindle away. Yet sitting in the little white headquarters house, Meade, seven corps commanders, and two division generals, weighed the situation and voted to "stay and fight it out" one more day, but not to take any offensive action.

As the meeting of the generals broke up Meade turned to Brigadier General John Gibbon (West Point, 1847), a division commander in the II Corps, and said, "If Lee attacks tomorrow, it will be on your front."

He could not have uttered a more profound, and, as far as General Lee was concerned, more ominous statement. Gibbon's division occupied the upper center section of Cemetery Ridge, and Meade, playing a little chess, reasoned that Lee, having found both the Federal flanks strong, would assume they must be strong only because he (Meade) had weakened his center.

General Lee held no council that night, but his mind was already made up to renew the attack as soon after daylight as possible. There was justification in this: his troops had fought splendidly. While they had not been entirely successful they had made inroads on both flanks of Meade's army, and morale was still high. One more push, this time a better-coordinated one, should topple the Army of the Potomac.

For most of the citizens of Gettysburg it was the same story as the night before. The Confederates had been eating them out of house and home, and now they were bragging that with the arrival of daylight they would put a finish to the Yankee army. One person, nevertheless, found there had been profound changes. He was Gettysburg's newest citizen, the little Rebel who had asked for asylum at the home of Billy Bayly. During the day he had been told by Billy's father he must come out of hiding and take his chances with the rest of the family, and in his borrowed clothes he had helped Billy pick cherries from the back orchard for his one-time, and much older, companions in arms, the insatiably hungry Confederates.

Physically tired and without the emotional anxiety of soldiering, the little Rebel slept soundly as a majestic moon, heavy with light, rose high in the heavens and pushed relentlessly across the sky.

Chapter V

Too Bad! Too Bad! Oh! Too Bad!

It was partially overcast, air hot and humid—a duplication of the preceding day—when the first streaks of light prodded the morning skies on Friday, July 3. Once more the salient military features were position and initiative.

Meade's council of war had ruled out any offensive operations for the Army of the Potomac. Initiative, then, was still in Lee's hands; but position highly favored Meade, and today there were going to be no mistakes about throwing an entire corps forward into an exposed deployment. And Little Round Top, as well as Big Round Top, was now held by a solid line of ready infantrymen.

Lee's plans for July 3 bore a marked similarity to those he had called the day before. Ewell's forces had a small toehold on the slopes of Culp's Hill. These forces, then, would renew the attack and force Meade's right. The main attack on July 2 across the Emmitsburg Road had almost carried as it progressed from Meade's left towards his left center. A grand assault, therefore, would be launched precisely at Meade's left center and carry Cemetery Ridge; and this time Jeb Stuart's cavalry would be employed to pile simultaneously into the rear of the Army of the Potomac, creating havoc and confusion upon a breakthrough.

The main assault was to be under the personal direction of Longstreet. Considering his record of the previous day, the delegation of command to Longstreet was at least risky; but then Lee had no other general with Longstreet's experience. On July 3, Longstreet was no more predisposed to offensive operations than he had been on July 2. There were bound to be delays.

Meade's first order of the day was to clear the Confederates off the slopes of Culp's Hill, thus eliminating the danger of the Rebels exploiting their slight hold on this part of his defenses.

Gettysburg National Military Park—Walter Lane

A view from another time when there were still the remnants of breastworks on Culp's Hill. The town of Gettysburg is in the distance—circa 1890.

During the night the Confederates had heard the rumble of shifting cannon and moving soldiers back of the Federal lines, and had held the hope that this indicated the Yankees were evacuating Culp's Hill. Daylight shattered any illusions about what the Yankees had been doing when the savage roar of a sudden artillery attack burst through the morning air. Far from giving up the hill, Meade had buttressed the position with all of the XII Corps and one brigade of the VI Corps, plus additional artillery. Thus, at daybreak on July 3, the Culp's Hill area was bristling with Yankees—a complete reversal of the situation encountered by the Rebels the previous evening when they were held off by a lone brigade.

Federal cannon flailed away into the woodlands of Culp's Hill, creasing and gouging into great oak trees which had often sheltered local picnickers from sudden summer rains. Now ground-hugging men from the South, nerves jarred and skittering, heard the high whine and din of exploding shells and the strange rustle, "like hail," of shattered branches and twigs and bits of metal cascading to the ground. The oak trees were being shot to death.

There was not very much the stubborn Rebels could do about the onslaught of Yankee artillery, as the dense woodlands of Culp's Hill precluded dragging up any support artillery to return the fire. They had to wait it out, each man in his own way, with his own thoughts, while a swirling hell of noise and metal burst about them.

All at once the cannonade stopped, and Yankee foot soldiers prepared to drive down on the supposedly stunned Rebels, pushing them back off the hill and across Rock Creek. To their surprise, the amazing Rebels suddenly stood up, took a bead on the crest of Culp's Hill, and started a charge of their own.

Bedraggled, grimy, and unshaven—there had not been much time for the everyday routines of civilization—but with none of the iron sapped from them, soldiers from Virginia, North Carolina, Louisiana, and Alabama, plus a regiment from the border state of Maryland, zigzagging past trees and underbrush, headed up the steep slopes of Culp's Hill. Waiting, atop the tree-lined summit, behind earthen and log entrenchments, were long rows of Federals, as begrimed as their adversaries and as determined.

Quickly regaining their balance, regiments from Connecticut, New York, Ohio, Pennsylvania and, significantly, also from the border state of Maryland, zeroed their muskets and let go in a blazing labyrinth of frontal and crossfire. This was rapidly followed by the nearby resurgence of artillery fire. The woods of Culp's Hill were again churned and battered in a riot of bursting

Volunteers from Maryland, a "border state," enlisted on both sides. The irony of this is demonstrated by these two monuments, one to a Northern regiment, the other to a Southern one. Both regiments were pitted against each other at Culp's Hill. Both were called the 1st Maryland. Both were recruited from the same section of Maryland. The Confederate regimental monument—right picture—has a very light engraving which reads: 1ST MD. INFANTRY CHANGED TO: 2ND MD. INFANTRY, C.S.A. At the time of dedication it was considered impossible to have two monuments bearing the same regimental numbers.

Walter Lane   *Lane Studio, Gettysburg, Pennsylvania*

shells and twirling bullets amid a turgid blanket of dense smoke. The Yankees were firing from positions of relative security, and they stopped the repeated efforts of the Confederates to get to the top of the hill.

One charge was led by a unique "soldier." Somehow a stray dog had wandered into the scene of fighting, and as a brigade of Confederates made another desperate attempt to wrest control of the hill the dog placed himself at the head of the attacking columns. The unfortunate animal was soon riddled in the counterfire. It was reported he licked somebody's hand before he died, and a Federal officer, regarding him as the "only civilized being" on either side, ordered him honorably buried.

As the fighting was pressed, a message arrived at Ewell's headquarters from General Lee with instructions to delay action until it could be timed to coincide with Longstreet's attack on the Federal left center. This was now, of course, impossible. Once more the major flaw, improper co-ordination, between the elements of the Army of Northern Virginia was in effect.

The sun rose high, casting a network of long, solid shadows in the smoke-filled woods of Culp's Hill, and still the Confederates tried vainly to claw their way into the enemy lines. Now and then, bowing their heads to a continued fusillade of musket fire, a group would manage to press up to the very edges of the entrenchments only to be battered back in a bloody repulse. Once, some seventy Confederates poked their way almost up to the muzzles of the guns of an Ohio regiment, but found it impossible to cover the last few feet. It would have been outright suicide to move forward, and just as bad to retreat. Somebody held up what was probably a white handkerchief as a flag of surrender, and the men from Ohio ceased firing. An outraged Rebel officer swung into the group, berating them, trying to stop the surrender. Honor and ethics of war were important and highly prized by both sides: if a man surrendered, you didn't shoot him. But by all the rules in the book he must stay surrendered. So the Yankee soldiers sent a flush of bullets ripping into the Rebel officer, toppling him over, and signaled the Confederates, now prisoners of war, into their lines.

Vicious punishment on the slopes of Culp's Hill was taking the steam out of the attack, but down to the southeast around the Spangler's Spring area, where the ground is fairly level, for a few moments the Confederates had things a little more their own way.

At one end of a little meadow were Rebels in strength. A Federal division commander wanted to know just how great this strength was, and sent a verbal order for pickets to be thrown forward and get a little information. By the

Gresham Hough,
a young Confederate
in the 1st Maryland,
which fought at Culp's Hill.

Confederate Museum, Richmond, Virginia

time the order reached the men in the line it had become a confused directive for an attack.

Aware there were many enemy troops concealed behind trees and rocks beyond the flat, open ground, a line officer remarked that it was "murder," but if the order called for an attack that was what it was going to be, and two regiments from Massachusetts and Indiana moved out with a loud cheer.

Hundreds of Confederate muskets were raised, sights brought to bear on the running Yankees. Somehow it was wrong: it had all the ease of a turkey shoot. *Fire!* A rain of bullets showered into the Yankees, crumpling some men into rag-doll heaps, while others, suddenly numbed into insensibility, stood upright, feet no longer moving at a run, and looked through dull eyes at a scene which had become a dream.

Two hundred and fifty Yankees felt Confederate lead before the attacking force was able to rush back to the cover of a stone wall, and in turn, quite surprisingly, beat off a counterattack.

Photographer Brady sits amid the freshly scarred trees of Culp's Hill.

With the repulse of the counterattack the Confederate offensive ground to a standstill, and by ten thirty the Rebels were forced into a sullen withdrawal from the slopes and southern base of Culp's Hill, and the precious waters of Spangler's Spring were once more in Yankee hands.

Legend, and there are lots of them connected with Gettysburg, has it that soldiers of both sides mingled around Spangler's Spring during the second night of the battle to fill their canteens. But Spangler's Spring rested squarely behind the Confederate lines at that time; and the story is apocryphal, "the faint memory of a dream," as one general many years later described his recollections of the battles and the war.

Despite the afterthoughts about Spangler's Spring, for fully fifty years, well into the early nineteen hundreds, great, moldering, dead trees covered the slopes where Meade's right defense had held—where the collective memories and thoughts of so many men of the South were terminated. Here for

126

many years woodcock, fluttering and darting through a skeletal woodland, were able to find a haven from fall hunters. Culp's Hill had become a spooky sort of place.

No legend, but fact, was the death of Virginia Wade, known as "Jennie," the only citizen of Gettysburg killed during the three days' fighting. As the rage of war centered on Culp's Hill, Jennie and her mother and two small brothers were at the home of Mrs. McClellan, Jennie's sister, on Baltimore Street, near Cemetery Hill. Mrs. McClellan's husband was away in the army, and Jennie and her family had good reason for staying with her instead of at their own house in another section of town—Mrs. McClellan was nursing her three-day-old son and needed care.

At the northern base of Cemetery Hill Confederate troops had occupied a few houses. With some of the walls knocked out in order to maintain communications left and right (the only major damage inflicted by the battle on the town of Gettysburg), sharpshooters using the second and third floors had been exchanging shots with Federal pickets up on Cemetery Hill. The line of fire sometimes swept by Mrs. McClellan's house.

The clock in the kitchen said eight thirty. Jennie and her mother and brothers and sister, and the new baby, too, had been awake at least three hours, and now Jennie was baking bread. Suddenly, a bullet cut through the kitchen door. It didn't stop until it entered Jennie's heart. In a pocket Jennie had a picture of her soldier fiancé. She never knew he had been mortally wounded two weeks earlier in the fighting around Winchester.

With the flash and fire of battle over around Culp's Hill, an eerie silence pressed down on the battlefield for a short time, only to be broken by a sudden resurgence of musket and cannon fire along the northern section of Ceme-

Virginia "Jennie" Wade, only civilian killed at Gettysburg.

Walter Lane

tery Ridge. Troops of both sides were fussing about a farm building between the lines. There had been a nasty squabble about the building the day before, but nothing had been resolved. This time, the problem was quickly settled: Federal troops moved out and set the structure on fire, burning it to the ground, leaving no more than smoldering ashes and no shelter for either Rebels or Yankees. Once more an uneasy quiet hung over the land, a quiet filled with an ominous sense of mounting urgency—a kind of swelling static energy, unstable, ready to explode in one great climactic burst.

Over on Seminary Ridge, General Lee had spent the morning hours conferring with General Longstreet, and Longstreet was proving as unenthusiastic as ever about attacking. Lee had expected, when he sent a message to Ewell to delay the assault on Culp's Hill, that Longstreet would be able to mount an offensive by 10:00 A.M. But it was well after this hour before Longstreet had troops arrayed for attack.

Lee's initial orders were for Longstreet to take his I Corps and place it in position to smash into Meade's left center along Cemetery Ridge following a softening-up artillery bombardment. There were three divisions in Longstreet's corps, and two, Hood's and McLaw's, both used in the previous

Northern Cemetery Ridge as Union soldiers saw it. During the battle Union troops were stationed behind the stone fence on the left. The ruts follow a line now covered by a modern road.

Gettysburg National Military Park—Walter Lane

day's fighting, were presently positioned about a half mile in front of Seminary Ridge opposite the Round Tops. According to Longstreet they could not be moved, as this would invite a wholesale flank attack by Federal troops. Therefore, only his third division, Pickett's, as yet uncommitted to battle, could be employed. Lee altered his orders on this advice: Longstreet was to take Pickett's division, plus a division and two brigades of A. P. Hill's III Corps —this would give Longstreet nearly the same strength as the entire I Corps— and assault Meade's lines.

Longstreet had had scouts out all night, and their reports were favorable to his one-track idea of moving the Army of Northern Virginia by a flanking march, thus forcing Meade to do the attacking. A somewhat too patient Lee listened, politely according Longstreet a latitude beyond military protocol. Lee, after all, was the commanding officer, and Longstreet was in effect telling him his plans were all wrong, that the Army of Northern Virginia could never win with Lee's tactics. Writing about it long after the war, Longstreet quoted himself as saying to General Lee: "I have been a soldier, I may say, from the ranks up to the position I now hold. I have been in pretty much all kinds of skirmishes, from those of two or three soldiers up to those of an army corps, and I can safely say there was never a body of fifteen thousand men who could make that attack successfully."

Longstreet next bitterly assailed the logic that troops could move successfully across fourteen hundred yards of open land while under fire from artillery on Little Round Top. An artillerist assured both Lee and Longstreet the Federal guns on this height could be silenced. It was an unjustified assumption, but it tended to dispel doubts on this question, and Lee finally closed Longstreet's digressions by pointing in the direction of Cemetery Ridge and saying: "The enemy is there and I am going to strike him."

For Pete Longstreet—forty-two years old, resolute and determined in battle (at the Second Battle of Bull Run and again at the Battle of Fredericksburg he had manifested his ability as an extremely capable officer), a former career soldier in the regular United States Army, a personal friend of Grant, an upperclassman when Hancock attended West Point—a great moment was arriving, and he was emotionally unprepared for it. The whole idea of an attack on Cemetery Ridge, in fact, as he later wrote, "depressed" him.

On Cemetery Ridge, back of the Federal lines, there was activity; but in a total over-all sense it lacked the urgency of the Confederates. With the troops at Culp's Hill obviously holding, attention swung to Cemetery Ridge. Meade had predicted that Lee's greatest effort would reach towards this section of his defenses, and before the morning was over it was quite apparent to the men lodged behind stone fences and earthen barricades beyond the crest of Cemetery Ridge that whatever was coming would crash off Seminary Ridge and slam across the long, superficial valley straight for their line. Over among the shaded woods of Seminary Ridge, and farther south, out in the open near the Peach Orchard, Lee had been hauling battery after battery into position without the slightest recourse to concealment until he now had a two-mile-long line of glinting cannon, muzzles inflexibly aimed at Cemetery Ridge.

Contemplative Yankee soldiers gravely placed their cartridge cases on stones, on the ground, anywhere that would afford easy access in loading, and waited. Behind them in fields and groves, out in front where Cemetery Ridge stretches down towards the Round Tops, the rumble of horses and limbers and caissons signified a build-up of the Federal artillery. Chief of Artillery General Hunt was bringing together a long line of massed cannon, arraying them to belch death and destruction at the Rebels.

Meade, now certain of Lee's intentions, was back in his headquarters attending to the constant flow of staff officers with this detail and that. But somewhere in this coming and going he looked up to see a civilian, and the civilian had an urgent problem. He wanted Meade to sign a paper which would give him claim on the Government in Washington for damages to his property. No one ever quite figured out how he had been able to barge his way into Meade's headquarters; but it seems Federal troops had been using his place as a hospital, strewing amputated arms and legs into his garden and burying the dead in his yard. Meade's nickname of Ol' Snapping Turtle was based in part on his lack of self-control, and a surprised civilian watched and heard Meade blow up: *If the battle were lost the civilian would have no government to apply to, much less any property which would be worth anything.* The civilian was hustled out of Meade's sight and wrath with the admonition that if any more were heard of him he would be given a musket and put in the ranks.[10]

About the time General Meade was venting his spleen on the unhappy civilian, General Hancock rode through the lines of his II Corps in front of Cemetery Ridge and met a little girl, about six years old. In some way she had strayed into the position held by Yankee pickets, and she staggered under the burden of a tightly clutched musket. When Hancock dismounted she fell

Brigadier General
John Gibbon,
division commander
in Federal II Corps.

Library of Congress

into his arms, and between convulsive sobbing blurted, "My papa's dead, but here's my papa's gun." When Hancock related this incident some years later, it was noted that his eyes were no drier than the little girl's had been.[11]

The time was shortly after noon now, and the sun burned off any haze left from early morning. With the sky bright and clear, the temperature was now in the high eighties. All across the battlefield the tenuous quiet persisted.

Lieutenant Frank Haskell, the officer who had wanted to shout when he saw the Rebels repulsed the day before, joined his superiors, Generals Gibbon (Haskell was his aide) and Hancock, and some other officers at an unexpected repast in a little orchard on Cemetery Ridge. Haskell had had no more than a drink of whiskey and a cup of coffee in the past twenty-four hours, and he felt the idea of food was an "extraordinary proposition."

Somebody had scrounged up a few chickens, which, according to Haskell, were "in good running order," some butter, and a loaf of bread. The chickens were stewed along with some potatoes, coffee and tea were brewed, and Haskell and his fellow officers fell to with great relish, enjoying as only soldiers can the magnificence of pot-luck food.

It was as the officers ate that General Meade and an aide rode up. A warm invitation went out for Meade and his aide to join them. An empty cracker barrel was located for the commanding general—the aide sat on the ground —and between all of them a quick end was put to the edibles. Afterwards, cigars were lit, and for a few moments there was talk about the probabilities of the upcoming fighting. Finally, Meade went back to his headquarters. General Hancock dictated some routine orders. Haskell, Gibbon, and some

131

staff officers puffed on their cigars and, as Haskell put it, "dozed in the heat and lolled upon the ground with half open eyes. . . ."

Overhead a bright sun beat away a few clouds. *The sun was, the textbooks said so, ninety-one million miles from the earth. And all the light, the energy of the sun, according to one theory, was kept going by vast numbers of meteors which rained down on its surface replenishing the central fire. . . .* The sun on the afternoon of July 3, 1863, stirred growing fields of corn and wheat. It was a hot afternoon.

To the west, despite the heat and the foot-dragging reluctance of Longstreet, arrangements for the attack were in the final phase. The last elements of the assault infantry forces were falling in among the woods of Seminary Ridge, along the "safe" reverse side of the ridge—the slight elevation of the ridge would offer some protection from Federal shells. And down the ridge, but on the forward side where a fold of land offered some concealment, an entire division of Virginians assembled.

In one brigade, twenty-one-year-old Lieutenant John Dooley waited with his men. They had been positioned in a field in which some apple trees were sprouting green fruit, and Dooley found himself joining his fellow soldiers in pelting one another with the small, unripe apples, a fact which Dooley later observed was rather ironic—that men could be "frivolous" when in a few minutes they would face death.

For all of the horseplay in the ranks, the "brass" was occupied with far more weighty details. Longstreet was explaining to his division commander, Major General George Edward Pickett (West Point, 1846), just what the operations called for. Pickett was to direct his division, plus the troops from A. P. Hill's III Corps, in the supreme effort. The plans were simple.

There was a "little clump of trees" over on the central section of Cemetery Ridge—General Lee had pointed it out to both Hill and Longstreet as the site upon which he wished the attacking forces to converge—and Pickett, after the artillery bombardment had silenced or weakened the enemy's batteries, was to order the troops to close in on the trees, smash through the Yankee lines, and take their positions.

And thirty-eight-year-old Virginia-born General Pickett, whose hair hung about his head in what were described as "long perfumed ringlets," prepared for the high moment of his military career.

General Lee, also, was busy. He rode along the length of massed artillery making certain everyone understood his plans—that the infantry was adequately prepared. *Was everything understood? Yes.*

To Colonel Edward Porter Alexander (West Point, 1857), chief of artillery in Longstreet's I Corps, fell the burden of controlling the artillery bombardment. Longstreet penned a note to Alexander which in so many words passed the buck to him: "If the artillery fire does not have the effect to drive off the enemy or greatly demoralize him . . . I would prefer that you should not advise Pickett to make the charge. I shall rely a great deal upon your judgment. . . ."

Alexander replied he would only be able to judge the effect of his artillery fire by the return fire of the enemy, and that it would take all his ammunition in this one effort, and that if there were any alternative to this attack "it should be carefully considered."

Longstreet sent a second note reiterating that Alexander was to make the decision as to whether the artillery fire on the Federal lines warranted the infantry attack, and then, according to the omnipresent British observer, Colonel Fremantle, moved off into some woods and went to sleep. And General Pickett, upon whom so much depended, penned a long letter to his fiancée.

Back on Cemetery Ridge Lieutenant Haskell basked in the peace and quiet of a lazy July afternoon. Spread out along the central section of the ridge were between nine and ten thousand men of the I and II Corps. Out near the Emmitsburg Road was a long, thin thread of waiting skirmishers. Waiting,

Major General
George Edward Pickett.

too, was the sun-baked artillery, eighty pieces in all, gun crews and horses idling in the bright light, the ammunition boxes of the caissons and limbers at "the ready."

12:45: Haskell reported: ". . . not a sound of guns or a musket [could] be heard on all the field."

12:55: Haskell had just looked at his watch. Returning it to his pocket, he contemplated going to sleep. Suddenly, he was jolted out of his reverie: "What sound was that? There was no mistaking it. The distinct sharp sound of the enemy's guns. . . ."

The Washington Artillery of New Orleans, attached to Longstreet's I Corps (the Washington Artillery would see distinguished service in World Wars I and II), had fired two shots, shattering the delicate stillness with a strident *bang . . . bang*. The signal for the guns along Seminary Ridge to begin their work! And as the echoes of the two swift explosions rumbled over the battlefield, up and down the line Confederate artillerists pulled lanyards. One hundred and twenty guns roared almost at once, sending solid shot and shell winging towards the Yankees.

An excited and wide-awake Haskell saw General Gibbon stand up and rush off on foot towards his division, followed by an excited orderly with Gibbon's horse. But orderly and horse all at once melded into a crimson flash and then reappeared through a billow of fleecy smoke, the horse still intact, the orderly quite dead, his chest ripped open by a shell fragment. A second orderly was luckier.

The effect of Confederate artillery on the rear portion of Cemetery Ridge. Note the dead horses. Meade's headquarters building is at the center right.

Haskell, in the meantime, ran for his horse, which was tied to a tree, and was surprised to find the animal "eating oats with the air of greatest composure," despite the fact that a nearby mess wagon piled into a heap as a shell exploded squarely on top of it, and a little farther on another shell tore a couple of mules carrying ammunition boxes into fleshy shreds.

Lieutenant Haskell spurred his mount and took out after General Gibbon as the skies, to all appearances, caved in around the Yankees in a tornado of staggering crashes. Infantrymen, ardently embracing the earth out beyond the crest of Cemetery Ridge, were escaping the full fury of exploding metal and bouncing solid shot. But artillerymen, unprotected and exposed, were catching lethal doses. Men and horses were going down, caught by shell splinters, bowled over by the ghastly crunch of cannon balls; and every now and then there was a wild blast which took in men and animals in swift carnage as a shell connected with a limber or caisson, blowing up the ammunition box in a geyser of splintered oak spokes and axles and metal fittings.

But it was the reverse side of the ridge, the rear area, which was catching unmitigated hell. The Confederates, either firing too long, or reasoning that Meade would keep his foot soldiers behind the slight protection offered by the barrier of Cemetery Ridge, were cutting the fuses of their shells to burst on the far side of the crest. With most of the infantry on the forward slope, it was a wasted effort; but noncombatants—orderlies, teamsters, medical corpsmen—were forced into a pell-mell scramble to get out of a place suddenly alive with Confederate metal.

And at Meade's little headquarters building it was quickly decided by both Meade and his staff that it was time to get out. Thumping shells—one observer claimed they were dropping at times at a rate of six a second—made it impossible to think. A shell crashed onto the roof. Another splintered the front steps. Around the building more than a dozen horses were quickly obliterated, or in the final kicking agony of death. A horse raced down the Taneytown Road on three legs in a rolling half-falling gait, the bloody stump of the fourth leg, raggedly amputated by a shell fragment, making obscene movements of futile co-ordination. General Meade and his staff retired, under extreme pressure, to the XII Corps headquarters of General Slocum at Power's Hill, three-quarters of a mile to the southeast.

And amidst this onset of the Confederate barrage, amidst the shrieking, howling, exploding iron, a regimental band on Cemetery Ridge struck up the strains of "The Star-Spangled Banner." Not then the National Anthem, it nevertheless created a stir among those who heard the music. General Han-

Confederate guns on Seminary Ridge which participated in the greatest artillery barrage ever fired in America.

cock, who was astride his horse, riding back and forth behind the men of the II Corps in a brave display of reassurance, found the music stirring enough to take off his hat and wave it.

Now, a new roar joined in with the music: the Federal artillery opened up full swing, cannoneers firing their pieces in headlong fury, sending angry metal back at the Confederates.

Artillerist General Hunt had wanted all the guns along Cemetery Ridge to withhold their fire for fifteen or twenty minutes and then fire slowly to conserve ammunition for the expected infantry attack. However, General Hancock, feeling he was in command on this front, gave the order for return fire— it wasn't good for morale to have to sit it out without replying—and eighty Federal cannon had opened a prolonged fire, their deep-throated roar adding a new weight to the incessant racket. All in all, fully two hundred fieldpieces were booming away at each other, and the flash and the thunder of a hundred summer storms centered on the thin ridges just below Gettysburg, sending up great banks of foul smoke to blot out entire sections of the landscape as effectively as fog rolling in from the sea.

The noise of the combined firepower, the mightiest roar ever heard up to that time on the North American continent, rumbled far. In Chambersburg, twenty-five miles away, it was heard faintly; but due to a freak atmospheric condition—probably an inversion of cool air above warm air, in which sound waves are sometimes "bounced" back to earth—there were reports that the bombardment, loud and distinct, had been heard one hundred and forty miles west of Gettysburg.

Over on Seminary Ridge, Confederate artillerist Colonel Alexander tried to watch the effect of the bombardment along Cemetery Ridge through his field glasses. Luminous flashes of light, muted to a deep orange color behind a layer of smoke, told him the Yankee guns were returning the fire; the crash and noise of exploding shells over his lines assured him the Yankee artillerists were fusing their shells all too accurately.

Alexander had intended to have his guns fire for fifteen minutes and then notify General Pickett to launch the infantry attack. But the fifteen minutes passed and there was no slackening of return fire. Twenty minutes. Thirty minutes. And still the Yankee cannon snapped back. For Alexander there were dire ponderables. Could his guns cripple enough of the enemy's artillery? Could his guns disorganize Meade's infantry? And ammunition—there was no plenitude—must be considered. This one barrage would have to be it. Alexander kept his guns going. . . .

Now, as the guns lashed out, another phase of Lee's operations went into effect: Jeb Stuart and the cavalry.

Stuart and four brigades, between five and six thousand cavalrymen, had moved east of Gettysburg about three miles. There were indications that Stuart planned to throw forward a strong skirmish line to occupy the Yankee cavalry while his main squadrons made a concealed flanking movement to strike the right and rear of the Army of the Potomac. But plans and coordination were, as with the infantry, difficult to institute in the mounted branch of the Army of Northern Virginia.

Stuart managed to get his troopers into some woods south of the York Pike. Beyond the woods to the east and southeast lay broad, open terrain. Due south,

Some of the guns which answered the Confederates. The 1st Connecticut Battery, shown here at the Battle of Chancellorsville, fired back at the Confederates from Cemetery Ridge and also helped break up the Confederate infantry attack.

Library of Congress

about a half mile, the Hanover Road cut through this expansive countryside, most of which was under cultivation, with fields of corn and wheat and great stretches of clover pasture land. Gathered on and around the Hanover Road and along a little country road which extended north and perpendicular to the Hanover Road were three brigades of Union cavalry, about five thousand men and horses. Under the leadership of thirty-year-old Brigadier General David M. Gregg (West Point, 1855), the blue squadrons were guarding Meade's flank on the right. The troopers were extended along the Hanover Road as far as Wolf's Hill, the largest hill in the area, a mile and a half southeast of Gettysburg.

Stuart sent a dismounted brigade forward out of the woods and had it move down into the open land to take position in and around the buildings of a farmer named Rummel. Almost immediately, Gregg ordered a New Jersey regiment to swing its men out of their saddles and with their carbines advance on foot towards the threatening Rebels. Some of Stuart's horse batteries opened fire and were instantly answered by hastily unlimbered artillery along the Hanover Road. Gregg sent another regiment of dismounted horsemen in alongside the New Jersey horsemen, and for a few moments the countryside resounded to the popping of carbines and muskets and roar of cannon fire.

With the Yankees busy contending with the Confederate skirmishers, by all rights the rest of Stuart's squads now should have been moving by the flank in a wild, clattering foray into Meade's main defenses. But no! The brigade thrown out to draw in the Yankees ran out of bullets and began to retire. Suddenly, out of the woods appeared dense columns of Confederate troopers.

The open land south of York Pike and the Rummel Farm buildings.

Walter Lane

Lieutenant General Wade Hampton.   Major General Fitzhugh Lee.

Whether this was due to a mix-up in orders or a natural wish to help their fellow soldiers, concealment and surprise were lost. In plain sight for General Gregg to see were squadron after squadron of Rebel cavalry.

In charge of the newly revealed horsemen were Brigadier General Wade Hampton and Brigadier General Fitzhugh Lee (West Point, 1856). Hampton, excellent horseman and soldier, and a wealthy plantation owner from South Carolina—at the start of the war he had raised and equipped at his own expense a command of artillery, infantry, and cavalry—was Stuart's most able and trusted officer. Fitzhugh Lee, nephew of Robert E. Lee, was a man after Stuart's heart, a devil-may-care horseman who liked nothing better than a good scrap.

"Fitz" Lee sent a Virginia regiment forward. Gregg countered with a Michigan regiment. Lee beefed up the Virginians with two additional regiments, and the Michigan horse soldiers were forced to retire. But in turn, the Confederates ran into flank fire and were obliged to withdraw towards the woods. Thus far it had been far from a classical cavalry action, all the fighting having been done by dismounted soldiers.

Then it came. Yankee horsemen looking towards the north saw a large mass of cavalry—the remaining portions of Hampton's and Fitz Lee's brigades—moving out in a close column of squadrons. It was headed due south. Troopers, horses gathered well under them, polished sabers glinting in the sun, held a steady line.

The movement at best was rash. The column was headed for the Hanover Road, which meant that as it crossed the open country, Yankee horsemen could strike it in a great broadside flank attack. Part of Gregg's artillery was along the Hanover Road, while a great portion of his troopers was strung

Company D, 3rd Pennsylvania Cavalry, part of the force that clashed with Stuart's men.

out along the little perpendicular country road. This meant the Confederate cavalrymen were moving inside from the top towards the bottom of a Federal deployment shaped in the form of the letter J.

Artillery caught the column from the front, emptying saddles, toppling horses, yet it came on, Wade Hampton's battle flag floating over the lead riders. General Gregg called upon a Michigan regiment to move in and strike the van of the advancing squadrons. Up moved newly commissioned Brigadier General George A. Custer. He would lead the countercharge. With his dry, flaxen hair flowing about his ears, Custer raised himself in his stirrups, held his saber outthrust, and cried to the men from Michigan, "Come on, you Wolverines!"

At a trot, at a gallop, the bombastic Custer, leading his Wolverines four lengths in front, reined his horse straight across the open land on a collision course as the ground gave off a muffled rumble where thousands of pounding hoofs were churning pasture lands into a mulch of dirt and crushed clover.

Finally, in a great tangle of men and horses, the Yankees and Rebels smashed head-on. "So sudden and violent was the collision," according to an eyewitness, "that many of the horses were turned end over end and crushed their riders beneath them."

The impact of Custer's troopers halted the front of the Confederate column, and in a swirl of milling and yelling, sabers twirled and hacked, turned red, and twirled again, pistols and carbines spurted at point-blank range and frantic horses, squealing with the wildest kind of terror, bit and kicked and threw their riders into a melee of grinding hoofs.

With Custer and his Wolverines chopping at the front of the Confederate column, other Yankee squadrons flailed in on the flank—in some instances the momentum of their attack carried horses and riders clear through massed Rebel troopers—and the fighting broke into a general free-for-all, the organization and forward movement of the squadrons of Hampton and Fitz Lee totally disrupted.

After a frenzy of saber slashing—Wade Hampton was severely wounded by a saber cut—imprecations, harsh demands for surrender, undaunted replies, charges and countercharges, the contestants called it a day. The Confederates retired to the woods whence they had come, leaving the field of combat to the Yankee horsemen.

Custer, whose life seemed to be charmed—by the end of the war the number of horses shot out from under him would total eleven—came through the foray unscratched. Certainly, his daring in leading the Michigan troopers straight at the Confederates had helped swing the tide. Custer's star, which had been rising, now began streaking across the skies. There was something about him. He didn't just plain like to fight, he loved it.

Both Stuart and Gregg claimed victory, but in what was accomplished the edge had to go to Gregg: his forces had stopped Stuart from reaching the Army of the Potomac, Stuart's initial objective.

Despite the fierceness of the fighting the casualties were relatively light compared to the number of men involved. On both sides the killed, wounded, and missing totaled slightly under five hundred, attesting in part to the somewhat exaggerated rhetorical remark passed around by cynical foot soldiers in both the North and South: "Who ever saw a dead cavalryman?"

On Cemetery Ridge and Seminary Ridge the cannons were still firing.

In battle, time is an elastic sort of thing. For some it stretches out to

A Union officer and his mount.

great length; for others it is short and concentrated. There is no one account which agrees precisely with another as to just how long the artillery duel lasted. Various times ranging from a half hour to two and a half hours have been cited; but a fair estimate places the length of time at about two hours.

From one until three, then, in a gigantic convulsion of jettisoning energy the guns sought to flatten each other, and in the process jarred many eardrums completely out of tune. (As long as two weeks after the fighting men who had been near the cannon found themselves almost deaf, or so acutely responsive to sound that the noise of a footstep was as vivid as a thunderclap.)

During the height of the artillery exchange Lieutenant Haskell and General Gibbon moved out beyond Cemetery Ridge. (A forward position was relatively safe since the trajectory of the Confederate fire carried the missiles high overhead and to the rear.) Haskell and Gibbon sat under the shade of an elm tree while spinning and tumbling shot and shell stirred the air into, in Haskell's words, an "ocean of noise." One type of Confederate shell, hexagonal in shape, made a noise fearful enough to set men's nerves fluttering. Fired from two long-range imported Whitworths over on Oak Hill, northwest of town, the intermittent and startling hiss of these shells carried a terrible finality in their trajectory sound alone.

Immediately to the rear of Haskell and Gibbon was a small grove of trees. A number of artillery pieces positioned in the grove were blasting the air, their operators frantically seeking to send more destruction to the Confederates than they received. In front of the grove was a long stone fence that made a sudden angle and ran in a perpendicular line some two hundred feet

A Whitworth cannon imported by the Confederates from England. The only breech-operated cannon on the field, it had an extremely long range. After the war, the United States Government sent Great Britain a bill for armaments sent to the Confederacy. The bill was paid. Among the items listed were the Whitworths.

Library of Congress

and then angled back once more to follow its original direction. Ghostlike and indistinct in the fog of smoke, soldiers from Pennsylvania, the Philadelphia Brigade, huddled behind the long fence, behind and along the zigzag of its angled contour.

As Haskell and Gibbon sat under the elm tree Gibbon reflected that while he was not a member of any church, he always assumed in battle it was in the hands of God whether he was hurt or not, and therefore he always went where duty called regardless of the danger involved. He didn't speak of his brothers at that moment, but it is possible he thought about them, for Brigadier General John Gibbon, U.S.A., had three brothers fighting for the South.

Shortly after two thirty Haskell and Gibbon noted that the artillery fire from the Federal lines was slackening, especially along the lower section of Cemetery Ridge, and both men decided to return to the lines.

General Hunt had taken it upon himself to order the guns slowly to break off their artillery duel and conserve long-range ammunition for the anticipated infantry attack. He was able to make his orders felt along lower Cemetery Ridge; but Hancock kept the guns of the II Corps, stationed farther up the ridge, going. When the infantry attack came Hancock's guns would be out of long-range projectiles. Hunt also ordered up replacements from the artillery reserve to fill up the gaps left by crippled or destroyed batteries. This would give the Federals practically the same firepower when the Confederates launched their infantry charge as they had possessed at the outset of the artillery bombardment.

On Seminary Ridge this slackening of the Yankee artillery alerted Colonel Alexander. He scanned the enemy's lines with his field glasses once more. The guns were still firing, but not so many of them. Maybe the barrage had done its work! He moved his glasses on "the little clump of trees." Alexander erroneously thought "the clump of trees" enfolded a cemetery, and in a note to Pickett at the beginning of the barrage told of eighteen guns still firing in the "cemetery." Yes! Eighteen cannon were moving out of the "cemetery." No doubt about it. If they did not return in five minutes he would give the word to launch the infantry. This could be the moment. It had to be the moment. Ammunition had been used at an alarming rate, and all batteries were now dangerously low. There could not be many more minutes of firing before they would be completely out.

The five minutes passed, and still the guns had not returned to the "cemetery." They were out of action! Alexander sent a courier dashing off through the smoke with a cryptic note to General Pickett: "For God's sake, come

143

quick. The eighteen guns have gone. Come quick or my ammunition will not let us support you properly."

The note reached Pickett while he was with Longstreet. Pickett read it and passed it without a word to his commander. Upon learning its contents, Longstreet remained silent. He gave no order. Then Pickett spoke up: "General, shall I advance?"

Longstreet made no reply. He bowed his head—more than anything, Longstreet did not want to make this attack—and nodded.

Pickett saluted and said, "I am going to move forward, sir." And the die was cast. And Colonel Alexander had made a catastrophic miscalculation about the eighteen guns in the "cemetery."

Quickly, the word was shouted up and down the line: "Pass the infantry to the front!"

The cannon along Seminary Ridge which so recently had filled the air with violence were suddenly mute, and as though in anticipation of a new and rising drama the Federal guns banked their fire, and the battlefield was stilled. The Confederate infantrymen who had hugged the ground of Seminary Ridge rose to their feet, but not all of them. The work of the Federal cannon had been singularly successful in some cases, and there were many who would never rise. Lieutenant John Dooley, who had joined the rest of his regiment in tossing green apples, saw two men lying prone trying to talk during the height of the bombardment when a shell cascaded through some trees and in an instant hatched into a crimson ball of light, spewing shell splinters over the ground. One of the men resumed talking, totally unaware the shell burst had killed his friend.

Through the thin line of trees on Seminary Ridge and past cannon with muzzles still red-hot moved the men upon whom Lee had placed his faith and hopes for victory. Out in the open, down off the mild slope connecting the

Brigadier General Lewis A. Armistead.　　　Brigadier General James L. Kemper.

ridge with the valley, the now grim foot soldiers assembled and lined up, their movements concealed by the still-lingering clouds of smoke. All of them steeled themselves as best they could for what they knew would be a desperate endeavor.

Eleven brigades dressed their lines and waited for the command to move out. The three brigades of Pickett's division, all men from Virginia, were under the command of Brigadier Generals Richard B. Garnett (West Point, 1841)—Garnett, buttoned to the neck in an old blue overcoat in spite of the heat, was really too ill to make the attack—James L. Kemper, one-time cadet at Virginia Military Institute, and Lewis A. Armistead.

For Armistead, this was to be the last of all days. An underclassman, but not graduate, of West Point, Armistead had become, nevertheless, an officer in the regular United States Army. And back when the war had just started and the "old army" was breaking up, Armistead had bade a tearful good-by to his close friend Winfield Scott Hancock at a farewell party in the officers' quarters of an army post at a little Pacific Coast town of four thousand people called Los Angeles. Armistead had resigned his commission along with some other officers to go with his native state, North Carolina, and the Confederacy, but he was truthful when he said to Hancock he would never know what resigning from the army had "cost" him. An officer's wife had sung "Kathleen Mavourneen" and there hadn't been a dry eye among the guests. It had been a sad party.

Now Armistead and Hancock were meeting again at a place called Gettysburg, separated by a valley and a different set of purposes.

Armistead took his hat and placed it on the tip of his upraised sword, while he pulled at the bridle of his skittery horse and spoke to the color bearer of a Virginia regiment: "Sergeant, are you going to put those colors on the enemy's works today?"

The sergeant said he was going to try.

The second division, under the command of Brigadier General James J. Pettigrew, was made up of men from Virginia, North Carolina, Tennessee, Alabama, and Mississippi. Brigade commanders were Colonel J. K. Marshall, Colonel D. B. Fry, and Brigadier General Joseph R. Davis, President Jefferson Davis' nephew, who had found the going rough on the morning of the first day's fighting.

Two additional brigades of North Carolinians were under the command of Major General Isaac R. Trimble (West Point, 1822). The brigade commanders were Brigadier General James H. Lane and Colonel W. L. Lowrance.

145

And two brigades of men from Florida and Alabama, commanded by Brigadier General Cadmus Wilcox (West Point, 1846) and Colonel David Lang, were positioned in reserve.

Fifteen thousand men were ready. An officer offered Pickett a swig of whiskey, but Pickett declined. He had promised "the little girl"—his fiancée—he would not touch the stuff.

War has an unjustifiable appeal to very young men. There are loyalty and duty; but equally, there are other notions: excitement, glory, uniforms, camaraderie—wonderful, mysterious, and new dingdong things. For many of the young men of the Civil War there was an added inducement: enlistment meant an opportunity, and probably the only one they would ever have, to get away from farms and small country towns, away from the often humdrum rural life. And so they went, filled with an enthusiastic awareness, a

With Seminary Ridge in the background—the line of trees—Union soldiers dug in behind the fence in the foreground fired at the advancing Confederates. The attacking columns extended on the open ground from the left beyond the farmhouse—the Codori farm—all the way to the right by the lone tree. This composite photograph was taken twenty

marvelous sense of the excitement of war. Down to the depots... *Good-by* ... *Good-by* ... down in puffing, slow, cinder-laden trains to the cities... over to the training camps. And the contemplation, the mystery—whatever it was—was lost in harsh orders, drill, the inglorious burden of camp dysentery, dry-mouthed fear of battle, the nauseating sight and sound of terribly wounded friends screaming and screaming....

The smoke lifted from the ridges below Gettysburg in an updraft of warm air, and what the rising smoke revealed sent the hearts of the Yankees along Cemetery Ridge right into their throats, sent a rippling murmur of admiration up and down the lines, kept the guns stilled. For the boys in blue who had gone off to war in search of many things, some of the mystery, the glory— whatever it was—suddenly came back to them. The stink, the awful hell of it, were momentarily forgotten in what their eyes beheld: a mile-and-a-half-

years after the battle and shows the land exactly as the Union soldiers saw it. The figure on horseback is Paul Philippoteaux, artist who painted a cyclorama of "Pickett's Charge" now in the new museum at Gettysburg. His assistant stands at the left on the fence.

long line of Confederates stood in front of Seminary Ridge; and they could have been assembled for a review, with glinting muskets at the right shoulder, officers with sabers unsheathed, and out in front their battle flags fluttering. The Yankees watched; they would never forget this electrifying vision of a far-flung battle line standing there in the open waiting for orders to move out. It was picture-book war, with all the glory and valor of the past. It was the first time, and last time, too, that Yankee soldiers ever saw anything like it.

Orders, unheard by the bluecoated soldiers along Cemetery Ridge, were shouted up and down the line. Skirmishers went first, swarming across wheat fields and meadows of swaying grass. Then double-ranged brigades moved out. Next, a second row one hundred and fifty yards to the rear stepped off, and if there had been regimental bands playing, it might have been a parade, lines all dressed and even. . . .

Now the misinterpretation of the guns in the "cemetery" is explained. The Yankees had withdrawn them only to make room for new batteries. The new batteries move into place. The gunners ram home the charges and wait grimly. The bombardment which had cost the Confederates most of their ammunition had been for naught. Cemetery Ridge, from Little Round Top to Cemetery Hill, bristles with loaded cannon, and thousands of cocked muskets hold a terrible finality in their muzzles. Pale and invisible in the bright afternoon light, Death is taking over the ultimate command. . . .

The Rebel ranks are beautifully aligned as they move across the valley. Red battle flags, bullet-torn from earlier battles, snap proudly. If will and endurance can do it, the flags will be waving over the enemy's lines before many minutes. The smooth columns keep moving.

Now Federal artillerists along the lower section of Cemetery Ridge make ready, as though suddenly aroused from their surprise at the spectacle of the fantastically arrayed enemy moving to overpower them. Out in the valley there is a first spatter of musketry as contending skirmishers shoot at each other. Suddenly the Yankee cannon let go in a mighty salvo on the Confederate right. Shot and shell rip into the ranks, tearing open jagged holes. The columns close in and the gaps disappear. The columns keep moving.

The Emmitsburg Road runs in a northeasterly direction, and the men under General Pickett, who are feeling the opening punch of Yankee artillery, reach the road first. There are split-rail fences on either side of the road, and alignment is lost as the fences are knocked down. Troops are halted and the lines dressed in the face of an infuriated enemy.

"Forward!"

The lines move out once more. "The little clump of trees" on Cemetery Ridge is ahead and to the left.

"Left oblique!"

The columns of soldiers, mostly in their uniforms of homespun butternut tan with here and there a regulation gray, pivot and carry diagonally to the left. The movement exposes the sides of the troops to flank fire. From Little Round Top the battery so laboriously brought up by hand the day before angles its guns and joins in with a savage roar. Shot and shell howl down on the massed troops, bowling over entire groups of soldiers like tenpins. The left wheel movement also offers another opportunity for the Federals, and General Hancock takes cruel advantage.

Hancock orders two regiments of Vermonters straight out into the field in a line perpendicular to Cemetery Ridge. Some Confederate artillery following in the wake of the infantry advance open on the repositioned Vermont regiments. It is the first time in battle for the men from Vermont. They ignore the Confederate artillery. Muskets are raised, their sights squarely on the flank of the moving columns.

Fire! And a torrent of bullets crashes out. Bull's-eyes are scored: again and again and again. . . .

Along the eastern side of the Emmitsburg Road are the farmhouse and buildings of farmer Codori. As co-ordinator and commanding field officer of the attack, General Pickett must remain to the rear of the attacking columns. Pickett reins his horse to a halt in the Codori farmyard and watches his troops advance. Despite the fact that they are receiving staggering punishment he sees they are still moving forward, and still maintaining splendid formation. If they can reach the Federal lines with enough troops, the attack should succeed. Pickett feels they will and sends a courier to Longstreet to advance the support brigades under General Wilcox and Lang. They are to follow the same course as the brigades now advancing.

"Green Mountain Boys." Soldiers from Vermont line up for the photographer.

The descendants of "the clump of trees."

Pickett's division, under Kemper, Garnett, and Armistead, keeps pressing for the "little clump of trees." Now the brigades of Kemper and Garnett stop and deliver their first volley of musketry at the Union lines. It is one-sided. Men in the open are not on equal terms with soldiers behind stone walls and barricades. A colossal flood of return musket fire stabs out from the Federals and the two brigades are dwindling faster and faster; yet they keep up a steady fire, and the Confederate marksmanship is good. Federal artillerists manning their guns behind the lines of infantry are taking a high rate of casualties, and here and there careless infantrymen find that the Rebels are as good with their muskets as they are brave. Courage alone, however, won't do it. The Confederates must bring enough men to bear on the area around the "clump of trees" to break through. As units of soldiers fire at the Yankees others move by the left. And there can't be a Yankee who doesn't realize that for sheer massed bravery there has never been anything like it. The Rebels, without more than occasional dips in the land to protect them, are maneuvering out in the open, offering their bodies as prime targets; and they are dropping in windrows, like leaves in a rainy wind. Flags fall. Are picked up. Fall again. And rise again. A captain stops to offer his mortally wounded son a drink from his canteen. There is nothing he can do. He moves on.

Lieutenant Dooley and his Virginia regiment are with Kemper's brigade. (Dooley will write it all down in his diary.) Dooley sees lines become "unsteady, because at every step a gap must be closed." The blood of the falling bespatters the faces of friends. More gaps appear. The lines press to the right or left. The gaps are closed, "while the bravest of the brave are sinking to rise no more." Dooley watches with breaking heart as volley after volley of churning bullets sweeps his regiment, mowing men down "like wheat before the scythe."

Up on Cemetery Ridge the mounted officers are by far the best targets for quick-shooting Confederates. Hancock is hit in the upper thigh. He is bleeding badly. Yet he will not leave the field in the face of the enemy. He is propped up and a tourniquet applied.

Two hundred yards more. One hundred and fifty. Now, one hundred. Garnett is down. Shot dead. Kemper has fallen. Lieutenant Dooley is knocked off his feet, a bullet through both thighs.

The remainder of Pickett's division is mingling with the left of the advance, the division under the command of General Pettigrew. . . .

At the outset of the grand advance, Pettigrew's men of A. P. Hill's III Corps had been as splendidly aligned as Pickett's on the right; but after an initial contact with a heavy body of scouts things began to go badly. The scouts turned out to be an Ohio regiment which swung back and let Petti-grew's men pass by, thus putting the Ohioans on the flank where they de-livered a steady terror of bullets from the side.

At this end of the attack formation the distance to Cemetery Ridge was shorter and, despite the enfilade fire which tended to bunch and herd Petti-grew's lines in on each other, the center section arrived before the Union en-trenchments relatively intact. But with the dogged soldiers was the Pale Rider, fleshless arms raised and pointing. Union cannon on this part of the front had used up long-range ammunition and were obliged to hold off until the enemy was close up to deliver short-range canister. The Union artillerists and infantrymen waited until the final moment, and then every last firearm on this part of Cemetery Ridge opened up at once and the entire division dis-appeared in an inferno of smoke. It was, literally, as if a solid mass had hit the Confederates broadside at high speed. Arms, legs, disembodied heads, muskets, canteens—a horrible collection of rubbish—went sailing into the air, and an audible groan, distinct amidst the roar of battle, was heard from Pettigrew's division. The lines, the formation, underwent an instantaneous transformation. The brigades of Mayo and Davis began to break up and go into retreat, and the other brigades started to drift towards the right. And as a final blow to keep the brigades off balance a New York regiment swung out in a perpen-dicular line to Cemetery Ridge, almost exactly as the Vermont regiments at the other end of the fighting front had done, and sailed into the assaulting brigades with a withering flank musket fire.

Now the Confederate advance, which once covered a front more than a mile in width, has been reduced by more than half, leaving a commingled mass of overlapping brigades and regiments, or what is left of them. Around them, among them, to the north, south, and rear, is a frightful mat of dying, wounded, and dead. Around them, among them, is the ghastly whine of bullets, the sickening noise of shot and shell. The number of dying, wounded, and dead is growing, growing.

Now the brigades of Lane and Lowrance under General Trimble are coming up behind the remnants of Pettigrew's division, only to be met in a wild storm of point-blank canister and musket fire. The lines stagger where great gaps are suddenly blown wide open; yet the rear elements push on tenaciously, straight for "the clump of trees," right up to the zigzag stone fence. They overlap the angle in the fence, and, suddenly, the Philadelphia Brigade behind the wall is caught in a murderous fury of bullets from the front and side.

And Battery A, 4th United States Artillery, positioned in the clump of trees to the rear of the wall, is falling to pieces. More than a score of horses are sprawled dead or dying as the result of both the earlier bombardment and the bullets of the approaching infantrymen. The commanding officer, First Lieutenant Alonzo Cushing (West Point, 1861), orders double canister to be rammed into the guns. A bullet catches Cushing in the shoulder. A second bullet stabs into his groin. He is still on his feet. He only has enough gunners left to man one gun. The gun is rolled forward, triple canister rammed into its muzzle. *Fire!* The gun belches its ugly contents and a final bullet plows into the commanding officer. Cushing drops over dead. Battery A is out of action.

The Philadelphia Brigade is firing back almost on a muzzle-to-muzzle basis at the Rebels, but with flank fire enfilading the position it is taking a severe beating; and from behind the wall the desperate Pennsylvanians can see a whole cluster of red battle flags converging directly in front.

There is no formation, no definition of this or that brigade, in the massed Confederates who have reached the wall, but the chances of success are gain-

Battery A, 4th United States Artillery. This photograph taken shortly after Gettysburg shows the effect of battle. The battery has only four guns instead of the normal six.

Library of Congress

A soldier from the ranks—
J. T. Jobson, who marched in
Armistead's brigade.

Confederate Museum, Richmond, Virginia

ing with each additional man who has managed to get this far. Now General Armistead, the last brigade commander of Pickett's division still on his feet—his horse was shot out from under him—leads what is left of his brigade up the gentle slope to the wall. His hat, which he had placed on the tip of his out-thrust sword, is rammed down to the hilt. Armistead pauses.

The Philadelphia Brigade back of the wall is giving way. The flank fire has pried it loose and the front is breaking. General Gibbon, who has been riding up and down shouting orders, is unhorsed with a severe shoulder wound. Lieutenant Haskell is the only mounted officer left in the sector.

Now General Armistead leaps to the top of the fence, crying, "Give 'em the cold steel, boys! Follow me!" And a hundred men of the South leap over the fence, and the defenders stream for the rear.

Haskell is in among the Pennsylvanians, pleading, cursing, ordering them to turn about and hold the line, but for a few minutes there is milling and general disorder as the triumphant Confederates take full possession of the angle of the stone fence. For the Federals the extreme moment has come. Haskell manages to get some of the defenders to rally in a new line and dashes off for help.

Down to the left the Federal line has completely checked the Confederates.

Haskell asks for reinforcements from this part of the front. With a yell, men from five regiments move out on the double, headed for the beleaguered angle.

At the angle there is a momentary lull. The Confederates look back anxiously to see if support is moving up to exploit the partial breakthrough. None appears.

The support brigades under Wilcox and Perry had moved out according to Pickett's directions, but in the confusion and smoke of battle they did not make a "left oblique" to follow the main assault line. Instead, they had moved straight ahead, and found themselves below and separated from Pickett's division and, more disastrously, below the two regiments of Vermonters

This statue on Seminary Ridge by Gutzon Borglum, creator of the Great Presidential Faces on Mt. Rushmore, commemorates the men from North Carolina at Gettysburg. North Carolina had fifteen regiments in "Pickett's Charge."

Walter Lane

thrown out by Hancock. The Vermonters immediately made an about-face and let loose with a devastating swarm of bullets on the lost brigades; then the artillery on Cemetery Ridge got their range and they were repulsed.

Now Haskell, with the reinforcements he needs, shouts an order: "Forward to the wall!" It is heard by the Confederates and an answering command to the few who have penetrated the Federal line goes up into the air: "Steady, men!"

Suddenly, the dismaying sound of hundreds of whining bullets catches the Confederates as the reinforcements and the routed defenders pour back into the breach. A Delaware regiment on Haskell's right bounds over the wall. Armistead goes down, mortally wounded, and all at once the Confederates are fighting not to advance but to get out. Too late! Most of them are killed or captured.

Out in front of the angle, out in front of Cemetery Ridge, is a hopeless tangle of Confederates occupying a space less than five hundred yards across. Dazed men who have passed beyond the limits of endurance are caught in a hurricane of frontal and crossfire, and there is nothing left to do but surrender, or, for those who can manage it, to start back to Seminary Ridge.

It is all over. The attack, which has lasted a little less than thirty minutes, has failed. Better than three thousand Confederates are killed and wounded and some two thousand are prisoners of war, along with twenty battle flags.[12]

When it is apparent what has happened thousands of grimy but exalted men in blue from Cemetery Hill all the way down Cemetery Ridge and up onto Little Round Top begin to cheer, some of them yelling: "Fredericksburg! Fredericksburg!"—a taunting reminder to the beaten Confederates that they have received some of the medicine handed out at the Battle of Fredericksburg, where the Federals had made a series of fruitless and bloody charges.

The moment had arrived for General Meade: counterattack!

Meade rode onto Cemetery Ridge as herds of prisoners of war were being shunted to the rear. Upon receiving word that the attack had been repulsed he let himself go momentarily to shout just once, "Hurrah!" But somehow this seemed to be the extent of his thinking—a natural sense of relief. He had planned to wage a defensive battle and the outcome had justified that decision; but this policy had become ingrained by now in Meade. Defense? Yes. Offense? That was something else.

As the wounded General Hancock was carried off the field he sent Meade a note in which he urged that along with the Confederate repulse "the defeat would be decisive" if a counterattack were launched. (Hancock a short time later would receive sad reminders that the war had broken forever old and cherished relationships: the dying General Armistead had been taken prisoner and had requested his watch and spurs be turned over to his friend General Hancock to see they were sent home.)

That a counterstroke was the obvious and expected military maneuver for Meade was much in evidence to the west along Seminary Ridge. A desperately calm General Lee sought to rally the disorganized remnants of his shattered brigades and get them into a hasty line of battle to fend off as best as possible a Federal thrust. To a nearly frantic General Pickett who could do little more than reiterate in anguish that his division had been destroyed General Lee spoke out firmly: "Come, General Pickett, this has been my fight and upon my shoulders rests the blame." To others he gave words of encouragement: "All will come right in the end . . . we want all good and true men just now." As magnificent in defeat as in victory, the nature of the man in whom every Confederate soldier placed so much trust and genuine devotion was manifest even at this critically anxious moment. A wounded Federal prisoner (probably a skirmisher captured when the charge was first under way) saw Lee passing astride Traveller and was prompted to shout, somewhat daringly, "Hurrah for the Union." General Lee stopped, dismounted, and walked over to a suddenly very worried Yankee. Lee extended his hand and said, "My son, I hope you will soon be well." The amazed Yankee soldier was so overcome he broke into sobs.

And Longstreet, slightly fortified with some rum proffered by the ever present British observer, Colonel Fremantle, was busily placing disoriented survivors in line. To a general who claimed he could not rally his men Longstreet replied testily, "Very well . . . the enemy's going to advance and will spare you the trouble." Old Pete, who had not wanted to make the attack, was ready, regardless, to do everything possible to forestall any attempt by the Federals to turn the repulse of his men into a total rout.

Longstreet's exertions were not necessary. The counterattack never came, although Federal cavalry officer General Pleasonton pointed out to Meade what should have been obvious: Lee had exhausted his available manpower and ammunition.

On the front from which he launched the attack, Lee had just three brigades—about fifty-five hundred men—in position. The survivors of the attack, totally disorganized, would require both time and redisposition before they could become effective. Lee had no reserves. General Meade had at his immediate disposal, with the idea of attacking straight across to Seminary Ridge, the troops which had beaten off "Pickett's Charge"—at least six thousand men —plus all the virtually unused fifteen thousand men of the VI Corps under General Sedgwick in reserve back of the Round Tops. Admittedly, it would take time to array these forces for a counterattack, but Meade did little more than make a tour of inspection to the sounds of cheering soldiers down Cemetery Ridge to Little Round Top. He would wait for Lee to make the next move.[13]

The day was not quite over.

A contingent of Union cavalry was stationed south of the Round Tops on the Union left flank. Under the command of Judson Kilpatrick—since the cavalry fight at Brandy Station Kilpatrick had been promoted to a Brigadier General—this cavalry was destined to provide a spectacularly anticlimactic, or at least ineffective, finish to the fighting.

An orderly came storming into the cavalry headquarters with news about the Confederate repulse on Cemetery Ridge and the astounding intelligence that "nine acres of prisoners" had been taken. Kilpatrick immediately ordered a foray into the Confederate rear. He assumed, without confirmation, that there would be a massive counterattack by Meade. His cavalry could do much to add to the confusion in the Confederate lines. It was a rash movement. The

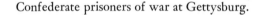

Confederate prisoners of war at Gettysburg.

The National Archives

cavalry would have to crash through the well-entrenched brigades of Hood's division, the same soldiers who had tried unsuccessfully to take Little Round Top and the lower section of Cemetery Ridge the day before.

Troopers of a West Virginia squadron went in first, hoofs pounding across green fields. Confederate infantrymen quickly broke up the charge and sent the West Virginians reeling back.

Kilpatrick ordered Brigadier General Elon J. Farnsworth to take a Vermont regiment and see what he could do. Farnsworth protested that it was suicidal. Kilpatrick asked Farnsworth if he were "afraid" to lead the charge. There was a nasty moment of silence, and then Farnsworth irately demanded Kilpatrick "take back" what he had said. Kilpatrick recanted, and Farnsworth went off on one of the wildest and most useless actions of the battle, and to his own death.

Jumping fences and galloping full tilt across meadowland, with all the vigor of a steeplechase, the regiment drew a withering fire from Confederates who considered them fair game all the way. Even so, the horse soldiers managed to get back of the enemy lines in a long circuit, and there Farnsworth was unsaddled with five bullets. For those who managed to get back to the starting point, the confusing question was: *Why?* Nothing had been proved and ninety-eight cavalrymen had been lost. The ride had drawn the fire of the enemy, and that was all. Kilpatrick had thought Meade would counterattack; his cavalry had tried to help—a fine question of military tactics and problems.

No one knew it yet, but the fighting at Gettysburg was over.

It was five thirty, the sun beginning to cast long shadows, when Farnsworth rode to his death and the fighting came to a final ending. Along the eastern seaboard families sat down to the evening meal—"supper" was an early affair in 1863. And across the tables there were anxious expressions of concern and

Brigadier General
Elon J. Farnsworth,
brigade commander,
Federal Cavalry.

Library of Congress

reassurance. *He's all right . . . don't worry*. And family clocks moved, pendulums swinging back and forth. *Past time. Present time.* In Washington, at the White House, there was anxious waiting for news from Gettysburg. *If things went wrong at Gettysburg . . . they can't . . . they just can't.* The pendulum of the upright clock in the hall swung back and forth. *Tick. Tock.* At his home in Richmond, Jefferson Davis, ill on this day, waited hopefully for word from General Lee. *A victory on Northern soil . . . a telegram with news of a victory would cure any sickness. Tick . . . tock. Tick . . . tock.* Out in Mississippi, outside the defenses of Vicksburg, it was four thirty in the afternoon and General Grant was holding a conference with his corps commanders. The commanding Confederate officer wished to surrender his army, and Grant was interested in hearing if his officers might have any suggestions for terms. The hour was four thirty. The hour was five thirty. *Past time. Present time. . . .* And both tolled doom for the Confederacy. . . .

Moonrise on the night of July 3 cast soft light on a scene which was becoming familiar at Gettysburg. Dead men. Wounded men. Exhausted men. Dead horses. Weary, head-down horses and mules. And a vast collection of debris scattered everywhere. But there was a change that night. As twinkling lanterns marked the movements of medical corpsmen looking for wounded, as campfires died in yellow embers, the war shifted fully in favor of the North.

A wound, staggering and eventually fatal, had been scored on the Army of Northern Virginia, and it could never again resume a grand offensive. The repulse of the last three days had been too costly in irreplaceable officers; and manpower in the South was no match for the vast reserves in the North. The North had at last won a major victory, and although losses in the Army of the Potomac had been high, they could be replaced. And whether it happened in the next few hours, the next few days, or in several months, there was an almost certain outcome for the Army of Northern Virginia, and for the war itself.

It was warm, with the moon high and full, as the summer night wore on. In the town of Gettysburg sleepy citizens, still unaware of how things had gone, could hear the shuffle of Confederate soldiers moving through the streets— General Lee was repositioning his army, pulling Ewell's II Corps back from the Rock Creek area near Culp's Hill and the streets of the town to a straight line along Seminary Ridge all the way up to Oak Hill. And when the Southern soldiers were awake enough to notice they might have gained the impression that housewives had forgotten to take in the household goods they had been airing that day. Mattresses, boxes, pieces of furniture, all had been placed outside windows, in front of doors, in an effort to stave off stray bullets and shell fragments entering the townspeople's homes.

And for young Billy Bayly, who had watched the opening of battle while picking berries, and who had been surprised to find a youthful Rebel seeking asylum at the front door, the night and the moon went unnoticed while he slept. The next day he and his new friend, the little Rebel, would watch Lee's discouraged legions march drearily out of Gettysburg.

For General Lee it was a mournful night. He, more than anyone, realized what had happened to his army. No thoughts now of offensive tactics. No alternatives. Retreat, and only retreat, could be considered.

An infinitely weary Lee rode into his headquarters area at about one o'clock in the morning. He had been up some twenty hours. One-time Virginia lawyer Brigadier General John D. Imboden, in charge of an independent cavalry brigade, was waiting for him. Lee had sent for Imboden to explain the details of the first stage of the retreat in which Imboden was to take charge of a wagon train of wounded and sick soldiers and head it out over the Chambersburg Pike.

A jaded Traveller was reined to a halt and Lee dismounted, so physically exhausted he had to throw his arm across the saddle and rest, his head bent, his eyes fixed steadily on the ground. In the bright light of the moon Imboden noted a sadness on General Lee's face he had never seen before and remarked: "General, this has been a hard day on you."

"Yes," replied Lee, "it has been a sad, sad day to us." Lee straightened himself up and with animation spoke of the magnificent effort of Pickett's troops and how the day might have turned out differently. He paused, and looking nowhere in particular, spoke out: "Too bad! Too bad! Oh! Too bad!"

The moon glided across the heavens heading endlessly west, and began to pale and grow watery behind a slow, high, thin layer of clouds.

Brigadier General
John D. Imboden,
brigade commander,
Confederate Cavalry.

Library of Congress

Chapter VI

Shoo Her Geese

President Lincoln:	"Do you know, General, what your attitude towards Lee a week after the battle reminded me of?"
General Meade:	"No, Mr. President, what is it?"
President Lincoln:	"I'll be hanged if I could think of anything else than an old woman trying to shoo her geese across a creek."

When President Lincoln made this pronouncement to General Meade, the Battle of Gettysburg had been over and finished many weeks earlier. It was a quasi-humorous summation of his bitter disappointment in General Meade for allowing Lee and the Army of Northern Virginia to withdraw from Pennsylvania and Maryland and escape into Virginia.

Lincoln's disappointment in Meade, despite the defensive victory at Gettysburg, resulted from his view of the events after the battle: the war was going to drag on with bloody attrition due to what Meade had *not* done.

After failing to follow up the repulse of "Pickett's Charge" with a smashing counterblow, Meade, nevertheless, for fully nine days after the battle, had had a great opportunity either totally to wreck the Army of Northern Virginia, or at least substantially to reduce it before it reached Virginia. But he had not grasped the possibilities; and Lee's forces, although battered beyond hope of ever fully recovering, had escaped. The tragic implications of Meade's failure to act can best be expressed by the fact that at the moment of Gettysburg the final costs of the war had been only half paid by North and South.[14]

A strange, continuing stillness hung over Gettysburg on the morning of July 4. Meade, ultra-cautious, stuck to his great "fishhook" perimeter and allowed his officers to precipitate no offensive operations. Cannon were mute, although here and there there were brief probing flare-ups of skirmishers and pickets; but on the whole it was quiet.

General Lee waited as preparations got under way to begin a mass retreat. Meade did not attack. Confederates eyed Cemetery Ridge for any signs of blue-jacketed soldiers moving out in assault columns. There was a feeling among the rank and file of the Confederates that if the Yankees attacked they would give them a hot reception. Still full of fight, the average Confederate soldier was not conscious of the great calamity which had overtaken the Army of Northern Virginia. No columns of Yankees appeared.

By midmorning the sky began to darken ominously as General Lee had his soldiers go through the motions of entrenching—"evidence" to deceive the Yankees into thinking that the Army of Northern Virginia was anything but on its last collective leg, and that it intended to remain on the field. To the west along the Chambersburg Pike General Imboden surveyed the growing lines of wagons assembling for the initial phase of the retreat back to Virginia.

And during the morning hours, 750 miles to the southwest, Major General Grant accepted the surrender of Vicksburg from Lieutenant General John C. Pemberton (West Point, 1837). Along with its capture of thirty thousand soldiers, the North now dominated the length of the Mississippi River and had split the South into two sections.[15]

With the twin victories at Vicksburg and Gettysburg there was a chance, an excellent chance, if General Meade acted decisively, that the Confederacy could be plunged into its death agony within a matter of days.

General Meade made two decisions of consequence on July 4. The first was to do nothing more than wait for Lee to launch another attack—he visualized this as a distinct possibility. The second decision took the form of an order to General French at Frederick, Maryland, to take his troops to the vicinity of Falling Waters and Williamsport and destroy the pontoon bridges across the Potomac River. (These were the same troops whose status at Harper's Ferry, seemingly so long ago, had caused General Hooker to ask to be relieved of command of the Army of the Potomac.) This order revealed that Meade had been struck with the startling notion that he might have Lee trapped: destruction of the pontoon bridges would be a further setback for the Confederates, both from the aspect of retreat and of securing supplies. Beyond this Meade did nothing. Caution, bred out of respect, was in all probability the basis of Meade's inactivity, and it all centered on Robert E. Lee.

Lee had bested every general, excluding Meade, that the North had pitted

162

against him since he had taken command of the Army of Northern Virginia. This thought alone was enough to shake the will of a general who had commanded his army for just seven days. That Meade had done a good job no one knew better than the Confederates; but Robert Edward Lee was near-by, and he had pulled victory out of defeat before. Meade did not attack. His army had done well enough, and while victorious, it had been pretty well mauled.

Around noon a light drizzle began falling from a steadily dimming sky. It continued for an hour, and then General Imboden, who was to write a graphic description of the retreat, found to his dismay "the very windows of the heavens seemed to have opened." A torrential onslaught heaved down on Gettysburg, and "meadows were soon overflowed, and fences gave way before raging streams." Falling in "blinding sheets," the rain drummed across hills and ridges and fields in a bouncing froth until the land oozed and became a muddy goo. It cascaded and sprayed off the backs of weary Confederates; ran down the glistening surfaces of rubberized ponchos draped over the bowed heads of Yankee cavalrymen; soaked into the sweaty, soiled blue uniforms of Yankee infantrymen. It splashed into Rock Creek, where a small

A wagon train of the Army of the Potomac ready to cross the Potomac River, too late: Lee and his army have escaped back to Virginia.

dam held back the water until it swelled out and began to drown some of the wounded. The downpour of that afternoon, that Fourth of July afternoon, continued without letup. It rained pitilessly.

At 4 P.M. mule teams lurched against their harnesses, and General Imboden's wagon train began rolling. Loaded with such Confederate wounded as could be moved, the van snaked out over the Chambersburg Pike, a morose and melancholy aftermath of an army which had marched into the North with such high expectations. Pushing out with the wagons were twenty-three pieces of artillery, a cavalry brigade, four thousand Yankee prisoners, and five thousand semisick and lightly wounded men, who, while incapacitated, were still able to walk. All through the grim, gray twilight of the late afternoon the wagons jostled and thumped over a road rutted in a quagmire of mud; wounded soldiers, tormented beyond endurance, cursed and screamed and begged to be taken from the wagons and put on the side of the road, more content to remain stationary in the driving rain than to submit to the exquisite torture of the springless wagons jolting raw wounds and splintered bones.

Nightfall overtook the lead wagons following a winding road through the South Mountain Range. General Imboden, whose orders were to continue moving regardless of the weather or the condition of the wounded—broken wagons were to be discarded—until the train reached Williamsport, had chosen a short cut which angled below Chambersburg. The road was narrow and tortuous; yet safety for the vulnerable convoy lay in the cover of darkness, and the wagons rolled on through the black, watery gloom in a procession of misery as near-gale winds and sudden flashes of lightning struck wild terror among the mule teams.

Yankee cavalry, flushed with its success at Gettysburg, did not seem to share Meade's caution, and patrols were out on the prowl, seeking anything of the enemy's it could wade into and smash. At three o'clock in the morning of July 5, on a serpentine road in the South Mountain Range, it found what it was looking for, and it struck. Hard.

Amidst a towering electrical storm a roving band of cavalry slipped in between the tail of the wagon train and elements of Ewell's II Corps, now on the first leg of the retrograde movement of the Confederate infantry. In a melee of shouts, gunfire, streaks of lightning and thunder, the cavalry succeeded in toppling a number of wagons into deep ravines and capturing fifteen hundred prisoners. It was a night in which General Imboden "realized more of the horrors of war than [he] had in all the preceding two years."

Dawn found the wagon procession rattling through the streets of Green-

164

castle, Pennsylvania. From end to end the wagons now extended into "seventeen miles of agony." And dawn brought further exacerbations.

Daylight revealed the stark plight of the Confederates. And some thirty or forty citizens of Greencastle, unable to resist the temptation to get in their own licks on a faltering enemy, seized axes and flailed into the wagon wheels. Smashing away at the spokes, they dropped a dozen vehicles before Confederate horsemen caught up with them and forcibly drove home the realities of war by carting them off in the rain as prisoners.

If the rain, the ax-wielding citizenry, and personal miseries were a bane, the Yankee cavalry was a whole flock of devils. Ranging in from fields and crossroads, packs of blue-uniformed horsemen began striking the wagons in a series of hit-and-run attacks which continued throughout the morning and afternoon of July 5. Pounding into unguarded sections of the convoy, they would tear things to pieces and gallop off to do the same thing all over again.

In spite of the forces arrayed against him, at five o'clock that afternoon General Imboden saw the first wagons roll into Williamsport. The Confederates were at the Potomac River. Across the river, on the far bank, was safety.[16]

But as though Nature were doing everything in her power to help the North put an end to things, the Potomac River, flooded by the continuous rain, was ten feet above fording stage. And a daring group of Yankee cavalry had swept in and broken loose the pontoon bridge, while just below, at Falling Waters, General French's troops had already destroyed the only other pontoon bridge. Imboden's wagon train, and for that matter the entire Army of Northern Virginia, was trapped—beyond two small ferryboats at Williamsport there was no way across the Potomac.

As his wagons jammed into the town streets, General Imboden ordered the citizens of Williamsport to open their homes to the wounded and supply such food as was available, and burial squads were formed to find suitable sites for the interment of those who had died en route from Gettysburg. There was nothing more to do now but wait. Wait for General Lee and the rest of the Army of Northern Virginia to come up. Wait for the waters of the Potomac to recede. The high water and the arrival of the rest of the army were beyond any immediate solution. They were a matter of time, but the problem of the Yankee cavalry was something else. It was acute and urgent.

At one o'clock in the afternoon of July 6, seven thousand Federal cavalry troopers, confident and filled with a sense of victory, closed in on Williamsport from the east and prepared to destroy Lee's wagons. If successful, this would end the Army of Northern Virginia as surely as an overwhelming defeat of its infantry. The South was not capable of replacing the wagons. Their value to Lee and his army was absolute—without them supply, logistics, would not exist.

In a little-known but one of the most brilliantly conducted minor battles of the Gettysburg campaign, General Imboden deployed his wagon men and such wounded as could use a musket—about three thousand in all—and along with his twenty-three fieldpieces held the Yankee horsemen off for the entire afternoon. By the clever stratagem of moving men from left to right and throwing his cannon forward he convinced the enemy he held Williamsport in heavy strength. At one point his artillery ran out of ammunition, but his luck held when ordnance arriving from Winchester was quickly ferried across the Potomac and brought to the field behind the guns.

As night closed in the Yankee riders suddenly had to make a run for it: Stuart's cavalry, belatedly approaching from Gettysburg, swept in and threatened them from two sides. It was very close, probably the nearest Meade's forces came to ultimate victory. General Imboden told just how close it was: "A bold charge at any time before sunset would have broken our feeble lines, and then we should have fallen an easy prey to the Federals."

The action, which came to be known as the Wagoneer's Fight, was a definite victory for the Confederates, and measured in terms of resourcefulness and courage they had earned it. Yet, even though they had not succeeded in their effort to reduce Lee's wagons, taking one thing with another, the Yankee horsemen were proving they had a fair notion of the state of Lee's army and wanted nothing better than to go after it.

The up-and-go of the Federal troopers, however, was hardly reflected by the "brass" back at Gettysburg. General Hancock, a proponent of wading into the Confederates, was out of it, bedded down in a field hospital with a painful wound, and the Army of the Potomac was behaving as if it were anything but victorious.

During the rain of July 4, General Meade penned a congratulatory order to the Army of the Potomac which in part explains what was happening at its brain center.

Meade thanked the army "in behalf of the people of the country for the glorious result of the recent operations..." And then went on to refer to a spurious notion with the words: "An enemy superior in numbers..." This belief was not a new one—it had rankled in the minds of the commanding

How the North heard the news. "Alert" telegraphers at Gettysburg.

generals preceding Meade—but analysis would have shown that the supposed preponderance of the Army of Northern Virginia consisted of one man. From the Federal point of view General Lee was a whole army in himself.

When President Lincoln eyed the commendatory order he was struck by one sentence and exclaimed in anguish: "Drive the *invaders* from our soil. My God! Is that all?"

Telegraphic communications direct from Gettysburg were restored within a matter of hours after the fighting, and President Lincoln spent a great deal of anxious time in the War Office Building reading dispatches and following the movements of the Army of the Potomac. As the clicking telegraph key relayed Meade's July 4 words to his army this sentence tumbled out: "Our task is not yet accomplished and the Commanding General looks to the

A "battery wagon" of the type used by the Army of the Potomac. These wagons, containing wet cell batteries to power telegraph lines, followed the army and were vital in maintaining communications with Washington.

The way the North "saw" the battle. Artist A. R. Waud sketches at Devil's Den. Photo-engraving had not been developed, and Waud's drawing would be painstakingly copied by hand engraving for publication.

Army for greater efforts to drive from our soil every vestige of the presence of the invaders."

With these particular words it was obvious to Lincoln that Meade viewed Lee's forces as mere interlopers on Northern soil. Unfortunately, Meade failed to realize that displacement of Confederate forces from Pennsylvania to Virginia did not alter the status of the soil—it was still American. The purpose and aim of the North was not defense, but rather maintaining the union of all states; and while it had been driven to defensive tactics at Gettysburg its final objective was the destruction of all the South's armed forces, thus rendering the Confederate States of America inexistent. Meade did not, or could not, envisage it this way.

True, Meade's army had suffered heavy casualties, but so had the Confederates. And proportionally these losses favored Meade. Final statistics would show Meade's army was reduced by slightly more than one quarter—3,072 killed, 14,497 wounded, and 5,434 missing or captured—while Lee's forces were reduced by almost a third—2,592 killed, 12,709 wounded, and better than 5,000 missing or captured.[17] Meade also had at hand the militia at Harrisburg, 20,000 men, the troops under General French at Frederick, 7,000, and the military garrison of Washington, which would give him if drawn together an aggregate total, including the Army of the Potomac, of at least 95,000. Lee, on the other hand, without the slightest possibility of gaining one additional man, had at best 50,000 combat-ready soldiers, and their effectiveness was limited by a very meager amount of ammunition. The problem of supply for Meade, although he laid great emphasis on the fact that his ordnance had been pretty well used up, was not much more than requisitioning it. His army, after all, was in the very heartland of the North—ordnance in quantity was available at Harrisburg, only thirty-five miles from Gettysburg. The fortunes of war had dealt Meade a pat hand—everything was in his favor—but he utilized it with the daring of a miser.

During the night of July 4–5, General Lee's infantry units succeeded in dragging themselves through a purgatory of rain from the battlefield without opposition. They headed out over the Hagerstown Road in a colossal jam of men, horses, mules, and artillery. Nightfall of the fifth found the columns pressing through Fairfield, Pennsylvania, and despite the weather and the prodigious problem of keeping an orderly flow, the undaunted men of the South were able to reach Hagerstown, thirty-four miles from Gettysburg, on July 6 and 7. With the Potomac flooded and all means of retreat cut off, Lee established a defense line southwest of Hagerstown covering the crossings at Williamsport and Falling Waters. The dictates of generalship indicated, in

The War Department office building in Washington, 1863.

what was an almost textbook situation, that Meade would soon be attacking. Lee made preparations to render battle as best he could—defeat was simply not part of his make-up as a man.

As the Army of Northern Virginia awaited its fate, the first news of recent events began trickling into the South. It was curious news. Based on no more than rumors and hearsay, it angled far afield from the facts.

A paper in Savannah captioned a lead story: *"The Best News of the War,"* and went on to tell of an "overwhelming defeat of the Yankees at Gettysburg. Forty thousand prisoners in our hands."

The Enquirer, a Richmond paper, announced it had a dispatch from the Southern Telegraph Company which read: "Lee has defeated the enemy. General Meade is retreating towards Baltimore. General Lee is pursuing."

The South had become too used to a victorious General Lee.

Early in the morning of July 5 Corporal William T. Livermore of the 20th Maine Regiment found himself walking towards the Peach Orchard in the direction of the Emmitsburg Road. The battle-scarred 20th Maine was on reconnaissance. General Meade, still uncertain whether "Bobby" Lee was really retreating or just playing possum, wanted some sort of confirmation.

Corporal Livermore, well inured to the sight of dead bodies and the debris

Corporal William T. Livermore, 20th Maine Regiment.

Oscar Hamlin and The 20th Maine
(J. B. Lippincott Company)

"Above and beyond the call of duty." A horse lies beside his wrecked caisson.

of battle, was a little overwhelmed by what he saw. In a letter to his brother, terse in its lack of punctuation and occasional misspelling, he told of a barn which had been burned. It was full of roasted corpses. (The barn at one point had been held by Federal troops until it was overwhelmed during the second day's fighting and caught fire.)

In a vast pageant of horror he found other morbid spectacles:

To speak safely there was a thousand dead horses that were all swolen and the smell of the horses and men was dreadful. That field as far as we went was as I might say covered with the dead of our own & Rebels . . . the ground every foot of it was covered with men, horses clothing cartridge boxes canteen guns bayonets scattered cartridges cannon balls everywhere. Caissons stood where horses were instantly killed by cannon ball and they piled up on the pole just as they were killed.

Along with these baleful relics of some of the components of battle Corporal Livermore and the rest of the 20th Maine soon found out what everyone in the ranks expected: Lee and the Army of Northern Virginia were gone.

By midmorning Meade finally became convinced the enemy had left. It now was fully forty hours since the last Confederate attack, and he issued orders to General Sedgwick to take his VI Corps and pursue Lee's columns, but *not* to bring on a general engagement. Sedgewick and his men were the first to take after the Confederates in what was to become an incredibly leisurely pursuit by the entire Army of the Potomac.

Meade was quite aware the Potomac River had flooded and that his forces had destroyed the pontoon bridges. However, even at the insistence of Brigadier General Herman Haupt (West Point, 1835), in charge of roads, rail-

Mutilated Northern casualty of the second day's fighting.

roads, bridges, and telegraph lines, that Lee could easily build new bridges with material which could be procured from barns, houses, and trees, Meade remained inflexible about doing anything which implied swift and adroit action. Meade's reply to a suggestion by General Haupt that he (Meade) should follow up his advantage and capture the remains of Lee's army before it crossed the Potomac was: "My army requires a few days rest, and cannot move at present."

Meade's attitude so upset Haupt that he commandeered a railroad locomotive and made a fast run into Washington to tell President Lincoln and General in Chief of the Army Henry Halleck his suspicions that Meade was allowing Lee to escape.

This information started the wires humming, and Meade throughout the remainder of the campaign was the recipient of urgent telegraphic proddings from an upset Lincoln and an apprehensive Halleck.

Meade himself made some noise over the telegraph calling for the erection of a pontoon bridge at Harper's Ferry, asking for command of the militia at Harrisburg, requesting troops from Washington. At least over the wires he gave indications he was preparing an attack of annihilation. But somehow Meade had set his sights too low.

From July 5 to July 12 the Army of the Potomac traveled seventy miles in a circuitous route which swung down through the Frederick area thence to a position north and east of Lee's defense line near Hagerstown.

On July 12 Meade arrayed his infantry and artillery in position to launch an attack. His cavalry was deployed far out on both flanks. (The fact that his cavalry was north of the Potomac and had not used the ordered pontoon bridge at Harper's Ferry to get south of the river and prevent Lee from effecting a crossing was an indication that Meade's attitude was far from that of a general about to administer a death blow.) Upon completion of military arrangements, he held a council of war with his top-ranking generals. Meade called for a vote: *Attack? No attack?* A majority voted not to attack, as it was felt Lee had had too much time to render his defenses formidable, thereby lessening the chances for a successful assault. Aware of the wishes of the men in Washington that he go after the Confederates, Meade himself voted in favor of an attack.

Upon hearing of the negative vote General Halleck sent an urgent wire from Washington telling Meade to attack, with the admonition: "Do not let the enemy escape."

Meade immediately reversed the decision of the council of war and ordered an attack for the following morning, Tuesday, July 14.

It was raining again when dawn broke on Tuesday, but battle flags were unfurled, bugles sounded, and Meade's army rolled forward—but found virtually none of the enemy.

The very thing General Haupt warned Meade about had happened. Confederate engineers had constructed a ramshackle pontoon bridge at Falling Waters, and during the afternoon of July 13 and on through the night into

Brigadier General Herman Haupt inspecting the work of a railroad construction crew.
Library of Congress

July 14 Lee's army used the swaying bridge to get south of the Potomac. Only a rear guard felt the brunt of Meade's attack and in a snarling little battle Confederate General Pettigrew was mortally wounded and Union cavalry captured fifteen hundred prisoners.

The Army of Northern Virginia had escaped and was headed for home. But the star of the Confederacy had moved into the first phase of a total and permanent eclipse.

Upon news of the escape of the Army of Northern Virginia, General Halleck sent off a wire to Meade in which he referred to the President's "dissatisfaction." Meade regarded the wire as a censure and promptly offered his resignation. It was just as promptly refused. And President Lincoln penned a long, strongly worded letter to Meade the same day explaining just why he was so dissatisfied. Lincoln neither signed nor ever sent the letter—it was a measure of working off steam—but one line summed up everything: "He [Lee] was within your easy grasp, and to have closed in upon him would, in connection with our other late successes, have ended the war. . . ."

Later, when Lincoln's disappointment had abated, he remarked: "Why should we censure a man who has done so much for his country because he did not do a little more?"

What was done. What was not done. What had happened. All were now history. Meade could have lost the battle and with it the war. He did not lose. Lee might have won. He did not win. Lee also tendered his resignation to Jefferson Davis on the basis that he was unable to accomplish what he had set out to do. It was refused: *Where was there another commander with greater ability?*

The way to Appomattox. A Federal pontoon bridge spans the Potomac River, and both armies have gone to follow the long road towards an inevitable destination.

And that was it. The bruised and bloodied armies trekked off into Virginia. There would be more battles, more marching, more heartbreak, more death, before it was all decided. And in that July the men and boys of both armies, men and boys of another time, a time when America was less sophisticated, moved off through a land of quiet little villages, down rural roads bordered here and there with split-rail fences and small frame houses with bluebells and hollyhocks in front, and kitchen gardens and sheltered wells and dusty barns, and back lots where the wind bent the timothy grass in long, opaque waves.

Looming over the horizon was the name of Grant. He would be brought in from the West, and with him would come new names: the Wilderness, Spotsylvania, Cold Harbor, Petersburg, and finally, when there was no place else to go, the roads would lead to a by-and-by of early spring flowers and surrender called Appomattox Courthouse.

And for many of the men of Gettysburg there were personal places. For "Uncle" John Sedgwick, the man who had led his VI Corps on a staggering march only to have it kept in reserve, there was a sharpshooter's bullet waiting at Spotsylvania. For Jeb Stuart, the *beau idéal* of Confederate cavalry, Fate would rush from a Yankee revolver at a crossroads designated on the maps as Yellow Tavern. For A. P. Hill the patient moment was in the barrel of a New England-made musket at Petersburg, Virginia. And there was something extra special for the cavalry officer who dressed like a "circus rider gone mad." The war wasn't going to get him, but far over the western horizon was a Sioux Indian Chief called Crazy Horse, and he was waiting for George Armstrong Custer at the Little Big Horn River. And John B. Hood, who had been wounded twenty minutes after he had led his division against Dan Sickles' III Corps, was going to suffer the chagrin of defeat when he led an army in defense of Atlanta by finding himself outfought, outmaneuvered, and tricked by a wily West Point graduate named William Tecumseh Sherman. For Lieutenant Haskell there would be a long, beautifully composed letter to his brother about Gettysburg, and then the finality of death at the Battle of Cold Harbor. And six months were left for Brigadier General John Buford, the man who flung his cavalry along a ridge west of Gettysburg and brought on the battle. He died in bed of exhaustion and the biggest killer of all—disease. And for two men, one a Rebel and one a Yankee, there was a place of bitter disappointment called Five Forks. The last big pitched battle of the war was going to be fought there, and both George Pickett and Gouverneur Warren were going to be relieved of their commands at Five Forks for what in essence was purported failure to fulfill their duties.

An old photograph of a small corner of Gettysburg and a faraway tragedy.

And old Pete Longstreet, who had never wanted the battle at Gettysburg, would stay with Lee to the end, and then find that Gettysburg was his special place. He spent the rest of his long life writing, corresponding, about the facts as he saw them at Gettysburg.

For all of those soldiers on the summer roads, men of the North and South, who though tragically at odds with each other were the kind of men America has always been so lucky to have, whether they lived a few days, a month, a year, or to be a hundred (some of them did), a time would come when every last one of them would be gone.

Do they know of a place called Gettysburg with thirty-five miles of graded roadways winding through fields and woods filled with monuments and statues?

There are drums sounding along those summer roads of '63. Rat-tat-tat. In the wind. Echoing off little frame houses and out through kitchen gardens. Rat-tat-tat. Echoing . . . fading. . . . By the barns. Ont in the timothy grass. Rat-tat-tat-tat . . .

Chapter VII

A Sea of Anguish

Long after the battle it was recorded that twenty-seven thousand muskets were picked up around Gettysburg. Dropped by the wounded and dead, or abandoned in a frenzied flight of fear, some of them bore a strange tale: rammed into the barrels were up to ten loads. In the heat of battle a lot of soldiers lost their heads, loaded, forgot to fire, loaded again, and so on. A few experts, intrigued with ratios and proportions, also recorded that in order to kill one man in the three days' fighting, each soldier would have had to fire away his own weight in lead.

Not recorded in these dispassionate statistics, but certainly bound in with them, was Gettysburg's final and, by any evaluation, greatest agony. Twenty-two thousand wounded Yanks and Rebels lay in fields, in ditches, in woods, in barns, in haystacks, in homes and churches—everywhere. And everywhere permeating the air was, as Cornelia Hancock, a young nurse who went to Gettysburg to help, described it, the "sickening, overpowering, awful stench" of unburied dead men and horses. Some of the miserable men, breathing the "nauseating atmosphere," had to endure the grinding torture of waiting as much as five days in the sun and rain for medical help.

So overwhelming were the numbers of wounded waiting attention that they had to be sorted according to their wounds. Those who were beyond help were separated from those who might be saved. In one woodland was a long row of unconscious men shot through the head. They were considered hopeless, and they lay there pathetically twitching and groaning, oblivious to the onlookers' wishes that they would soon die. Nearby, amidst frantic screaming and yelling, were soldiers who would soon have to take stock once again of their courage for the coming ordeal of crude surgery.

There was no over-all pattern to the profusion of suffering and makeshift care. A turn in any direction and a new and different horror fell into place like some malignant kaleidoscope containing nightmare mosaics. Cornelia Hancock entered a church which had been converted into a giant litter; boards had been placed across high-backed pews and the wounded piled on top. With the wounded thus elevated and jammed together almost on a level with her face she felt as though she were standing "breast-high in a sea of anguish."

Mrs. Sallie Robbins Broadhead, a townswoman who had gone to give aid in a building converted into a temporary hospital, discovered that the variations in misery were almost endless: "Such a sight I had never seen and hope never to see again . . . his leg was covered with worms . . . I fed one poor fellow who had both legs and an arm taken off. . . . [During the heavy rains on July 4 and 5, the basement of the building had flooded.] I found that I had only seen the lighter cases and worse horrors met my eyes on descending to the basement of the building. Men wounded in three or four places, not able to help themselves the least bit, lay swimming in water. I hunted up the lady I had been helping and told her to come and see how they were situated. When she came down, she reverently exclaimed, 'My God! They must be gotten out of this or they will drown!'"

Lieutenant John Dooley, who had been captured after he was wounded in "Pickett's Charge," saw a fellow prisoner: "Here is a poor wounded Confederate who is walking up and down, anywhere his cracked brain directs him.

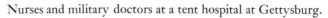

Nurses and military doctors at a tent hospital at Gettysburg.

Library of Congress

A makeshift tent hospital immediately after the battle.

Just on top of his head and penetrating his brain is a large opening made by a shell in which I might insert my hand."

And in the middle of all this, surrounded by it, sweating, overworked surgeons, wiping bits of bone and blood from dulling surgical saws on their bloody smocks, holding scalpels in their mouths, resolutely performed operations. They cut and sawed and stitched, and cast aside the horrible relics.

In one area there was a long table around which surgeons and ill-trained attendants labored. "This was the operating table," wrote Cornelia Hancock, and went on to register with grisly emphasis, "and for seven days it literally ran blood. A wagon stood near rapidly filling with amputated legs and arms; when wholly filled, this gruesome spectacle withdrew from sight and returned as soon as possible for another load."

In another section of the field it took three hundred surgeons five days to perform the necessary amputations. And in most instances, even from the viewpoint of mid-nineteenth-century medicine, it was pretty crude surgery: a great many of the doctors of the Civil War were men whose background

Two doctors of the Army of the Potomac.

consisted of little more than a rudimentary medical knowledge, gained either by apprenticing or in some diploma mill, and along with their more learned colleagues they did not have the slightest concept of antisepsis.

The first few days after the battle, the little country town was manifestly the seat of unparalleled disaster. A medical officer summed up part of it when he described those first days as "an occasion of the greatest amount of suffering known to the Nation since its birth!"

For the wounded soldier who underwent an amputation and who might not have had the blessing of chloroform (in many instances it ran out in the first few hours after the battle), there was the rasping agony of cold metal biting into responsive bone, the fiery slash through convulsive and wildly signaling nerves. And of course the numb grief in realizing what had happened.

If the patient were lucky, or rather survived the shock of surgery and loss of blood, there would be a daily inspection of the stump. This meant looking for "laudable pus," considered a good sign, and a testing of the ligatures, the small threads used to tie everything up. As many as thirty of them would hang from a stump. A few would have little knots in them to indicate they tied off an artery or vein. After a few daily inspections, the ligatures should all pull out, indicating that the tissue had rotted sufficiently and that the inside of the wound was healing. Often a tug on one of the knotted ligatures was followed by a gush of blood; this was a "secondary hemorrhage," where the blood vessel had not closed off. The wound then had to be reopened and the blood vessel tied higher.

A daily inspection of the stump also meant looking for dreaded "mortified flesh"—gangrene. If the "mortified flesh" were there, then radical cauterization with nitric acid was the prescribed treatment. A Southern physician who, while not at Gettysburg, had a flair for the graphic intermingled with professional tones, described this treatment: "Pouring the acid on the 'proud' flesh, you would see smoke rise, the flesh sizzle and crisp up and, all the time, the patient screaming in agony." It very seldom worked, and the only alternative was higher amputation; that is, if the gangrene had not become too massive, or if there were anything left to amputate.

And there was septicemia. The only remedy for this was a chaplain—blood poisoning was fatal.

That amputation occupied the major attention of the surgeons eloquently shows the type and scope of medicine practiced at Gettysburg. Very little could be done for a man wounded any place but in his extremities; almost all surgery, and that in the form of amputations, took place on the arms and legs.

A few managed to survive an injury such as a shattered jaw and eventually wound up in a soldiers' home. In ten years, maybe a little more, medical

Surgical instruments used by Civil War doctors.

reports would show in terse lines: "mandibular disfunction . . . general debility. Patient given two ounces of brandy daily." (The simple fact was that the patient could not chew.) For some the Battle of Gettysburg was an endless affair. . . .

In all the turmoil of the immediate days after the battle, outside help reached Gettysburg, slowly at first, but in an ever increasing amount. Two organizations, the Sanitary Commission and the Christian Commission, filling roles similar to the modern Red Cross and Salvation Army, sent nurses, doctors, medicines, and whatever else they could. And individual citizens from all walks of life arrived in wagons, in horse buggies, by train, by foot—the best way they could—bringing food, supplies, or just their hands.

The one railroad which had been sacked by Jeb Stuart's horsemen was put in working order so that by July 10 thirty trains a day were arriving in Gettysburg. They carried with them huge quantities of medicine, tents, and other equipment. With all of this welcome relief, the immediate crisis abated somewhat, allowing at least a little more effort for the depressing task of getting bodies into temporary graves. But it would be a long time before all the misshapen cadavers could be buried. They were everywhere—behind stones and rocky crags, in fields, in woods, upon the hills . . . everywhere.

Burial details swung out and managed to get most of the things which had once been men into hasty graves. But without any system it was rather slapdash and perfunctory. Inverted muskets, their bayonets rammed into the earth, or pieces of board penciled with brief information, or just stones, marked the sites of superficial graves. And in a short time the woods and fields at Gettysburg became a hodgepodge burial ground. But for the time being it was all that could be done.

In this neat field hospital with the town of Gettysburg in the background, death was an everyday occurrence for many weeks after the battle. *Library of Congress*

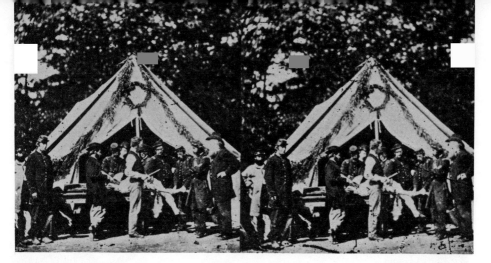

An early stereo-photograph of a Civil War surgeon about to operate at a tent hospital back of Cemetery Ridge.

As the burial parties went on with their dreary missions, vast tent hospitals were erected and units of the Pennsylvania Militia (the same ones who were so hastily pulled together when General Lee began his invasion of the North) were brought in to stand guard duty. They were just in time.

The curious, if also understandable, problem of visitors besieging the area struck Gettysburg with the impact of a fire after an earthquake. Thousands of them swarmed into town and about the tent hospitals looking, seeking, hoping for information about *their* soldiers. In an effort to keep some sort of order and regulation, the Pennsylvania Militia was forced to set up a curfew— after 4 P.M. all visitors had to leave the tent hospital areas.

It was a gloomy business for many of the visitors, and often as not they were too late. Mrs. Sallie R. Broadhead found that sorrow had a way of extending itself when she was called upon to bear the sad tidings to a young wife who had arrived in Gettysburg just after her husband had died of his wounds: "I never pitied anyone as I did her when I told her he was dead. I hope I may never again be called upon to witness such a heart-rending scene." For these unhappy people there were quick and anguished arrangements with a civilian embalmer. And he was not difficult to locate. A whole slew of them had descended on Gettysburg in the high spirit of profit. Setting up their places of business within a macabre distance of the field hospitals, they did not wait long for a flourishing trade. A plank across a couple of barrels made a handy establishment.

With their formaldehyde beside them, the embalmers pumped the bereaved for all the cash they could get and then pumped in their preservative. Probably they tried to look solicitous as an untroubled body was placed in a pine coffin for the long, sad, last trip home to a quiet cemetery and eventual dust under a mossy and one-day-to-be-forgotten headstone.

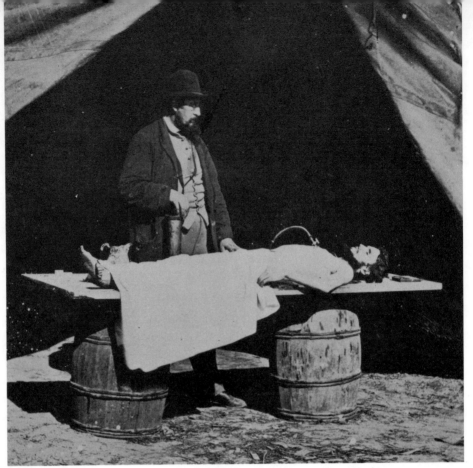

A Civil War embalmer plies his trade on a Union soldier.

Some of the visitors would have to wait a bit before consulting an embalmer; others, thankfully, would escape this unfortunate task; and still others would never find *their* dead—there were hundreds of unidentified bodies around Gettysburg.

Towards the end of the third week in July, six hospital trains a day were leaving Gettysburg, taking with them those soldiers well enough to be moved. Sixteen thousand men were thus transferred, and with this exodus of wounded the strain of accommodating the visitors eased. Those who had learned the "bad news" were gone; and a great percentage of those who had created a secondary crisis at Gettysburg were now able to maintain their bedside vigils at permanent hospitals in York, Harrisburg, Baltimore, and Washington.

For the first batches of wounded transferred to the permanent hospitals, the ride on the train must have been like a nightmare, a mirror of the suffering they had already undergone. With no attendants, the wounded were placed in box cars which, as one officer described it, were "filthy from the business of transporting cattle and freight." Without water, without straw to lie upon, without sanitary facilities, the miserable soldiers jogged along rackety tracks in unclean cars without springs.

The hospital trains were under the supervision of civilian operators who, as one irate medical inspector exaggerated, "got the only profit of the battle." In reality, the civilian operators did the best they could, bringing in all the rolling stock possible as soon as the Army Engineers had repaired the tracks; but as railroad men, without proper equipment, much less background, they were in no position to render service in the form of hospital trains. Finally, the Army pushed its authority and, with the help of the Christian Commission, introduced such essentials as water coolers, bandages, bedpans, medicines, bunks where possible, and a medical officer with each train, and in the end the transportation of the wounded was fairly well handled.

Remaining behind in the tent hospitals were four thousand wounded, still too weak to make almost any trip. But many of these were eventually forced to leave. Cornelia Hancock watched one of them pack up and leave one afternoon on the last day of August: "Rufus M. is in the process of dying.... I have taken every care of him; his leg commenced bleeding and he cannot last long...."

Little by little, day by day, out of the bedlam of pain, screams, amputations, anguished visitors, the dead and the dying, order came back to Gettysburg.

Wounded Union soldiers in Armory Square Hospital at Washington.

Not the everyday order of the past, but an order which at any rate pointed towards normalcy.

But if the worst of it were over, there was, nevertheless, the pressing concern of decent burial for the soldiers who were going to stay in Gettysburg forever. And that it was a pressing matter was starkly evident after each rainfall. Shallow graves would wash bare, revealing mute and grisly specters, macabre reminders that there was no comfort in a hasty grave, especially for the living.

From the myriad and widespread burial sites across the battlefield, it was obvious a better place—a central cemetery—would have to be evolved, and that as rapidly as possible.

With this end in mind Pennsylvania's Governor Curtin appointed David Wills, a Gettysburg attorney, as his special agent to purchase the necessary land. Agent Wills selected seventeen acres of cornfield on Cemetery Hill, just beyond the civilian cemetery, where the Army of the Potomac had made its desperate rally on July 1.

At Governor Curtin's suggestion, Attorney Wills approached the governors of the eighteen Northern states whose men had participated in the battle, and after negotiations and much correspondence, it was agreed that all of these states would share the cost of building and maintaining a cemetery and that a Board of Commissioners would implement and carry out all plans.

From the projection of William Saunders, landscape gardener with the United States Department of Agriculture, a semicircular design for burial was adopted. This allotted each state a portion of land for its dead radiating

Baltimore Pike after the battle. Tents belong to state militia brought in to guard hospital areas.

Governor Andrew Curtin
of Pennsylvania.

Library of Congress

outward from a central point—a symbolic arrangement suggesting the national government with its sovereign yet attendant states.

The actual work of preparing the cemetery carried faint overtones of politics, a certain dalliance over details, and red tape. As it was strictly an affair of the states—the government in Washington supplied only the coffins—the governors perhaps could be forgiven taking a little time in which to display due concern over the fate of the fallen for home consumption. And so it was not until October 27 that the actual work of exhumation and reburial began. Strangely, it was to become a difficult thing to fix a date when the last body found final rest in the Soldiers' National Cemetery. By the following March the task was formally finished, but a long time after this a farmer plowing his fields unearthed the remains of three Union soldiers. Easily identified by their brass buttons, they were reburied with their comrades on Cemetery Hill. The year was 1914.

For the men who went north with General Lee and stayed there, it was another story: They were placed in mass graves throughout the battlefield without identifying headstones. Later on, after several years, they would be transferred to decent cemeteries in the South to rest with friends. But now there were long trenches covered with earth and marked by wooden signs: "58 Rebels Here." "70 Rebels Here." Nothing else. In other times, another age, their value to all Americans would be felt and understood—but at Gettysburg it was too soon, too near the edge of misunderstanding, and these men from "way down south in Dixie" were far beyond all of this anyway.

Chapter VIII

A Few Appropriate Remarks

And so it all passed—the summer, the problem of the wounded. And suddenly, one day over at Rock Creek the mallards were gone, and tiny, fragile insects—"skaters"—darted in a thousand nimble ways over blue-black water. At Devil's Den red-leaved sumac molted into rusty stalks; and on nights when the air was sharp and still, high migratory geese honked an old secret about time and change. . . .

Deep fall had come as the moment arrived for the formal dedication of the cemetery. Political pundits, wise in the vagaries of men in public affairs, saw Governor Curtin's success in creating the cemetery as nothing more than "politicking," and now with formal invitations out to governors, senators, congressmen, President Lincoln, and members of the President's cabinet, it was more than "politicking"—it was a downright "show."

And there is indeed strong indication that it was all of this. It was a joint state effort creating a nice panoply in which the office-holders could display themselves before the public. But why, if the war were still going on and men were dying on other battlefields, single out a cemetery in Pennsylvania? The motives were those of political practicality, brushed with overtones of mysticism.

Edward Everett, the foremost classical orator of the time, was asked to deliver a dedication speech. A superlatively learned man, he had been Phi Beta Kappa at Harvard, a United States Senator, Professor of Greek at Harvard, President of Harvard, Governor of Massachusetts, a member of Congress, Secretary of State under President Fillmore, and Minister to Great Britain. His lectures and speeches over the years had brought him more than $150,000, all of which he had turned over to charitable causes.

At the request of Edward Everett, the dedication day was set back from

Edward Everett,
greatest orator
of his day.

The National Archives

October 23 to a later date in order for him to prepare his oration. Thursday, November 19, was selected and seemed to meet with everyone's approval.

Attorney Wills of Gettysburg sent President Lincoln a second and more informal invitation in which he stated the purpose of the dedication and finished by saying: "I am authorized by the Governors of the various states to invite you to be present and participate in these ceremonies, which will doubtless be very imposing and solemnly impressive. It is the desire that after the oration, you, as Chief Executive of the Nation, formally set apart these grounds to their sacred use by a few appropriate remarks."

It was noted by a member of the Board of Commissioners long after the ceremonies that "the [second] invitation was not settled upon and sent to Mr. Lincoln until the 2nd of November, more than six weeks after Mr. Everett had been invited to speak, and but little more than two weeks before the exercises were held . . . the question was raised as to his [Lincoln's] ability to speak on such a grave and solemn occasion." The decision, then, to invite Lincoln to speak at the dedication was an afterthought.

A legend talked almost into fact claims Lincoln wrote his speech on the back of an envelope or on some scraps of paper while aboard a train en route to Gettysburg. There is no evidence for this. He probably penciled some alterations, but if he did it was on a speech already written and for the most part finished.

The dedication and his speech were very important to Lincoln. With half his cabinet indicating disapproval of Governor Curtin's dedication ceremonies by declining invitations, Lincoln, sensing in some intuitive way that it was to be more than a "show," that it would have a special significance, shaped and

The first draft of the Gettysburg Address. The first page, with the letterhead of the Executive Mansion, was written in ink, the second in pencil on foolscap. In this draft (there are six copies of his speech in Lincoln's handwriting) there are 239 words.

ted to the great task remaining before us—
that, from these honored dead we take increased devotion to that cause for which
they here, gave the last full measure of devotion— that we here highly resolve these
dead shall not have died in vain; that
the nation, shall have a new birth of free-
dom, and that government of the people by
the people for the people, shall not per-
ish from the earth.

molded his speech. He was aware, too, that there would be extensive newspaper coverage. This was important. The war was still dragging on. The dedication ceremonies would afford an opportunity to convey the purpose of the war and what all the sacrifice meant to a great many people.

His final draft was written and completed in Gettysburg the evening before the dedication from an original composed on two pages. The first page was on White House stationery and the second foolscap.

Lincoln spoke twice at Gettysburg—a formal speech at the cemetery, and earlier to a group of serenaders who called him for a few words after he had arrived in town. He addressed himself to them by saying:

"In my position it is sometimes important that I should not say foolish things. [A sarcastic voice called out: "If you can help it." There was laughter.] It very often happens that the only way to help it is to say nothing at all. Believing that is my present condition this evening, I must beg of you to excuse me from addressing you further." The serenaders did not think much of it and moved on to call on more oratorically inclined guests.

The weather was mild and clear the next morning as Lincoln, in a black suit, high silk hat, and white gloves, mounted a large chestnut horse and waited for

Marching out to the new military cemetery to listen to orator Edward Everett and President Lincoln at the dedication ceremonies, November 19, 1863.

Some of the crowd at the dedication ceremonies. The structure in the left background of photograph is the gate to the civilian cemetery.

the parade out to the cemetery to begin. The time was ten o'clock, and, as with most parades, it took an hour to get started.

Bands, governors, mayors, a regiment of troops, hospital corpsmen (there were still wounded soldiers at Gettysburg), fraternal orders, the press, fire departments, telegraphers, and citizens of Pennsylvania and other states listened to booming cannon and saw lines of troops standing at attention as they all marched over to Cemetery Hill.

The parade took fifteen minutes, but Edward Everett was late. The crowd of fifteen thousand gathered at the cemetery grew restless. Bands began playing, and a man with a large, bulky camera took some photographs with his "wet-plate" films of chemically treated panes of glass, and, as always, boys "got into the act" by prominently disporting themselves and gazing very uncandidly into the lens. (Other generations would appear, but recorded on a piece of photographic glass plate was the time, a precise moment, when they were boys on a November day in 1863.)

At noon Edward Everett at last arrived. Everything was ready. On the speaker's platform were honored guests, governors, mayors, Edward Everett's daughter, Governor Curtin of Pennsylvania, Generals Abner Doubleday and John Gibbon from the Army of the Potomac, members of Congress, foreign ministers, a few members of Lincoln's cabinet, and President Lincoln.

The only known photograph of Lincoln at Gettysburg. It was "discovered" recently by Josephine Cobb, Archivist in Charge at the National Archives. (This is a highly enlarged section of a long-range panoramic photograph taken at the dedication ceremonies.)

A chaplain offered an invocation. Edward Everett was introduced. He acknowledged President Lincoln and began:

"Overlooking these broad fields now reposing from the labors of the waning year, the mighty Alleghenies dimly towering before us, the graves of our brethren beneath our feet, it is with hesitation that I raise my poor voice to break the eloquent silence of God and Nature. But the duty to which you have called me must be performed. Grant me, I pray you, your indulgence. . . . As my eye ranges over the fields whose sods were so lately moistened by the blood of gallant and loyal men . . ." He spoke on in the high-flown style of his day, full of allusions and classic metaphors laced with adjectives and adverbs.

It was an oration embodying the art form which Edward Everett had perfected to its fullest, and it represented Edward Everett's greatest effort in a long career of oratory. As a speech it was first rate. It lasted two hours, and was well received, although two hours tended to dampen any wild response.

An ode sung by the Baltimore Glee Club followed Everett's delivery. The dedication was almost over. President Lincoln stirred in his chair.

The crowd was slightly smaller than it had been at the opening of the exercises. It was noted during Everett's speech that members in the back reaches of the audience had a tendency to wander off. An entire group of convalescent soldiers who had come to listen to the "speechifying" had drifted away down onto the battlefields and observed carcasses of still unburied horses, and looked across the fields, remembering what they had seen and done in them. . . .

One newspaper would write: "We pass over the silly remarks of the President, for the credit of the nation we are willing that the veil of oblivion shall be dropped over them and that they shall no more be repeated or thought of."

Another: "Mr. Lincoln did most foully traduce the motives of the men who were slain at Gettysburg. . . . Readers will not have failed to observe the exceeding bad taste which characterized the words of the President. . . ."

The *London Times'* correspondent would write: "The ceremony was rendered ludicrous by some of the sallies of that poor President Lincoln. . . . Anything more dull and commonplace it wouldn't be easy to produce."

Lincoln himself would feel his speech was a failure. In a remark regarding his effort he would say it did not "scour." A word used by farmers: if wet soil stuck to the plow it did not "scour."

The correspondent of the *Chicago Tribune* would be among the first to recognize something special in Lincoln's oration: "The dedicatory remarks by President Lincoln will live among the annals of man . . ."

The Baltimore Glee Club finished its ode. President Lincoln adjusted his metal-rimmed spectacles and took two sheets of paper from his pocket. They contained in his own handwriting the final draft of his address.

Somewhere in an audience already growing anxious to get things over, the photographer began setting up his apparatus to take a close-up picture of the President. He poked his head under a large hood at the back of the camera and fussed with the lens. Now the tall, angular man with the sad face whose background included less than one year of formal education began to speak

In memory of Lincoln's Gettysburg Address. The only monument in the world commemorating a speech.

Walter Lane

Wounded citizen fighter John Burns after the battle, with crutches and the flintlock musket he used in the first day's fighting.

in a high, thin, and what a contemporary termed "unlyrical" voice. When he had spoken 266 words in slightly under three minutes the dedication was over.[18] The hour was a few minutes after two. A bronze sun cast long, slanting rays over a politely applauding audience and President Lincoln left the speaker's stand. The man with the camera fussed once more with the lens, but Lincoln was gone. There had not been enough time to get a picture.

After the ceremonies Lincoln had lunch with Governor Curtin and other dignitaries at Attorney David Wills' home. At five o'clock he walked with old John Burns to a patriotic meeting scheduled in a town church. At six thirty he was aboard a train bound for Washington. Over on Cemetery Hill the wind stirred rattling leaves, and an infinite star-swept sky glinted and sparkled through the brittle air. It was another fall night at Gettysburg. . . .

The Wills' house, where Lincoln stayed while at Gettysburg.

"I am in height, six feet, four inches, nearly; lean in flesh, weighing on an average one hundred and eighty pounds; dark complexion, with coarse black hair, and grey eyes..." is the way Lincoln described himself. This photograph was taken November 15, 1863, a few days before he went to Gettysburg.

Chapter IX

The Long Encampment

On November 23, 1863, the last wounded soldier left Gettysburg. The speech-making was over. In the west the haze along the South Mountain Range had dulled into a gray-blue, and sometimes there were snow flurries which swept over fields and meadows with the promise of bleak days. Up on Cemetery Hill rows of soldiers, who would never have to rise for morning reveille, never march or fight, were bivouacked down for their first winter at Gettysburg. They would not have to bother with the Second Battle of Gettysburg.

The battle had to be fought once more, this time in the hearing rooms of the Joint Committee on the Conduct of the War.

That redoubtable politician general, Dan Sickles, was up and about, bounding around Washington on crutches and, in the winter months of 1864, led a flank attack on General Meade. Supported by generals Doubleday and Butterfield—on Sunday, July 5, just after the fighting at Gettysburg, Meade had relieved Butterfield as Chief of Staff, a fact which did little to engender cordial feelings—Sickles waded into the leadership at Gettysburg. *Meade had proposed retreat at the very outset of the battle.* (On the morning of the second day of battle Meade had written a standby order of retreat. It was no more than a measure of precaution in case things went bad; but Sickles pulled it out of context from the rest of the operations and tried to make it appear that Meade was ready to retreat before he was ready to fight.) *Meade had used Hooker's campaign plans. Meade had no battle plans. Meade had given the III Corps no orders; and Meade had thrown away a golden opportunity in not smashing Lee.*

Only in the latter allegation was there strong logic; but Dan Sickles, smarting under the suggestions that his almost disastrous move at Gettysburg was anything but right, had begun what was to prove a lifelong attempt to justify

General Dan Sickles, "hero" of Gettysburg, minus the leg he lost on July 2 near the Wheat Field.

The National Archives

his claim that *he* had won the battle. (Dan was singularly unaware of the fact that had he not suffered so grievously at Gettysburg, General Meade said he would have made him stand court-martial for disobeying orders and imperiling the safety of the Army of the Potomac.)

The Joint Committee on the Conduct of the War came up with no positive answers, yet it was so patently evident General Meade had done a good but not outstanding job at Gettysburg that Lincoln kept him on as general of the Army of the Potomac.

As Sickles sniped at General Meade, the Gettysburg Battlefield Memorial Association was formed to purchase the land where so many had fought and died and where so many had lived on in anguish. There was to be a permanent park, a place to remember.

In the spring of 1864 General Grant was elevated to the rank of lieutenant general and made general in chief of all Northern armies. Making his headquarters with the Army of the Potomac, Grant directed the North's over-all military strategy. He specifically directed both General Meade and the Army of the Potomac in the campaign and battle tactics which eventually, and at a staggering cost, battered General Lee's Army of Northern Virginia into surrender.

By the late spring of 1865 the war was over. President Andrew Johnson was in the White House after Lincoln's assassination. And on the Fourth of July, 1865, the cornerstone was laid for the National Monument, the first commemorative work at Gettysburg. The events of the past four years now belonged to yesterday.

At Gettysburg on May 30, 1868, a memorial service was held at the National Military Cemetery. It marked the beginning of the observance of Memorial Day in America.

In March, 1869, General Grant took the oath of office as President of the United States. And the following year General Robert E. Lee died at Lexington, Virginia, where he was serving as president of Washington College. General Lee was sixty-three years old. The South—the whole country—lost one of its truly great men.

And at Gettysburg some of the cannon used in the battle had been brought back to rest in the fields and woods they had helped transform into a hallowed battleground. Ultimately, they would grow rusty and old, evidence for the curious of a once-upon-a-time unhappy rage.

In 1872 General Meade died at the age of fifty-seven. His horse at Gettys-

Lincoln's casket moves through Washington, April 21, 1865.

The VI Corps marching down Pennsylvania Avenue, Washington, D.C. in a grand review at the end of the war, May, 1865.

Library of Congress

Union soldiers at the National Military Cemetery, July 4, 1865, for dedication of the cornerstone of the National Monument. The upright wooden slats indicate graves—gravestones had not yet been fully placed about the cemetery.

Formal invitation to "Monumental Dedication."

Culver Service, New York

The children of Sergeant Humiston. This photograph was found in the hands of their dead father near Cemetery Ridge. Copies of the photograph were sold to found an orphanage at Gettysburg for dependent children of Federal soldiers.

A sad aftermath. Orphanage and orphans of Union soldiers at Gettysburg—circa 1875.

Gettysburg National Military Park—Walter Lane

"Strike the tent." The chapel and campus of Washington College during the funeral of General Lee, October 15, 1870.

burg, Baldy, who had nearly carried him into the Confederate lines, walked in the funeral parade carrying an empty saddle with Meade's boots set in the stirrups in reverse.

It was in the year 1876 out in Montana that Chief Crazy Horse caught up with George Armstrong Custer and his 7th United States Cavalry. Where the Big Horn River connects with the Little Big Horn, Chief Crazy Horse annihilated Custer and the 7th United States Cavalry to a man.

By the fall of 1884 General Grant had less than a year to live, and at Gettysburg some of the commemorative monuments now dotting the land were becoming weatherbeaten from winter snows and driving fall rains. . . .

As night fell, the rain, which had started in the late afternoon, continued without letup until the mired surface of the land oozed beneath sidings and flaps of the encampment tents. The rain, however, did not visibly dampen the bustle and orderly confusion of hundreds of Union veterans. At eight o'clock official activities were proceeding normally, and the veterans witnessed the dedication of the 106th Pennsylvania Regimental Monument, while thousands of raindrops reflected, in quick golden beads, the filaments of several of Thomas Edison's new incandescent lamps. Strung out from a special generator car of the Cumberland Valley Railroad, they marked the first time an encampment had ever been lighted by electricity.

It was Thursday evening, August 13, 1885, and ever since the preceding Sunday the annual reunion of the Pennsylvania Department of the North's combined veterans' organization, the Grand Army of the Republic, had been under way at the site of the greatest single battle in American history. And, while not all of the assembled veterans had fought at Gettysburg, none was unaware of the importance of those three sanguinary days in 1863.

There would be larger reunions at Gettysburg, yet for these veterans, most of whom were in their late thirties and early forties, the quicksilver of youth was not entirely gone, and thus far at their encampment, Camp U. S. Grant, named in commemoration of the President's recent death, things had lived up to their expectations of a lively get-together.

On Tuesday there had been a full-dress parade with brass bands and fife-and-drum corps heading up file after file of men in the official uniform of the GAR—wide-brimmed hats and dark blue jackets and trousers. And they all marched with vigor and purpose, yet veterans with tutored eyes realized somehow that their ranked columns did not quite have the crisp alignment, the spit-and-polish, they remembered when they were soldiers. *But it had nothing to do with age. No! Just out of practice. That's all.* However, the spectators, including an honorary reviewing officer, Colonel W. F. Beasley, president of the Confederate Home Association of North Carolina, agreed it was a bang-up parade.

And Wednesday had been a big day. All the bands and fife-and-drum corps from the encampment thumped down Baltimore Street, the usual contingent of "recruits"—barking dogs and excited children—in tow, and wheeled into the town square where a temporary duplex arch in honor of the reunion had been erected. They were there to greet excursions of veterans arriving from

The 106th Pennsylvania monument, dedicated at the reunion of the Pennsylvania Department of the Grand Army of the Republic in 1885.

Walter Lane

Headquarters of the Pennsylvania Department of the GAR reunion, 1885. In the center is a veteran in the white uniform and helmet of a Prussian officer. He probably fought with the XI Corps of the Army of the Potomac.

Battle-scarred trees on Culp's Hill, twenty-two years after the battle.

With Culp's Hill in the background, Pennsylvania veterans wait for something to happen near their encampment.

Gettysburg National Military Park—Walter Lane

In the foreground a patient wife and daughter wait while "Papa" gets instructions. And "Papa," over by the tents, learns the picnic will be on East Cemetery Hill.

near-by towns, and their fanfares, coupled with the antics of the "Owls" and "Sunflowers," organizations of GAR men all bent on much tomfoolery, were greatly appreciated, although all of this certainly disrupted the normal, quiet tenor of downtown Gettysburg. But the folderol and swirl were infectious, exhilarating; and, after all, it didn't happen every day.

That evening there had been a fireworks display followed by a sham battle on East Cemetery Hill. Old cannon belched defiant noise and smoke in the direction of Culp's Hill, where the visible remnants of real battle, the hundreds of dead trees covering its slopes, loomed gaunt and melancholy. And for a few minutes, as the cannon crashed and spewed out sulphury fumes, the veterans again tasted the salty chill, an emotional reincarnation, of a one-time horror. But it quickly passed when the music of a band concert filled the night air, and all in all, when it came time to turn in the veterans viewed the day as well spent and lots of fun.

But it had not been all parades and concerts and horseplay. There were other things. Highly important was the deep regard the veterans held for the spirit of Gettysburg and what it represented. A vote had been passed on increased appropriations for maintenance of the land, and an endorsement by the entire reunion for the Battlefield Memorial Association's action to allow Confederate markers and statuary to be placed on the field also had been passed. And on Wednesday morning, while the bands and the fife-and-drum corps had whooped it up at the town square, a few members of the Battlefield Memorial Association went over to McPherson's Ridge to inspect the site of a new road which would follow the battle line of the first day's fighting. McPherson's Ridge really had not changed since that July morning twenty-two years earlier when all hell had broken loose. There were a few stone markers where regiments and companies had made a stand, or repulsed a determined charge, but McPherson's barn was still there and small wild-life still hopped about in the woods where General John Reynolds had been killed fifteen minutes after he arrived and took command of the Union forces. *It hardly seemed possible twenty-two years had passed.... Was it all just a fable? Something that had been dreamed while young? Was there a yesterday where a Lincoln existed? Where a Lee, astride his gray horse, rode into Pennsylvania? Twenty-two years ... it hardly seemed possible....*

The National Band closed the dedication ceremonies on Thursday evening with a spirited interpretation of "The Girl I Left Behind Me." The rain which glinted in the light of Edison's lamps finally slackened, and by nine o'clock it was little more than a residual mist. The evening was still young, and band members volunteered to give an impromptu concert for the citizens of Gettysburg.

Things to come. Here atop a temporary arch erected in the town square for the 1885 Reunion of the Pennsylvania Department of the GAR is the first electric light at Gettysburg. Draped from the arch are corps insignia of the Army of the Potomac.

Gettysburg National Military Park—Walter Lane

The Globe Hotel.

Lining up in front of the Globe Hotel at the town square—the "di'mond," the villagers called it—the band opened with the martial notes of "Tramp, Tramp, Tramp, the Boys Are Marching." A gathering crowd, no doubt augmented by breathless boys who had successfully pleaded to "go hear the music," greeted the band with delighted enthusiasm.

Powered by the same generator car which supplied electricity to the encampment lights, a single incandescent lamp atop the duplex arch cast its strange, nebulous illumination across the square to die in dark shadows, or to glisten on the disturbed surface of a black puddle. Its amber glow held a prophecy of bright rooms and cities of light—but tonight there was the music and the present, and the past. The band swung into the frankly sentimental ballad "Lorena." During the war it had been very popular. Thoughts glided back to other times, to a mood long gone:

> *The years creep slowly by, Lorena*
> *The snow is on the grass again*
> *The sun's low down the sky, Lorena*
> *The frost gleams where the flowers have been ...*

The spell held for a moment and then shattered as the band abruptly

Members of the 17th Connecticut Volunteers dedicate their monument.

changed to the upbeat tempo of "Dixie." And just for a few moments, blan-
keted in the mantle of night and the crisp notes of the South's "national
anthem," Gettysburg could have been almost any small Southern town.

Probably a stir of disappointment crept across the boys listening to the
music when the band began the soft strains of "Tenting on the Old Camp
Ground." They marked the end of the concert:

> *We're tenting tonight on the old camp ground,*
> *Give us a song to cheer*
> *Our weary hearts, a song of home*
> *And friends we love so dear . . .*

The light on the arch went out. Tomorrow the reunion would be over—
all that remained was a short service at the National Military Cemetery. In a
little while, after some wind and rain, nothing would be left to indicate there
had ever been a reunion. The music coasted into the night air, softly,
slowly . . . echoing, dying . . .

> *. . . Tenting tonight, tenting tonight,*
> *Tenting on the old camp ground . . .*

If Gettysburg could have been viewed from a stationary position in time, as on an animated map, its landscape would be seen burgeoning forth with stretching roadways following the battle lines and an ever increasing profusion of statuary, terminal cannons, and stone markers. Man's artifacts were conditioning the Pennsylvania farmlands into vistas and re-remembered facts and minute data.

General Sickles was a visitor time and time again. He had become convinced, now more than ever, that his role in the battle had resulted in a Union victory. (He must have had some doubts at times, however, as he spent many hours writing letters in support of his views.)

The loss of a leg had proved anything but a hindrance to Dan. It was visible proof that here was a hero who had given his leg for his country; and if all the facts were known, a man who had turned the tide at Gettysburg when he gave that leg. The relic of the leg, if anyone cared to see it, was on view

The shattered leg bone of Dan Sickles.

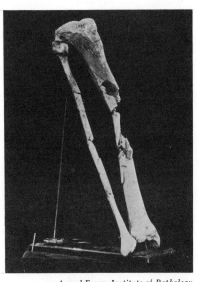

Dan Sickles holds still on his one leg long enough for the photographer to take this picture at Gettysburg in 1893. At Sickles' right is Colonel E. P. Alexander, who was in charge of Longstreet's cannon during the bombardment on the third day's fighting. Immediately at the right of Alexander is General J. B. Carr, brigade commander in Sickles' III Corps. The long-bearded gentleman third from the right is General C. K. Graham, who served in the III Corps and was captured by the Confederates at Gettysburg.

Gettysburg National Military Park—Walter Lane

at the Medical Museum of the Library of Congress in a little wooden coffin, a gift to the Government from Dan himself. Dan went to see it many times.

As head of the New York State Monument Commission (created solely for overseeing the erection of the Empire State's monuments at Gettysburg), Sickles became a familiar figure hobbling about on his crutches through the battlefield and streets of the town where men once had waited for an ordeal they fortunately could not foresee.

In 1893 Dan was elected a congressman from New York City and started pushing for legislation making the battlefield Federal property. And by 1895 Dan Sickles' efforts in Congress were rewarded: the Gettysburg Battlefield Memorial Association deeded its holding to the United States Government and Congress enacted legislation making the battlefield a National Military Park.

The silvery notes of a bugle coasted into the air softly, slowly, at one o'clock in the afternoon of Tuesday, July 1, and as their echoes died out in the woods of Seminary Ridge, thousands of men in uniforms of gray and blue officially began the Fiftieth Anniversary Reunion of the Battle of Gettysburg.

The year was 1913, and the bright tempers and sharp animosities of a time when American valor clashed with itself had softened and dulled under the gentle pressure of a half century. Whatever the past, since June 28, as friends, the graying men of both the United Confederate Veterans and the Grand Army of the Republic had been arriving at Gettysburg as guests of the State of Pennsylvania and the national government.

Union veterans go to quarters near Cemetery Ridge.

Culver Service, New York

Gettysburg National Military Park—Walter Lane

Arriving at Gettysburg after an "air-conditioned" trip. Open windows and plenty of wind were the railroad's solution to summer heat in 1913.

Maintaining a dignity befitting their average age of seventy-two years, fifty-four thousand veterans observed the fellowship and tolerant fraternity which those who have passed from the day into the evening of life seem to understand so well. Before the reunion was over the Confederates gave their Yankee comrades permission to make the fearsome sound of the "Rebel Yell," and both the Grand Army of the Republic and the United Confederate Veterans introduced a joint resolution calling for the construction of a Peace Memorial at Gettysburg.

When the formalities of the opening ceremonies were at an end, a few hardy veterans boarded what is today a relic of a bygone era—an open trolley car which ran between the battle lines to Devil's Den.

With low-powered good humor they clutched their hats and hung onto the seats as the clanking and swaying machine rolled down a dusty roadbed. And the swirling wind mussed white hair and smarted watery eyes and turned mellowed battle ribbons. These men were not ghosts . . . they were old veterans. Out by the woods and ridges the ghosts of youth might linger, but these were flesh-and-blood veterans. The trolley slowed—on the right was the Codori farmhouse—and the wind moved on to bend a few bushes and test the grass in a broad wave where the resolute legions of Pickett had charged into legend.

They had almost done it. For one exalted moment up at the crumbling stone wall they had breached the line and planted the Confederate field flag, the Stars and Bars, squarely within the Union works. But only for a moment. And when it was all over one regiment, the Confederate 7th Virginia, found

Open trolley ready to move down the tracks on a scenic tour of the battlefield past Fiftieth Reunion tents. No longer in existence, the trolley ride was once a feature attraction of the battlefield.

it had been driven back by the Federal 7th West Virginia. Confederate Lieutenant Lockwood of the 7th Virginia had been wounded and captured. His uncle, Lieutenant Colonel Jonathan Lockwood, commanded the 7th West Virginia.[19]

And afterward, when the burial parties had begun their grim work, they found a woman had been killed in "Pickett's Charge." It had been assumed by the Confederates that she was a young boy, serving with his father in the Army of Northern Virginia. The "father" had been her husband, and both were killed in the attack.[20]

A half century after. Members of the Philadelphia Brigade Association and Pickett's Division Association, both organizations of survivors of the two forces which clashed head on during "Pickett's Charge," greet each other over the stone wall which they once bitterly contested.

Walter Lane

The grinding wheels of the trolley picked up speed and moved on. They passed Bloody Run, a leisurely little stream which once, for a few sad hours, had flowed red, tinted with the blood of wounded soldiers—its water was clear now and only became discolored in a storm or an early spring flood. In the distance was the Peach Orchard where on a hot July day disbelieving young men had clutched the pulpy stump of an arm or leg, and slowly, under the small green peaches, had grown cold, while somewhere far off, familiar doors silently closed forever. And there was the Wentz farm. During the fighting on the second day a Confederate artillery sergeant set up his cannon in the yard of the Wentz farm, and then went into the house for a few minutes to talk with the owner, a man he had not seen in many years—his father. And below the Wentz farm was the Wheat Field, which had been beaten flat by charges and countercharges. Up ahead was Devil's Den.

Despite the hundreds of stone markers and monuments set in geometrical patterns amidst the haphazard profusion of rocks and trees, it was almost inconceivable that there had ever been an intermission in the quiet of Devil's Den, a moment when it had hissed and crackled with the violence of a volcano, when bursting shells erupting from the crest of nearby Little Round Top had sent hot, jagged metal ripping through cloth and flesh.

But it all had happened, once upon a time, on a terrible day, when there

Monument of the 7th West Virginia.

Walter Lane

Devil's Den.

Walter Lane

was a nightmare during the afternoon and Americans had killed and maimed one another. In the Peach Orchard . . . at the Wheat Field . . . among the rocks of Devil's Den . . .

A remote bugle heralded evening "mess," and the cursory trolley coasted to a grinding halt. The trip was over. The motorman changed poles, adjusted his control bar, and in a few moments the trolley with its pensive occupants headed back towards the camp.

The field kitchens set up throughout the two-hundred-and-eighty-acre tent city dispensed ample and well-prepared meals, with generous portions of pie, ice cream, fruit, and freshly baked bread; and there was real coffee in large tin cups instead of a watery brew stretched out with chicory as it so often had been during the war; and there were cigars, too, for an after-meal smoke.

Tobacco and coffee—two simple items which had resulted in much "between-the-lines" wartime swapping among the soldiers of the North and South. This bartering—Yankee coffee for Confederate tobacco—had been an unsophisticated illustration of the interdependence of both sections of the

A perfect shot of GAR veterans at "mess."

Gettysburg National Military Park—Walter Lane

"Pickett's Charge" of July 3, 1913. Old veterans assist a cameraman with an idea and run across wheat fields where friends died fifty years before.

country. The Confederates had the tobacco, and the Yankees had the ships necessary to transport coffee from South America. But war, once started, has a way of becoming its own master.

For the veterans, the gaudy illusions of the war had long since burned away; its bright promises, if any, were locked in the graves of those who had died in its battles. War, somehow, does not belong to old soldiers who, having fought and lived and grown older, go to reunions and listen to heroic speeches and serene bugles. War, more properly, belongs to the young whose memories include only a long childhood.

When night slipped over the land of Gettysburg, young soldiers of the regular United States Army walked the streets of the encampment on internal guard duty and watched the glow of lantern-lit tents and subdued activity slowly fade into quiet darkness. Thousands of old veterans dreamed old dreams while hundreds of young soldiers kept a constant vigil. Within four years the young soldiers would go off to fight in the Great War "to make the world safe for Democracy."

After the opening ceremonies on Tuesday the reunion seemed to meld into a rapid movement of events and time. (*Was it the getting older? The body slows, and in some sort of inverse ratio time begins to move with the throttle wide open.*) Wednesday came and went like a whirlwind. Old General Dan Sickles had croaked a flowery speech about his III Corps and its part in the battle. And there had been a parade and an evening band concert, and then it was time to sleep again.

Thursday lasted a little longer. After the usual meetings, dedications, and resolutions, there were sight-seeing trips in open automobiles—"touring cars," they were called—and some of the veterans rode over the freshly oiled Han-

Walter Lane

Monument to General Custer in
the middle of farmlands.

Culver Service, New York

"Hell, the whole battlefield is my
monument." Dan Sickles' answer to
the fact that no monument has ever
been erected at Gettysburg to
honor him. Sickles is in his nineties;
the woman behind him is his
"housekeeper."

over Road to East Cavalry Field, where Jeb Stuart's horsemen had clashed
with Yankee cavalry and a young general named Custer had yelled, "Come
on, you Wolverines!" There were statues and monuments in the middle of
green cornfields and pasture lands. And it was odd; but the statues were proof
there once had been a crazy scene of galloping rows of cavalry plowing into
each other across rolling fields with an audible thud.

By eleven thirty Friday morning the reunion was well into its last hour.
Earlier in the morning President Wilson had arrived with his staff on a special
train. He reviewed the encampment, and then spoke to about fifteen thousand
veterans in a great tent set up near the Codori farm. He told how as a small
boy he had seen both Confederate and Union soldiers marching through his
home town of Staunton, Virginia. And then, almost before anyone was
aware of it, Wilson, his staff, and his special train were gone.

And there had been a brief ceremony honoring a group of elderly women
who had served as nurses during the war. A few remembering veterans recalled a time when they were young and the women were young . . . in shaded
wards, in the flickering, yellow lantern light of hospital tents. . . .

Friday was also the Fourth of July, and as high noon closed in on Gettysburg, idling citizens turned and stood motionless. An expectant calm quickly fell apart when the bells of town clanged out the hour.

A bugle sounded and somber flags fluttered to half mast. Erect soldiers, Boy Scouts, and local militia brought hands to foreheads in rigid salutes. Aging veterans with faraway eyes pressed trembling fingers to their brows. Out on the battlefield a battery of cannon began firing in a steady, slow cadence—in memory of other people and other times.

At the end of five minutes the solemn toll stopped and the bugle sounded again. When its high, thin tones disappeared in the green hills and valleys,

President Woodrow Wilson, flanked by a Union and a Confederate veteran, arrives at the Fiftieth Anniversary Reunion.

Walter Lane

Civil War nurses at the Fiftieth Anniversary Reunion.

Walter Lane

Special guests—sons and grandsons of Confederate generals. Left to right: 1. James Longstreet Welchel, grandson of General Longstreet; 2. Major Robert Lee Longstreet, son of General Longstreet; 3. George Edward Pickett, grandson of General Pickett; 4. E. J. Stackpole, Jr.; 5. John E. Welchel, grandson of General Longstreet; 6. Christiancy Pickett, grandson of General Pickett, and 7. Albert Stackpole.

the flags were raised and the Fiftieth Anniversary Reunion of the Battle of Gettysburg was over.

With the dispatch of a circus "breaking up" while the finale takes place, the United States Quartermaster Corps, the outfit which had done most of the work and made it all possible, started dismantling the vast tent city and arranging transportation for the veterans aboard special trains. By the time the engine of the train carrying the last of the veterans got up a full head of steam, it was late Sunday afternoon, July 6; and the evidence of recent events was slowly disappearing. Mule-drawn army wagons (mechanization still be-

"Come on, Henry, our car is down here." Veterans leaving the Fiftieth Reunion and Gettysburg, most probably forever.

longed to the future) had been hauling tents and equipment to neatly stacked tiers along the railroad tracks, and a great many of the young soldiers, their gear already inspected and packed, waited for orders to move out. There was a restive air of impermanence about it all, a pervading nostalgia, as though the past and things departed held exclusive possession of Gettysburg.

A blast on the whistle, a quick thrust of steam to skidding drive wheels, and the train moved off. In a few minutes the noise of the pounding engine receding into the distance was all that was left of the veterans.

In 1914 Dan Sickles, who had survived the shattering ordeal of losing a leg at Gettysburg, died. (He had survived quite a few other things, too, among which was the squandering of five million dollars on women and bad investments when he was in his early seventies. This money was an inheritance derived from his father, a man who had hung onto his money tenaciously, and not only did not trust Dan but was unkind enough to live to an extraordinarily ripe old age.)

Also in the year 1914 Joshua Chamberlain, the college professor from Maine who had called for an attack when the odds were all against him and saved Little Round Top and the Army of the Potomac, died. In 1864 he had received a staggering wound at Petersburg and was told he would die. The wound eventually killed him, but Chamberlain, strong physically and mentally, endured fifty years before succumbing to his war injury.

At Gettysburg a few seasons passed. A long winter with quiet snow over cool graves. A quick fall and the unheard rustle of leaves behind some forgotten stone which once had sheltered, but not well, a grim terror. Gettysburg waited, waited through the warmth of endless days in July and the damp winds of spring. . . .

The pounding noise of an overburdened engine moving along in the distance very well might have been a frustrating sound for a young captain in the United States Army. It easily could have symbolized the constant problem he had with makeshift equipment and meager supplies.

Standing near the ground where General Lee had seen his un-co-ordinated attacks on the Union lines smashed and repulsed, the young officer listened to the underpowered engine of an imported French Renault Whippet Tank, the only operational tank in the United States.

The year was 1918, and an America that had gone to war prepared with little more than a small regular Army and millions of untrained civilians had to settle for the Whippet at Camp Colt, Gettysburg, the first tank corps training center in United States history.[21]

When the captain had arrived at Camp Colt to assume command, it was early spring, 1918, and out on the soggy ground where Yanks and Rebs had once clawed and mutilated each other, six thousand new soldiers were living in overcrowded tents. Adequate shelter, fuel for heat, and food were in short supply.

The new commandant ordered details of khaki-clad soldiers to search the countryside for any items, including hay for bedding, which would help ameliorate the lack of necessities—an action reminiscent of the boys in blue and gray, the greatest foragers of all. As morale, which had reached almost zero, visibly rose and the camp took on the look of rough plenty, the business of turning out tank engineers swung into high gear.

By midsummer of 1918, graduates of Camp Colt were overseas successfully operating tanks, although their training at Gettysburg had been for the most part theoretical and simulated—no tank other than the two-man Renault Whippet reached Camp Colt until after the Armistice in November, 1918.

From the encampment area the tank trainees could see the majestic Virginia Memorial on Seminary Ridge. Dedicated only the year before, it marked the first monument erected by any Southern state on the battlefield. But somehow, despite the undeniable beauty of the Virginia Memorial, it did not significantly alter the tenuous, lost aura of Seminary Ridge, as though time had flowed by

Camp Colt, 1918. Seen here is area where fifty-five years before Pickett's legions had swarmed into history. In upper center is the Codori farmhouse.

The National Archives

Over in Europe a war is raging, and these
"doughboys" on the Pennsylvania Monument
are ready to go.

The Virginia Memorial viewed
from Seminary Ridge.

Soldiers of Camp Colt inspect a French Renault "Whippet" tank at Gettysburg.

Lonely sentinels of the past still holding the line on Seminary Ridge.

and left it to drowse lonely and undisturbed in another era. Bland, patient cannon, whose deadly destinies had been fulfilled, still lined the crest of Seminary Ridge pointing towards a long-departed foe, and graceful rows of trees clung to the haunted ground where in the heat of a summer afternoon Confederate soldiers had set out to reach the stars, and in a meteoric shower of exploding iron and hissing lead advanced towards Cemetery Ridge, slightly less than an impossible mile away. A lot of them had never come back, and Seminary Ridge was still waiting.

It is most probable as the young captain viewed the Virginia Memorial, the low, rolling ridges and swiftly banked hills of the battlefield and the distant blue haze along the South Mountain Range, that he wondered just what his role would be when he went to join the American Expeditionary Forces in France; but when he received his overseas orders and prepared to leave his command with a brand new commission as Lieutenant Colonel the war ended, and twenty-six years would pass before Dwight David Eisenhower set foot in France with an American army.[22]

The view from Oak Hill of the blue-hazed South Mountain Range rimming the western horizon like a giant half-bowl and the sweep of the low, rolling ridges and swiftly banked hills of the battlefield were as they had been twenty-five years ago and fifty years before that. The change, the long, slow change, was not in the land nor in the spirit of Gettysburg, but in the men— the hand of time had brushed better than ninety years on their faces.

Sitting in a specially constructed grandstand, some eighteen hundred very old, white-haired men of the Grand Army of the Republic and the United

Confederate Veterans waited for President Franklin D. Roosevelt to signal the unveiling of the Eternal Light Peace Memorial on Oak Hill, July 3, 1938.

Since 1933, when the park authority had been transferred from the War Department to the Department of Interior, the new commemorative works had numbered less than five on a site which held some two thousand monuments, tablets, and stone markers; and now with the Peace Memorial the once flourishing dedications were all but over.

Gathered on the broad, slightly inclined plain in front of the Peace Me-

The commandant of Camp Colt, front row, third from the left, poses with his fellow officers.

Ira Williams

morial were thousands of people who had come to see the dedication and the veterans, as they observed the seventy-fifth anniversary of the Battle of Gettysburg. Although there were almost eight thousand survivors of the War Between the States in 1938, the men waiting in the stand were all who could make the trip to Gettysburg for the last reunion of the Blue and Gray.

From their position on Oak Hill, the veterans could not quite see the buildings and streets of Gettysburg, but when they had ridden out to the dedication ceremonies in giant busses, they were able to look back and view the panorama of the small crossroads town whose name was so indelibly marked in history.

At the north end of town, spread out over the flat, open fields, were the boardwalk streets and tents of the reunion encampment. Beyond, over by Rock Creek, was Barlow Knoll, the low knob of land where the Federal line had cracked first on the opening day of the battle. Young General Barlow, "the boy general," had been badly wounded near the knoll, and when the Confederates overran the position he was given aid by Georgia lawyer, Brigadier General John B. Gordon. Barlow asked Gordon to notify his wife, a nurse with the Army of the Potomac. A courier under a flag of truce was sent through the Union lines and brought her back to her badly hurt husband. In the wake of battle General Gordon saw no more of Barlow, but assumed he would die. Under the constant care of his wife Barlow survived, and one

Early morning a long, long time afterwards at Gettysburg.

Walter Lane

"Yessir, saw Abe Lincoln as plain as you." Boy Scouts and veterans talk of a time seventy-five years earlier.

"Nice to see you, suh." An old Reb and Yank exchange greetings over the stone wall where twenty-five years earlier handshaking veterans had met, and where, fifty years before that, they, as boys, had shot and clubbed each other.

Gettysburg National Military Park—Walter Lane

America's past and the future arm in arm. A Boy Scout and a Confederate veteran walk past friends at the reunion encampment.

day he read the sad news that General Gordon had been killed. Twenty years later, during a banquet in Washington, at the speakers' table Barlow was introduced to a man who looked vaguely familiar. It was the Gordon of Gettysburg—the General Gordon who had been killed was another man— and both men, each having believed the other was dead, had an emotional reunion.

Due south of Barlow Knoll, below downtown Gettysburg, was the hill which had been the anchor of the Union line. And that hill turned a few memories to a long-ago scene of a land touched to silver under a bright moon and General Meade, astride his bay horse Baldy, making a midnight reconnaissance through the little village cemetery atop the hill. A sign at the gatepost ironically had proclaimed a five-dollar fine for anyone using firearms within the cemetery limits.

Next to the village cemetery, where soldiers had once fallen in noisy death among the tombs, was the National Military Cemetery. Placed in neat, con-

226

centric rows, the eternal boys rested beneath the silent grass, dreaming perhaps of their unfinished lives. On a faraway day, when death was still new, a tall, sad man had delivered a short oration over their graves, and the boys and the words and the sad man became immortally bound at Cemetery Hill.

To the left and slightly beyond Cemetery Hill was Culp's Hill, the right end of the Union line way back in '63. There was a story about Culp's Hill: how a young lad had left Gettysburg before the war and gone south. When he had come back he was with General Lee's army. During the battle he had called on his mother and then gone off to be killed on Culp's Hill. His name was Wesley Culp. The hill had belonged to his great-grandfather. . . .

Somewhere overhead an airplane engine rippled the air into a washboard of

The National Military Cemetery on Cemetery Hill.

Gettysburg National Military Park—Walter Lane

The possibilities of just what these fine-looking old veterans were saying are limitless, but they seem happy about it.

sound, and then eased and lessened and disappeared. Sunlight flowed softly over the land of Gettysburg, mellowed by the late hour of the day. It was six o'clock in the afternoon, and from an elevated stand newsreel photographers aimed their cameras and set reels spinning. President Roosevelt threw a switch, and a huge garrison flag cascaded from the shaft of the Eternal Light Peace Memorial into the waiting arms of a Northern veteran and a Southern veteran and two National Guardsmen attendants. Instantly, from an urn on top of the shaft, a perpetual flame flared, and the monument petitioned for twenty-five years earlier had become a reality—a symbol of peace eternal in a nation united.

After receiving the deed for the monument from the governor of Pennsylvania, President Roosevelt's cultured voice was carried across the nation on radio and to the farthest spectator by loudspeakers:

"Governor Earle, Veterans of the Blue and the Gray, on behalf of the people of the United States I accept this monument in the spirit of brotherhood and peace.

"Immortal deeds and immortal words have created here at Gettysburg . . ."

The exact moment of the unveiling of the Eternal Light Peace Memorial.

President Roosevelt addresses Confederate and Union veterans at Oak Hill.

A misty recollection moved down a long corridor to a moment when life was fresh, to a moment when the nearby thunder and crash of battle sounded and a little drummer boy waited in vain for an order, never given, to join in battle and play a rat-tat-too on his drum . . .

President Roosevelt's voice flowed on, "But the challenge is always the same . . ."

Yesterday there was a parade. They said it was the biggest parade ever held at Gettysburg—over seven miles long—with soldiers from the World War and a few men from the Spanish-American War, and United States Army soldiers with steel helmets. And there were airplanes and tanks . . . No . . . no . . . the airplanes and tanks were supposed to be tomorrow . . . things and events were confusing . . .

The lowered voice of President Roosevelt concluded, "May we live by the wisdom and humanity of the heart of Abraham Lincoln." The dedication was over.

The next day, July 4, the regular United States Army enacted a series of demonstrations with tanks, artillery, and horse cavalry (so soon to be relegated to the limbo of canister, smooth-bore cannon, and muskets). And in the late afternoon, exactly on schedule, bomber and fighter planes from Langley Field, Virginia, appeared in the skies over Gettysburg. As did the soldiers who had guarded the reunion encampment twenty-five years before, the young men of the planes and tanks and cavalry and artillery in four years would go off to war—a war of "unconditional surrender."

That evening, most of which went unnoticed by the tired veterans as they slept for the last time in the tents at Gettysburg, there was a band concert

Gettysburg National Military Park—Walter Lane

In five years the helmets and guns will be different. Members of the Regular United States Army parade at Gettysburg during the Seventy-fifth Anniversary Reunion of the battle.

Gettysburg National Military Park—Walter Lane

Two gentlemen from "Dixie" demonstrate "how it's done" to attentive National Guard attendants.

followed by a giant searchlight display, and down by the depot the short-and-long hoots of incoming trains sounded far into the night. In the morning the trains would carry the old Rebels and Yankees home.

A bugle sounded taps when the last trainload of veterans glided onto the "main line" and picked up momentum down the clicking tracks. The special reunion trains had been pulling out since early morning, and now, as the final train moved away, the living link with this part of America's past faded. The ancient soldiers who had once clutched hands with Destiny when they were young—the boys, friend and foe alike, who in a welter of misery had given America the gift of their youth—were gone.

The old, old men, men who quite literally had outlived their times, on that last trainload leaving the last of all possible reunions were bound for a far land, where their comrades of long ago waited. The long encampment was almost over.

Some early morning, perhaps, after a long night's vigil, a tired, old voice would sigh, a few birds would twitter in the first dawn light, and somewhere a telegram: *Grandpa died*. And somewhere in time and space, before Gettysburg had become a land of flaky cannon and winter-chipped monuments, before it had become an American legacy of imperishable bronze and granite statues, it was still July, 1863, at . . .

Gettysburg.

Walter Lane

Principal References

Ballard, Colin R. *Military Genius of Abraham Lincoln.* Pp. 160–71. New York: The World Publishing Co., 1952.

Battles and Leaders of the Civil War, Vol. III. Pp. 244–440. New York: The Century Co., 1884–87.

Boatner, Mark Mayo III. *The Civil War Dictionary.* New York: David McKay Co., Inc., 1959.

Bruce, Robert V. *Lincoln and the Tools of War.* New York: The Bobbs-Merrill Co., Inc., 1956.

Catton, Bruce. *The Glory Road.* Pp. 158–361. Garden City: Doubleday & Co., Inc., 1954.

Davis, Kenneth S. *Soldier of Democracy.* Pp. 174–80. Garden City: Doubleday & Co., Inc., 1952.

Dooley, John. *John Dooley, Confederate Soldier, His War Journal,* ed. Joseph T. Durkin, S.J. Washington: The Georgetown University Press, 1945.

Doubleday, Abner. *Chancellorsville and Gettysburg, Campaigns of the Civil War,* Vol. VI. New York: Charles Scribner's Sons, 1882.

Downey, Fairfax. *The Guns at Gettysburg.* New York: David McKay Co., Inc., 1958.

Eisenschiml, Otto and Newman, Ralph. *The Civil War, The American Iliad.* Pp. 457–506. New York: Grosset and Dunlap, 1956.

"Electric Lights," *Gettysburg Compiler,* August 4, 1885, p. 3, col. 2.

"The Encampment and Funeral," *Gettysburg Compiler,* August 11, 1885, p. 3, col. 2.

Freeman, Douglas Southhall. *Lee's Lieutenants,* Vol. III. Pp. 20–166. New York: Charles Scribner's Sons, 1944.

———. *R. E. Lee,* Vol. III. Pp. 107–36. New York: Charles Scribner's Sons, 1935.

Fremantle, Arthur James Lyons. *Three Months in the Southern States, April–June, 1863.* London: William Blackwood and Sons, 1863.

"The G.A.R. Encampment," *Gettysburg Compiler,* August 18, 1885, p. 3, col. 2.

"Gettysburg, Town of," *Encyclopaedia Britannica,* Vol. 10, p. 318. Chicago: Encyclopaedia Britannica, 1957.

Grimm, Herbert L. and Roy, Paul L. *Human Interest Stories of the Three Days' Battles at Gettysburg.* Gettysburg: Times and News Publishing Co., 1927.

Hancock, Cornelia. *South After Gettysburg: Letters of Cornelia Hancock,* ed. Henrietta Stratton Jaquette. New York: Thomas Y. Crowell Co., 1956.

Haskell, Frank Arteas. *The Battle of Gettysburg,* ed. Charles W. Eliot. (Harvard Classics, Vol. 43.) New York: P. F. Collier & Son, 1910.

Hatch, Alden. *General Ike.* Pp. 77–82. New York: Henry Holt and Co., 1944.

Henderson, G. F. R. *The Civil War: A Soldier's View,* ed. Jay Luvaas. Pp. 225–53. Chicago: The University of Chicago Press, 1958.

Hoke, Jacob. *The Great Invasion of 1863.* Dayton, Ohio: 1887.

Jacobs, Michael. Weather conditions during the Battle of Gettysburg compiled by Prof. Michael Jacobs, member of the Faculty of Pennsylvania (now Gettysburg) College, 1863.

Lyman, Theodore. (Letters of Theodore Lyman.) *Meade's Headquarters 1863–1865, From the Wilderness to Appomattox,* ed. George R. Agassiz. Boston: Atlantic Monthly Press, 1922.

McMaster, John Bach. *A History of the People of the United States During Lincoln's Administration.* Pp. 398–400. New York: D. Appleton and Co., 1927.

Miers, Earl S. *Robert E. Lee.* New York: Alfred A. Knopf, 1956.

—— and Brown, Richard A. *Gettysburg.* New Brunswick: Rutgers University Press, 1948.

Mitchell, Joseph B. *Decisive Battles of the Civil War.* Pp. 144–59. New York: G. P. Putnam's Sons, 1955.

The Photographic History of the Civil War, ed. Francis Trevelyan Miller. 10 vols. New York: 1911.

Pullen, John J. *The Twentieth Maine.* Pp. 82–148. Philadelphia: J. B. Lippincott Co., 1957.

Roy, Paul L. *The Last Reunion of the Blue and Gray.* Gettysburg: The Book Mart, 1950.

Sandburg, Carl. *Abraham Lincoln: The War Years,* Vol. II. Pp. 452–77. New York: Harcourt, Brace and Co., 1939.

Smith, Leroy E. *Illustrated Gettysburg Battlefield Map and Story.* Gettysburg: 1955.

Stackpole, Edward J. *They Met at Gettysburg.* Harrisburg: Eagle Books, 1956.

Steele, J. Dorman, A. M. *A Fourteen Weeks Course in Astronomy.* New York: A. S. Barnes and Co., 1869.

Storick, W. C. *The Battle of Gettysburg.* Harrisburg: J. Horace McFarland Co., 1954.

The Story of Gettysburg in Pictures, Gettysburg: The Book Mart.

Swanberg, W. A. *Sickles the Incredible.* New York: Charles Scribner's Sons, 1955.

Tilberg, Frederick. *Gettysburg National Military Park, Pennsylvania.* Washington: National Park Service Historical Handbook. Series No. 9, 1954.

Tucker, Glenn. *Hancock the Superb.* New York: The Bobbs-Merrill Co., Inc., 1960.

War of the Rebellion. Official Records of the Union and Confederate Armies. Series I, Vol. XXVII, parts I, II, III. Washington: Government Printing Office, 1889.

Wellman, Manly Wade. *Rebel Boast: First at Bethel—Last at Appomattox.* Pp. 111–37. New York: Henry Holt and Co., 1956.

Wiley, Bell Irvin and Milhollen, Hirst D. *They Who Fought Here.* P. 224. New York: The Macmillan Co., 1959.

Williams, T. Harry. *Lincoln and His Generals.* Pp. 251–71. New York: Alfred A. Knopf, 1952.

Notes

[1] The states of South Carolina, Florida, Alabama, Georgia, Louisiana, and Texas seceded first and formed the Confederate States of America with a provisional capital at Montgomery, Alabama. The Confederacy was then joined by the states of Virginia, North Carolina, Arkansas, and Tennessee, and the capital was moved to Richmond, Virginia. Missouri, a border state, was claimed by the South as part of the Confederacy, but its status throughout the war was indeterminate. The governor wanted to secede the state, but a vote by the State Senate passed a resolution not to secede. Federal troops occupied and held Missouri, thus keeping it under the jurisdiction of the North.

[2] Winfield Scott, born in 1786, had been appointed general in chief of the Army in 1841 and held that position when the Civil War began. Old and infirm in 1861, he retired in November of that year in favor of General George B. McClellan, who in turn was replaced by Major General Henry W. Halleck. Halleck was down-graded to chief of staff when Ulysses S. Grant was made general in chief of the Army in 1864.

[3] Lee was at the time of the Seven Days' Battle military adviser to Jefferson Davis. He took over the command of the Confederates defending Richmond when their commanding officer, General Joseph E. Johnston (West Point, 1829), was wounded. It was under Lee that this army became known as the Army of Northern Virginia.

[4] The bounty system became very involved. The Government in Washington introduced a draft, but exerted extreme pressure upon states to fill their quotas by volunteers. The states in turn began offering bounties, and this in turn created many "bounty jumpers." Men would enlist, get their bounty, and desert, enlisting somewhere else. And there was the substitute in the draft: following a custom set up in Europe, a draftee could hire, usually for three hundred dollars, somebody to take his place.

[5] Part of this campaign was the Seven Days' Battle, in which Lee forced a general retreat on the Federal forces.

[6] In the Missouri Compromise, 1820, part of the legislation designated that all territories accrued in the Louisiana Purchase north of parallel 36° 30′, except for the then-to-be-admitted state of Missouri, would be "free," all below "slave." This demarcation was so close to a boundary established in 1763–67 by surveyors named Mason and Dixon between Maryland and Pennsylvania that it eventually was called the Mason-Dixon line, and it became a symbolic east-west line dividing all the country.

[7] There is no accord on whether Buford's men actually had Spencer carbines—one very eminent Gettysburg historian feels there is little concrete evidence that Buford's

men had Spencers—but most contemporary writers credit the Spencers as a factor in the opening of the battle. Lieutenant Colonel H. E. Dana, Union officer, wrote that "the firing was rapid from our carbines," when he described the opening fire along McPherson's Ridge. In light of the fact that Buford's men were able to contain the Confederates although outnumbered, there seems to be a strong case for the presence of the Spencer repeating carbines.

[8] This hardly would have finished the Army of the Potomac. General Meade at this time still planned to fight the major battle at Rock Creek and he had all of his artillery reserve, plus five infantry corps and most of his cavalry, and despite overwhelming annihilation of the I and XI Corps he would still have had better than sixty-five thousand troops. Much has been made of this as Lee's "lost opportunity" to win the Battle of Gettysburg. A successful attack on Cemetery Hill would have deprived the Army of the Potomac of the high ground, but it is exaggerated to assume it would have automatically meant a victory over the Army of the Potomac.

[9] Based on figures given on the brigade tablets at Gettysburg, the Confederate strength at dawn of July 2, including 10,350 men of the First Corps, was about 40,000. Added to this was the strength of 58 batteries, averaging 85 men per battery. Also at hand was Jenkins' brigade of cavalry. This made a total figure of 45,400. Meade had at Gettysburg at the same time the remnants of the I and XI Corps, numbering about 10,000; the II Corps, three miles south of Gettysburg, 12,744; the III Corps, less two brigades, 10,500; the XII Corps, 9,961; and the two brigades of Buford's cavalry, about 3,200; an aggregate of 46,405.

[10] There is no record of any property owner around Gettysburg ever having received any compensation for damages inflicted by the battle from the United States Government. Mrs. Leicester, owner of Meade's headquarters building, received only the price of the bones of dead horses in her yard. They were made into fertilizer.

[11] This incident was reported in a column entitled "Camp Fire Notes" in *The Grand Army Review*, Vol. 1, Number 9, page 142, Col. 2. There is no explanation of how the little girl happened to be in the Federal lines, nor of the circumstances relating to her father's death, i.e., whether he had been a soldier, etc., or what became of her.

[12] Of the 14 Confederate division and brigade commanders, 3 were killed—Armistead, Garnett, and Marshall; 2 were wounded and captured—Trimble and Fry; and 2 were wounded but escaped capture—Kemper and Pettigrew. In Pickett's division there was only one officer above the rank of major who hadn't been either wounded or killed. A North Carolina regiment was left with 8 men and one officer out of 100. Of the Confederates, 3,060 were killed and wounded in the attack, and 2,260 were captured or listed as "missing." Union casualties were 2,200 dead and wounded, with 112 listed as "missing."

[13] When Hancock suggested a counterattack, he had in mind sending the V Corps, plus the VI Corps—at least twenty thousand men—in a flank attack around the lower end of Lee's lines on Seminary Ridge. Upon the failure of "Pickett's Charge," Meade was presented with two or three tactical possibilities, all, which if pursued with speed and vigor, probably would have succeeded.

[14] In terms of lives lost the Civil War was the costliest in American history. The combined mortality rate for North and South was 529,332, a greater figure than that

of World Wars I and II combined. In World War I the figure was 116,516, and in World War II it was 405,229.

¹⁵ When the North captured New Orleans in April, 1862, by joint army-naval operations it then controlled all of the Mississippi River except at Vicksburg. Here Confederate cannon dominated the river, preventing Union boats from passing. In what some historians consider the most brilliant campaign of the Civil War, Grant laid siege to Vicksburg on May 22, 1863. Forty-three days later, at ten o'clock in the morning of July 4, Vicksburg was surrendered. Strategically, the victory at Vicksburg was as important to the North as Gettysburg.

¹⁶ Immediately south of Williamsport is West Virginia, admitted to the Union on June 20, 1863. Once part of Virginia, it withdrew from the state by declaring void the Virginia Secession Convention which took Virginia out of the Union on April 19, 1861. Long at odds with the eastern portion of Virginia over representation at the state capital, the western section met at Wheeling, June 11, 1861, and set up a new "state government" of its own. West Virginia, in the summer of 1863, while declared officially as a state in the Union and therefore part of the North, was regarded by the South as still belonging to Virginia. It supplied men to both sides.

¹⁷ An updated casualty compilation, including killed, wounded, missing, and captured, indicates the Confederates suffered the loss of twenty-eight thousand. Based on this figure, Lee's army was reduced by *more* than one third.

¹⁸ The speech as delivered by Lincoln was recorded by Charles Hale of *The Boston Advertiser*. Lincoln wrote out at least four additional copies, one of which he gave to Edward Everett. Everett was among those who realized Lincoln had composed a magnificent speech and he requested a copy. The first draft composed in Washington contains 239 words. The fifth and sixth additional copies contain 272 words.

¹⁹ Many of the human-interest stories about Gettysburg are regarded as not based on fact. This story, cited in *The Civil War Dictionary*—"Brother Against Brother," page 89—is in all probability true. The 7th Virginia was part of Kemper's brigade, which was in "Pickett's Charge," and the 7th West Virginia belonged to Carroll's brigade, Hancock's II Corps, which bore much of the brunt of the attack on July 3.

²⁰ A Union burial detail discovered "a female dressed in a Confederate private's uniform." She had been killed when grabbing for the flag falling from the hands of her companion, also shot. By piecing evidence together—Confederate Captain A. R. Fitzhugh afterwards recalled how singularly impressed he was by a "boy" and what he thought was a "father" guarding him; others had noticed them, too—it was established they were husband and wife.

²¹ Camp Colt first was established in May, 1917, to train infantry soldiers. At the beginning of 1918 it was made into a tank training center.

²² With a wartime brevet commission of lieutenant colonel, Eisenhower received his orders to report to Fort Dix, New Jersey, for overseas duty beginning November 23, 1918. With the Armistice, November 11, 1918, his overseas assignment was automatically canceled. In 1928 he was awarded the Distinguished Service Medal for his work at Camp Colt. In 1951 General Eisenhower established his permanent residence at Gettysburg, a short distance from the battlegrounds.

Index